316-1
2

REFLECTIONS ON VALUES EDUCATION

Reflections on Values Education

Edited by John R. Meyer

Canadian Cataloguing in Publication Data

Main entry under title:

Reflections on values education

Bibliography: p.
ISBN 0-88920-031-9 bd.   ISBN 0-88920-030-0 pa.

1. Moral education — Addresses, essays, lectures.
I. Meyer, John R., 1934-

LC283.R44   370.11'4   C76-017065-7

Wilfrid Laurier University Press
Waterloo, Ontario, Canada

ISBN—0-88920-030-0—Paper
ISBN—0-88920-031-9—Cloth

CONTENTS

PART THREE: THE LEARNING & HELPING FACILITATOR

EPILOGUE

FOREWORD

Someone has remarked that contemporary life is a "white on white jigsaw puzzle." The same might be aptly applied to what is becoming known as "values education." The territory is terribly comprehensive and the boundaries within and without are often blurred. In some respects it is unfortunate that a title or label lends specificity or separateness to such a noble endeavor that has many interrelationships. On the other hand, it is not particularly helpful to simply say that all education *is* values education or social education *is* values education. Hence, it is a challenge to provoke continuous discussion on an emergent emphasis in education.

The authors have generously responded to the invitation to keep us informed on the very recent discoveries and thinking on this matter. To the contributors I owe the profound expressions of gratitude. I have attempted to gather soundings on the more theoretical aspects of the field with some attention to the impact of change on value systems and various professionals.

In some respects this may be a sequel to an earlier work. It should provide material for a fairly wide range of non-specialists and those who are continuing to pursue the topic in greater depth. As "reflections" the contents are subject to a tentativeness. The implications for education and the influences upon persons as learners are weighty. J. K. Crossley, Director of Teacher Education and Certification, Ministry of Education, Ontario, reminds us:

> Most of us have formulated our beliefs and our goals and our values into codes of behaviour, into ways of thinking, and into procedures for solving problems and for dealing with other people. None of us is absolutely consistent in our behaviour—life is too complex and we're too imperfect. Our beliefs are not firm enough, our minds can't handle all the implications, or the other guy won't let us do it our way anyhow.
>
> But the implication for public schools is this—teachers and other educators concerned with public education have a special responsibility in teaching the children of all the people. Children come in a wonderful diversity—in a multitude of talents and backgrounds—and we must be careful, very careful indeed, with the influence and the power that we have over them.

It is a special pleasure and privilege to leave the final words to a person who has expressed a significant interest and support for values and moral education in this Province as the current Minister of Education. It is my hope that the essays in this volume will complement and supplement the efforts of many named and unnamed who have and continue to labour in the "vineyard." It is to the leaders and to the dedicated practitioners that credit is due for making most of this a reality.

John R. Meyer

PREFACE

It seems to be an inescapable fact of life that values direct and govern the actions of people, institutions, and society. The school, as a major extension of the home in our contemporary culture, cannot avoid its share of the responsibility, or its significant opportunities, in developing positive attitudes and thinking in the moral and values dimension.

Among the various factors that act as a basis in this development are the broad social and moral principles that are found in the ideals of a society's heritage. Important, too, are the examples set by responsible people, such as school staff, and the example of the school itself as an institution. There is also, on a more individual basis, the necessary ingredient of acquiring attitudes and skills that contribute to the analysis of everyday values issues and moral decision-making. The combination and interaction of these factors tend to make the whole matter rather complex.

The series of essays in this publication contributes in learned and significant ways to a recently growing body of literature on this complex topic. There is satisfaction for me, as Minister of Education for Ontario, to see the cooperative efforts of various experts, including an impressive number from this Province. It is also gratifying to recognize the interest and contribution of the editor, as well as that of Wilfrid Laurier University Press, in making the publication a reality.

The greatest satisfaction may be in that this book should help parents, teachers, educational administrators, and teacher educators acquire further background and theoretical understanding of the complexities of moral and values education.

Thomas L. Wells
Minister of Education
Province of Ontario
Canada

PART ONE

THEORETICAL PROBLEMS

PHYSICAL SCIENCE AND MORAL CONFUSION

Guy Debrock
Faculty of Natural Sciences
University of Nijmegen, Holland

Our age is an age of confusion. This confusion expresses itself primarily in the realm of ethics. We still make moral judgments but by and large, we have lost the ability to say *why* we judge actions to be right or wrong.

Yet, there is no doubt that this is the century in which science and technology triumph. There exists something like a scientific world-order, while the world-order of morality has vanished. In this respect, Nietzsche's words have a ring of prophecy: "The entire history is the refutation by experiment of the principle of the so-called moral world order."[1]

If this is really so, then the problem of twentieth century man can be summarized as follows: twentieth-century man is a scientific and technical giant, but a moral idiot. The scientific and technological giant also has the power of a giant, and therefore, for the first time in the history of mankind, does a global moral idiot have giant power. The possible consequences of this contradiction are frightening.

In this essay, I would like to investigate how this opposition between our moral confusion and our scientific superiority has arisen historically. If we know how the problem arose, it may become less difficult to provide possible answers to the problem.

Man is a being of paradox. A quick glance at history reveals an almost lawful relationship between man's scientific knowledge and man's moral consciousness: the greater his scientific knowledge, the smaller his ethical certainty. Man's history coincides with the history of the improvement of his scientific thinking. Even though the word "improvement" in science may be subject to various interpretations, it may be asserted that, in general, a particular theory is considered to be better than another theory, if it allows for more accurate predictions of a greater number of phenomena. It is because of this progress in his capacity to make predictions that man has acquired an ever increasing power. Francis Bacon expressed it very convincingly: "Human knowledge and human power meet in one: for when the cause is not known the effect cannot be produced."[2] Even in primitive cultures, the power of an individual is always related to his capacity to predict events.

[1] F. Nietzsche, *Ecce Homo*, tr. by A. M. Ludovici (New York: Russell & Russell, 1964), pp. 133-134.

[2] Francis Bacon, *The Great Instauration,* in Edwin A. Burtt, ed., *The English Philosophers from Bacon to Mill* (New York: The Modern Library, 1939), p. 28.

Since man knows ever more in an ever shorter period of time, his power also increases in an ever shorter period of time. We experience a scientific acceleration which makes us dizzy. This dizziness is due to the fact that it has become impossible for an individual to know everything, or even to know everything within one branch of science. The more mankind knows, the less a man knows. It is typical of our age that we have become afraid of the possibility that science and technology can no longer be controlled by man. We find ourselves in a spaceship steered by various scientific disciplines, but it becomes more and more difficult for one helmsman to know what the others are doing. Therefore, the more we know, the less we know, not only in content, but also in the direction we are taking.

Yet, in spite of this, man's history does coincide with the history of an ever increasing scientific certainty. On the other hand, his history also coincides with the history of a decreasing *moral* certainty. This must now further be examined.

What is unknown, remains unloved, and, in most cases, the unknown is to be feared. These two properties, ignorance and fear, characterize every primitive culture. Ignorance, however, is not the same as uncertainty. Indeed, it is another paradox of the human condition that the more man knows, the less he becomes certain of what he knows (certainty becomes more and more a question of probability), and the *less* we know, the more we vocally try to express our certainty. That is why dogma is always necessarily vocal; its ground is uncertainty.

No one has better expressed this paradox than Socrates, when he told his accusers that his wisdom was due to the fact that he alone knew nothing with certainty, while others hastened to expose their uncertainties as truth.[3] But Socrates by this expresses nothing more than the typical attitude of the real man of science: an attitude of *skepsis*, i.e., of a contemplating investigation. This is the reason why through Socrates, mankind makes the transition from superstition to scientific thinking, and with this transition begins the dialectic of scientific thought; each new certainty carries with itself a greater uncertainty.

But our immediate concern is with moral certainty, i.e., with the certainty of the criteria according to which we ought to *act*. This certainty has a greater existential import. Descartes already noticed that while we can afford to doubt whether or not something is true or not, such a doubt is not possible, when we must act.[4] For even not to act is the result of a choice.

In a superstitious culture, the criteria of actions are described and understood with great precision. Primitive man is a man who has no power over nature, but is overpowered by nature. The consciousness of primitive man is a

---

[3]Plato, *Apology*, 21-22.

[4]". . . while reason obliged me to be irresolute in my beliefs, there was no reason why I should be so in my action." R. Descartes, *Discourse on the Method* and *Meditations*, tr. by L. J. Lafleur (New York: Bobbs-Merrill, 1960), p. 18.

consciousness in which fear plays an important role. This fear is less a fear for the power of nature than for the unpredictability of its power. Even now, we sometimes find ourselves in circumstances where nature overpowers us without warning. In such events where we cannot count on nature, we wish to be able to count on each other. The written or unwritten law is a guarantee that I can count on my neighbors' behavior. The language of the law, however, is peculiar because it describes what *will* happen. Our description of facts is always a description of what has happened, but the language of laws is always written in the future tense: "Thou *shalt* not steal." Yet, it is not possible to describe what is about to happen, unless we limit ourselves to the language of probability. To say that tomorrow, the weather will be nice, is nothing more than to say that there is a reasonable *probability* that tomorrow the weather will be nice. The law, however, does not tolerate such limitation to probability. What the law prescribes, *ought* to happen.

How can anyone be sure of what "shall" happen? How can anyone be certain that his neighbor will not come and steal his possessions. This certainty can be achieved only by *making* it certain. This in turn can only be achieved by making it clear that if someone steals, something far worse will happen to him. If he steals what belongs to me, his hands will be cut off. But perhaps the other is much stronger than I am. I do not have the power to punish the other. It becomes therefore necessary that someone have the power, and exercise that power. The moral law must ultimately come from someone who has power over everyone. The moral law must be in the hands of someone who governs everyone and everything.

We find a remarkable illustration of this situation in the Mesopotamian conception of the world as an organized network of divine wills which obey an absolute will. The Mesopotamian moral law was conceived in political terms. Politically, the cities were governed by free people. The daily business was overseen by a gathering of elders, while in emergencies, the general assembly delegated absolute power to a certain member of the community, who for a short time became king. The Mesopotamian realm of the gods had almost the same structure. Nature too was a political state, with a general assembly of gods under the leadership of Anu, the God of heaven, and his assistant, Enlil.[5] The gods address their absolute leader as follows:

> What thou hast ordered (comes) true!
> The utterance of prince and lord is (but)
> what thou hast ordered, (that with which) thou art in agreement.
> A Anu! Thy great command takes precedence,
> who could say no (to it)?
> O father of the gods, thy command,
> the very foundation of heaven and earth,
> what god could spurn (it)[6]

[5]H. Frankfort *et al., Before Philosophy. The Intellectual Adventure of Ancient Men* (Baltimore: Penguin Books, 1968).

[6]Quoted in Frankfort, *Before Philosophy,* p. 153.

In this text, the emphasis is entirely on the absolute power of Anu. This power is at the origin of the moral law, which in its turn is expressed by the will of human rulers, who receive their power from the gods.[7]

The same, or similar ideas are to be found in many texts, not only in the Middle East,[8] but also in the far East[9] and the Far West.[10] In all these texts, it

[7]See for example how Hammurabi exercises his power by delegation of Marduk, the god of Babylon:

> When lofty Anu, king of the Annunanki, and Enlil, lord of heaven and earth, who determine the destinies of the country, appointed Marduk, the firstborn son of Enki, to execute the Enlil functions over the totality of the people, made him great among the Igigi, called Babylon by its exalted name, made it surpassingly great in the world, and firmly established for him in its midst an enduring kingship whose foundations are (as) firmly grounded as (those of) heaven and earth—There did Anu and Enlil call me to afford well-being to the people,
> me, Hammurabi, the obedient, god-fearing prince, to cause righteousness to appear in the land,
> to destroy the evil and the wicked, that the strong harm not the weak and that I rise like the sun over the black-headed people, lighting up the land.

Quoted in Frankfort, *Before Philosophy,* p. 208.

[8]The Bible provides many examples of the same attitude: man's salvation and security lie in God's power. One example of this is provided by the beginning of Psalm 37:

> Do not strive to outdo the evildoers
> or emulate those who do wrong.
> For like grass they soon wither,
> and fade like the green of spring.
> Trust in the *Lord* and do good; . . .
> Depend upon the Lord,
> and he will grant you your heart's desire.
> Commit your life to the Lord;
> trust in him and he will act.
> He will make your righteousness shine clear as the day
> and the justice of your cause like the sun at noon.
> Wait quietly for the Lord, be patient till he comes;
> do not strice to outdo the successful
> nor envy him who gains his ends.
> Be angry no more, have done with wrath:
> strive not to outdo in evildoing.
> For evildoers will be destroyed,
> but they who hope in the Lord shall possess the land. . . .

The New English Bible (New York: Oxford University Press, 1970). The attitude which underlies this and other psalms is explained with admirable candor in the words of Tertullian: "The God whom he cherished is the inflexible and jealous Judge who has established fear (*timor*) as the basis for man's salvation." Quoted in V. J. Bourke, *History of Ethics* (Garden City, N.Y.: Doubleday, 1970), Vol. I, p. 79.

[9]The following Indian text from the Ṛg Veda puts the emphasis on the guilt which the sinner has before Varuna, the highest of the Aryan gods.

> Let me not go to House of Clay, O Varuna!
> Forgive, O gracious Lord, forgive!
> When I go Tottering, like a blown-up bladder,
> forgive, O gracious Lord, forgive!
>
> Holy One, in want of wisdom I have opposed you.
> Forgive, O gracious Lord, forgive!
> Though in the midst of waters, thirst has seized your worshipper.
> Forgive, O gracious Lord, forgive!

appears that the unpredictability of nature is compensated by the certainty and the reliability of the moral law. In such a moral structure, obedience is the greatest virtue.

The transition from the superstitious vision of the world to the scientific understanding of this world happens in Greek culture. This transition is characterized by a search for the lawfulness in nature; and little by little, the emphasis on personal powers is replaced by an emphasis on causes which are to be found in the structure of nature itself. Obviously, this process was slow, and our Western view will for a long time be dominated by an attempt to marry a new scientific with a religious understanding of the universe. Moreover, there is no doubt that even in Greece, the attempt to replace divine wills by natural causes was received with great suspicion. The example of Socrates clearly shows the fear with which the new scientific attitude was received. When he was accused of impiety, the accusation stemmed at least in part from his association with the new scientific ideas imported from the Milesian school.

Yet, when Socrates understood that knowledge of nature was useless without knowledge of self or without moral consciousness, he turned more and more to an exclusively moral interpretation of the world. It is all the more remarkable that he raised the problem which is at the heart of every religiously oriented moral conception. If the origin of the moral law lies in an absolute will, then the question arises why this will determines certain things to be good, and certain things to be evil. Why does God forbid murder? Either he forbids it because he chooses to consider it evil, or he forbids it because murder is evil. But neither of these answers is satisfactory, for in the first case, God is arbitrary, and ultimately a tyrannical God; while in the second case, the thinking is circular and moral authority remains groundless.[11]

We can understand why Socrates and Plato tried to create a new world vision from which a non-arbitrary, yet absolute ethic would emerge. By wedding the moral with the scientific view, it became necessary to create a world that was both absolute and unchanging. This was Plato's vision of the Ideal world, which ultimately found its origin in the concept of the Good. The Good is the origin of all that is,[12] but at the same time it also is the goal of all human action.[13]

Whatever sins we mortals have committed, against the people of the gods,
if, foolish, we have thwarted your decrees,
O God, do not destroy us in your anger!
Quoted in A. L. Balsam, *The Wonder That Was India* (New York: Grove Press, 1959), pp. 237ff.

[10]In the American-Indian legends and myths, the emphasis is usually more on the divine influence on nature. But even there too, the sense of morality is inspired by supernatural wills. See, e.g., an account of the origin of violence of man towards nature in Luis Rosado Vega, *El alma misterioso del mayab* (libreria y Ediciones Botas).

[11]Plato, *Eutyphro,* 8b-10a.

[12]Plato, *Republic,* Bk. VII, 517.

[13]Plato, *Symposium,* 211 a2-b2. In this text, the goal of the human activity is described in terms of the beautiful which is the object of love.

Yet, it was Aristotle who would connect in a definitive manner the moral vision of man's experience with a scientific theory of the structure of the world. This deserves closer examination, for ultimately the moral confusion of the twentieth century will appear to be largely due to an unwarranted adherence to part of his philosophical insights.

First, it should be remembered that precisely the connection between, on the one hand, the physical and metaphysical interpretation of the structure of the world, and the moral interpretation of man's experience on the other hand, is central to the contribution of Greek philosophy to our Western thought.

In Oriental philosophies, the central problem is always the moral experience of man. The basic teachings of Hinduism and Buddhism are rooted in the one observation that everything is suffering. Even though some of their concepts, such as the Pratityasamutpada in Buddhism,[14] are metaphysical, even these have an almost exclusively moral function, and contribute little or nothing to a conceptual understanding of our world. Even in Lao Tzu, who is perhaps the most metaphysical Oriental thinker, the concept of Tao, which seems to be derived from our experience of the physical world, is important only because it contributes to ethical consciousness. Moreover, in the last analysis, it is clearly derived from moral presuppositions. The following text from the sublime *Tao Te Ching* illustrates this very well:

> Heaven lasts long, and Earth abides.
> What is the secret of their durability?
> Is it not because they do not live for themselves
> That they can live so long
> Therefore, the Sage wants to remain behind,
> But finds himself at the head of others;
> Reckons himself out,
> But finds himself safe and secure.
> Is it not because he is selfless
> That his Self is realized[15]

The text seems to teach that the wise man always acts in the same manner as nature. The thinker sees a relationship between nature and what man's behavior ought to be. But there is no real effort to discover the secrets of nature. There is merely a beautiful, and simple description, which seems to demonstrate that man can learn something from the behavior of nature.

Yet, a closer investigation allows us to see that the appearances of Lao Tzu's method are deceiving. He does not limit himself to describing how nature manifests itself. Lao-Tzu says *why* nature lasts. It lasts because heaven and earth do not exist for themselves. But such statement is obviously not the result of an

---

[14] The doctrine of *Pratityasamutpada* or of 'Dependent Origination' asserts that in the empirical world, everything is relative, conditional, and dependent. See e.g., Chandradhar Sarma, *Indian Philosophy: A Critical Survey* (London: Rider & Co., 1960), pp. 72-75.

[15] Lao Tzu, *Tao Teh Ching,* tr. by John C. H. Wu (New York: St. John's University Press, 1961), p. 9.

accurate observation. We can only describe heaven and earth as selfless, if these physical phenomena are considered as moral beings. It seems as if heaven and earth were pious men who had taken the decision not to live for themselves, and who, as a reward, or as a result of that behavior, obtain eternal life.

Our first impression was mistaken. The moral vision of man appeared first to be an application of a simple and beautiful description of the physical world. But now we discover that this so-called simple description of the world has its explanation in a more fundamental moral conception of the universe. The text of Lao-Tzu contains, in logical language, a circular argument. It contains two arguments, which presuppose one another. They can be formulated as follows:

> Arg. 1. He who does not live for himself, abides.
> Heaven and earth do not live for themselves.
> Therefore, heaven and earth abide.
> Arg. 2. Whoever lives like heaven and earth, abides.
> Whoever does not live for himself, lives like heaven and earth.
> Whoever does not live for himself, abides.

The moral prescription, "Do not live for Thyself," is derived from the description of nature, and the description of nature in turn rests on the moral prescription. It is no surprise, therefore, that reality must remain unintelligible. This unintelligibility of reality is expressed in the first of Lao-Tzu's poems:

> Tao can be talked about, but not the Eternal Tao
> Names can be named, but not the Eternal Name.
> As the origin of heaven-and-earth, it is nameless:
> As "the Mother" of all things, it is nameable.
> So, as ever hidden, we should look at its inner essence:
> As always manifest, we should look at its outer aspects.
> These two flow from the same source, though differently named;
> And both are called mysteries.
> The Mystery of mysteries is the Door of all essence.[16]

There is in this text a mysticism of non-being. All being is semblance, therefore, non-being must be reality. The ground of reality must be indescribable and unnameable. This thinking—with a few exceptions—has been contrary to the Western perspective.

From the very beginning, Greek thought rejects this cognitive pessimism. The clearest example of this rejection is to be found in Aristotle's thinking, which will ultimately influence our entire Western outlook on reality.

It is not a mere coincidence that it was Aristotle too who was the originator of logic in the formal sense of that word. Even though he did not call the logical discipline by its present name, there can be no doubt that the concept of *logos* was central to his thinking. *Logos*, that extraordinarily rich word, not only meant proportion, word, sentence, or reason, but also "that whereby everything happens." In Heraclitus, we read that "all things originate according to this

[16]Ibid., p. 3.

Logos."[17] The central position of the Greek vision of the world is that the world and human reason exist for each other. Reality is essentially intelligible, and whatever is intelligible, is also real. Without this presupposition, we cannot understand Parmenides, for whom "Thought and the object of thought are the same,"[18] or, even more strongly, "Thinking and being are the same."[19] This belief was only strengthened by Plato and Aristotle, and it will remain the backbone of Western philosophy, and of Western science up to this day.

Aristotle, however, went beyond a mere statement of principle. He tried to reveal the structure of the physical world which constitutes the world of our human experience. In that sense, Aristotle was the first major scientist. He will also be the first to derive a moral system from a scientific understanding of the world.

It must now be seen, briefly, how he attempts to do this, before we can understand that he too will fall into the anthropomorphic fallacy, which was illustrated in Lao-Tzu's text. Aristotle's physics ultimately rests on a moral intuition. His physics will be rejected in favor of classical Newtonian physics. Since his moral system rests on his physics, the rejection of his physics will entail the rejection of the basis of his ethical system.

Aristotle begins his metaphysics with the well-known words: "All men by nature desire to know."[20] The word he uses, *eidenai* (to know) is related to the word *eidos* (image). To know is to have an image, to have a sight. We have a sight of reality when we form an image of the structure of reality. For Aristotle, the desire for this *eidos* is expressed by asking what the cause is of what appears. He carefully demonstrates that, although his predecessors were implicitly looking for causes, he is the first one to clearly discover all the causes. Some thinkers before him had asked for material causes, some for efficient causes, and some for formal causes. He adds the necessity of final causality.[21]

In Aristotle's analysis, the most important cause is the form of a thing.[22] To the question, "What is this?" the answer—provided it is a true answer— corresponds with whatever makes the thing so, and only so. The reason why a mussel is a mussel, rather than a turtle, is its principle of organization, which is unique to mussels. But this form can be known only when the mussel is full-grown, and this full-grownness in turn, is the goal of everything the mussel does. Therefore, the questions, "What is a mussel" and "What is the goal of the mussel" are inseparable questions.

Moreover, for Aristotle, as for his teacher Plato, the question, "What is

[17]Heraclitus, Fragment 1.

[18]Parmenides, Fragment 7,8.

[19]Ibid.

[20]Aristotle, *Metaphysics*, BkA, 980 a21.

[21]Ibid., 988 a34-b16.

[22]Ibid., BkZ, 1091 b.

this?" demands an unchangeable answer. Just as the answer to the question, "How much is five times six?" is unchangeable, so also the question, "What is a mussel?" demands an answer that will never change. The form or the nature of the mussel must be unchangeable.[23]

In Aristotle's philosophy, the important doctrine of the immutable nature of things is born. This doctrine was to have an inestimable influence on the scientific as well as the common sense thinking of Western man. Many are the expressions which begin with the words: "By nature, man is. . . ." Such expressions imply that there is in man something which never changes. Science as a whole has been mostly the collective answer to the question: "What is the nature of the totality of the things which constitute the physical universe?" The layman still asks, "What is an atom?" and by that very question shows that he believes there is an unchangeable answer to that question, i.e., that atoms have an unchangeable nature.

Only against the background of this doctrine of the nature of things can we understand Aristotle's ethical views. Only by understanding the nature of things, can one understand what is good for them. For indeed, the nature and the goal of a thing determine each other. Its goal is what it ultimately wants, it is its good.[24] In the case of a human being, this goal is called man's happiness.[25] Whatever enhances happiness will therefore be moral. Man's happiness, for Aristotle, consists in the exercise of the activity which best expresses his nature.[26]

Our concern here is merely to point out how closely Aristotle's ethics is based on his physics. This dependence of ethics on a physics has the great advantage of unifying the vision of the human experience. This unity of vision did profoundly impress the medieval theologians who rediscovered Aristotle's writings.

When the teachings of the gospel spread in the West, great emphasis was put on the moral doctrine of Christianity. There was little concern for reconciling those moral principles with scientific concepts. But slowly the demand for rational understanding grew. The development of Christian theology went from Tertullian's *Credo quia absurdum*[27] to Augustine's *fides quaerens intellectum,*[28]

---

[23] Ibid.

[24] Aristotle, *Nicomachean Ethics,* Bk I, 1094 a3.

[25] Ibid., 1095 a.

[26] Ibid., 1098 a.

[27] The expression itself is incorrectly attributed to Tertullian. But its spirit is undeniably that of Tertullian. See, e.g.,: "What indeed has Athens to do with Jerusalem? What concord is there between the Academy and the Church? What between heretics and Christians? . . . Away with all attempts to produce a mottled Christianity of Stoic, Platonic and dialectic composition. We want no curious disputation after possessing Christ Jesus, no inquisition after enjoying the Gospel. With our faith, we desire no further belief. . . ." Tertullian, *On Prescription Against Heretics,* Ch. VII.

[28] *"Si non potes intelligere, crede ut intelligas; praecedit fides, sequitur intellectus."*

and on to Aquinas for whom reason, despite its limitations, was able to know truth.[29] Even though man could not grasp the mysteries of God's nature, he could know without the help of faith, not only the structure of the world, but also the basic principles of moral conduct.

The entire doctrine of natural law and of the *ratio recta* is ultimately based on Aristotle's vision.[30] Just as man naturally knows the fundamental laws of reasoning, so he also knows naturally and by means of a mysterious faculty, called *synderesis,*[31] what is good and what is bad. We know *a priori* that we ought to pursue the good and avoid what is evil. Whether an action is good or bad is determined by the degree by which we respect the nature of things. And since the nature of things is expressed by their goal, everything which respects and furthers that good, will be good, while whatever thwarts that goal, will be bad. Similarly, some things are naturally tuned to other things, and there exists a natural suitability (*convenientia*) between them, as in the case of man and woman who are naturally suited to have sexual intercourse.[32] It is evident that there were still remnants of this ethical way of thinking, as for example, in the arguments which have been used to condemn the use of contraceptives. Taking a pill which prevents a woman's pregnancy is an immoral interference with immutable nature.

The concept of natural law is evidently the heritage of the Aristotelian philosophy. The consequences of the collapse of Aristotle's physics can now better be understood. If a pillar which supports a roof is taken away, then either the roof collapses, or it remains in a state of dubious suspension. The first case is tragic, because without a roof there is no house, but the second case is more dangerous, because the illusion of safety persists, while in reality catastrophe may be near. Ever since the Renaissance, the second case has more or less prevailed. The roof is still there, but it has lost its support.

The collapse of Aristotle's physics has left his ethical system groundless. Two factors, in particular, have hastened the collapse of his physics: first, the fact that Aristotle's physics ultimately depended on an anthropomorphic concept, and secondly, the fragility of the concept of final causality.

Knowledge, for Aristotle, was essentially knowledge of causes. The Greek word for cause, *aitia*, is related to the verb *aitiesthai* (to accuse). *Aitia* is in the

("If you cannot understand, believe so that you may understand; faith precedes, understanding follows.") Augustine, Sermo 118, 1. *PL* 38, 672.

[29] For a discussion of the relation between faith and reason in the Middle Ages, see E. Gilson, *Reason and Revelation in the Middle Ages* (New York: Charles Scribner's Sons, 1938).

[30] The doctrine of right reason is central to Medieval thinking. For a discussion of these theories, see V. A. Bourke, *History of Ethics,* Vol. I, Chap. 5.

[31] The term *synderesis,* maybe first used by St. Jerome, was discussed by several medieval philosophers, notably by Bonaventure, who gives a rather clear description of its meaning. See St. Bonaventura, *In II Sententiarum,* d. 39, 2,1; in *Opera Omnia,* ed. crit. (Quaracchi: Collegio di San Bonaventura, 1882-1902), vol. II, p. 910.

[32] See Bourke, *History of Ethics,* Vol. I, p. 142.

first place "responsibility." When someone knocks over a cup of coffee, we say it happened through his fault, and this indeed means he was the cause, i.e., the moral cause. When, therefore, Aristotle says that everything has a cause, he means in the first place that something is responsible for whatever is. For example, the sculptor is the cause of the statue, which means that he is responsible for its coming into being. The totality of things has its origin in something with absolute responsibility otherwise there cannot be anything.[33] There is but a small step from Aristotle's ultimate cause to the absolute reason of Stoicism, and to the concept of God's absolute Providence. But modern physics has slowly tried to dispense with this anthropomorphic concept of causality. If we still speak of causes, it is no longer in the sense of responsibility.

But there is another reason yet why Aristotle's physics eventually collapsed. Aristotle, who by temperament was a biologist, considered final causality to be most important. The final cause is a goal. But it is evident that the language of goals does not come from an accurate observation of nature in general. Things in nature cannot be observed to have goals. Only human beings have goals. A student may have the goal of becoming a biologist, but a tree can hardly be said to have the goal of growing this or that way. Why then did Aristotle ascribe goals to everything? He did so precisely because his concept of causality in general, and therefore of final causality, contained the concept of responsibility, and therefore ultimately rested upon the assumption that whatever holds for man also holds for all reality. The ultimate cause of everything must, e.g., lie in a consciousness, in a *noesis*.[34]

But modern physics has an aversion for whatever cannot be measured, or verified or tested. A goal can neither be measured, nor verified, except when the goal has been reached, and at that point it no longer is a goal. But if the concept of final causality is rejected, then the concept of nature which depends upon the notion of final cause, must be rejected as well.

This rejection, however, never occurred. In our world, the sciences have discovered and used a new mathematical language to describe reality. On the other hand, man has continued to believe in the myth of the nature of things, and to speak the language of that myth. We must indeed speak of a myth, of which the ground is Aristotle's idea of man's nature, i.e., of man's unchangeable final cause.

In spite of the predominance of this myth of human nature in our Western culture, there have been some prophets who saw its weakness. The brilliant thinker of the Renaissance, Pico della Mirandola, was such a prophet. In one of the very beautiful texts of that period, he wrote:

> Finally, the Best of Workmen decided that that to which nothing of its very own could be given, should be given, in composite fashion, whatsoever had belonged individually to each and everything . . . and He spoke to him as follows: We have

[33] Aristotle, *Metaphysics,* and *Physics,* Bk. 8, 258b10f.

[34] Aristotle, *Metaphysics,* 1074 b 33.

given thee, Adam, no fixed seat, no form of thy very own, no gift peculiarly thine, that . . . thou mayest possess as thine own the seat, the form, the gifts which Thou Thyself shalt desire. . . . In conformity with thy free judgment in whose hands I have placed thee, thou art confined by no bonds and thou wilt fix the limits of thy nature for thyself. . . . Neither heavenly nor earthly, neither mortal nor immortal have We made thee. Thou . . . art the moulder and maker of thyself. . . . Thou canst grow downward into the lower natures which are brutes. Thou canst again grow upward from the mind's reason into the higher natures which are divine.[35]

In this text, still entirely inspired by religious images, Pico attacks the notion of a given human nature, by showing that man is an exceptional creature, precisely because he received nothing but possibilities, from which each of us is supposed to forge his nature, whereas all other things still receive a nature of the Aristotelian type. The theme which Pico suggests here will become central in the writings of Kierkegaard,[36] and of the existentialist thinkers of our century.[37]

What then are the consequences of the collapse of the notion of the nature of things? So far, it has been shown that (1) the Aristotelian description of reality was rooted in the idea of the nature of things; (2) the concept of nature was connected to the concept of goal; (3) only man has goals; (4) therefore, the concept of nature is ultimately based on an anthropomorphism; (5) finally, man precisely has no nature, and therefore the concept of the nature of things is based on a wrong anthropomorphism. In the last analysis, then, the logical interdependence between the moral and the physical description of the world experience which we found in Lao-Tzu's writings finds its counterpart in Aristotle's philosophy, for there too, the assumption which underlies the description of the physical world order presupposes a moral world-order, which in turn *appears* to follow from the physical world-order.

The concept of the nature of things has become so essentially a part of our thinking that even after the new physics was introduced, it was adhered to more fervently than ever. Even after Hegel and Darwin had, for very different reasons, introduced a dynamic vision of reality, philosophers who tried to introduce new ethical theories could not divest themselves from an underlying theory of human nature.[38]

---

[35]Quoted in P. O. Kristeller, *Renaissance Thought: The Classic, Scholastic and Humanist Strains* (New York: Harper Torchbooks, 1961), p. 129.

[36]See e.g., Kierkegaard's discussion of truth as subjectivity in S. Kierkegaard, *Concluding Unscientific Postscript,* tr. by David F. Swenson and W. Lowrie (Princeton University Press, 1962), pp. 173-182.

[37]See e.g., J. P. Sartre, *Being and Nothingness,* tr. by Hazel E. Barnes (New York: Philosophical Library, 1956), pp. 21-35.

[38]In this respect, it is worth noting that, even though Hegel wrote separate books on the philosophy of history, or religion, and of art, he has no explicit philosophy of man, precisely because the moments of the human experience do not constitute a "human nature." Kant, on the other hand, shifted the emphasis from the permanence of human nature to the unchanging character of reason: ". . . the basis of obligation must not be

Two languages therefore characterize our view of the world: on the one hand, the language of physics, which is entirely indifferent to absolutes, and does not need to commit itself to a belief in the nature of things; on the other hand, the language of a system of values, in which we have implicitly or explicitly held on to the concept of the nature of man. But precisely because our basic allegiance has shifted to scientific certainty, and because science has nothing to say any more about what is ethical, *nothing in our ethical view is any longer certain.*

To put it in other words, the old physical view of the world was rooted in the concept of an absolute world order, in which time played but an accidental role. This absolute world order contained an absolute moral order. The old physical vision of the world has collapsed, and therefore the moral vision which depended on it has lost its support. The old physical vision has been replaced by a new and sturdier vision. The moral vision, however, was not replaced.

Two possible attitudes can be and have been taken towards this fact. One consists in a repeated and dogmatic assertion that there is but *one* and absolute moral vision; the other consists in the assertion that there is no moral order, and that everyone can determine his own values. But in the first instance, the illusion prevails that as long as one is sufficiently convinced of it, the roof will not and cannot collapse. In the second instance, human experience becomes impossible. Whatever is good for one person, may be evil for someone else, and consequently, no one can count on anyone else. But the fabric of human relationships is made possible by the fact that human beings do count on one another.

It is obviously impossible to provide a quick answer to this painful dilemma. Yet, a few suggestions can be made that may provide at least a direction in which the answer may possibly be sought.

1. As some thinkers, among whom Heidegger,[39] have shown, the original

sought in the nature of man, or in the circumstances in the world in which he is placed, but *a priori* simply in the conceptions of pure reason. . . ." See I. Kant, *Fundamental Principles of the Metaphysic of Morals,* tr. by T. K. Abbott (Indianapolis: Bobbs-Merrill, 1949), p. 5. With regard to post-Hegelian philosophers, two influential moral thinkers stand out: J. S. Mill and K. Marx. Both try to avoid the traditional conceptions of morality, but neither one can free himself from the concept of human nature. In the case of Mill, "human nature" is implied in his discussion of the concept of happiness, as that which is desirable, and he makes explicit reference to human nature: "Meanwhile, the feelings exist, a fact in human nature. . . ." See J. S. Mill, *Utilitarianism,* in Edwin Burtt, *The English Philosophers from Bacon to Mill* (New York: The Modern Library, 1939), p. 918. Marx tries to redefine human nature, but the implication is still that this nature never changes: "Man is directly a natural being. As a natural being, and as a living natural being he is, on one hand, endowed with natural powers and faculties. . . . On the other hand, as a natural, embodied, sentient, objective being, he is a suffering, conditioned and limited being, like animals and plants." Karl Marx, *The Economic and Philosophical Manuscripts,* in Karl Marx, *Early Writings,* tr. by T. B. Bottomore (London: C. A. Watts and Co., 1963), p. 206. The process philosophers, on the other hand, notably Bergson and Whitehead, avoid the concept of the nature of things, but their discussion of the ground of moral judgment remains sketchy. This is even the case in Bergson's *The Two Sources of Morality and Religion,* where the concern is precisely with tracing the origin and the genesis of morality, but not with the ground of moral judgment.

[39]M. Heidegger, *An Introduction to Metaphysics,* tr. by Ralph Manheim (Garden City, N.Y.: Doubleday & Co., 1961), pp. 11ff.

meaning of the Greek concept of nature (*physis*) has largely been lost. The verb *phuo* is close in meaning to the word *gignomai*, from which we have the word "genesis." In that perspective, nature is not something immutable, but essentially becoming. Reality, too, must be seen primarily as a becoming, while the facts of reality are merely hardened fossils of reality.

2. There is a tendency to consider science, and more particularly, the exact sciences, as a new religion. But if science is primarily concerned with facts, then this new religion rests on a limited vision of what reality is. The following analogy may help to understand this. When a painter makes a painting, then he is judged *through* his painting. The work he makes is the *fact* about which we can speak. But the reality of the painting, its *physis*, its becoming is obviously more than this fact. To reduce art to that about which art critics speak or write, is to have a limited and distorted idea of the reality of art. Similarly, to reduce reality to whatever scientists speak about is to have a limited idea of reality.

3. Yet, just as it would be absurd to speak about art without speaking of works of art, so it is absurd to speak of reality without speaking of facts. Facts are the methodological starting point of our description of reality. We know there is art because there are works of art. We know there is reality because there are facts. Facts are the objects of the exact sciences. These sciences have been extraordinarily successful, not merely in the sense that they were useful, but in the sense that they have been able to give the picture of a world order. Moreover, this success occurred as soon as scientists abandoned the language of absolutes, and addressed themselves to the limited reality of facts. This does not mean that—as is often assumed—they rejected the absolute, but merely that the language of absolutes was no longer part of their method. Neither did the abandonment of the language of absolutes mean that scientists relativized everything. Nobody would argue, for example, that Newton's theories were inferior to those of Descartes.

In other words, scientists are able to determine whether one theory is better than another, without deciding the question of what constitutes absolute truth. It is not within the scope of this essay to examine the criteria whereby scientists do determine the superiority of one theory over another. But ultimately, these criteria point to the necessity of a creative element. A superior theory is a theory which creates new possibilities. It can be tested more strictly, it allows one to explain more phenomena more consistently, etc.

Perhaps the answer to the question of the basis for an ethics is to be found in that same direction. It may be time to stop the dogmatic language of moral absolutes. But this should not mean that therefore ethics is relativized. We may not be able to determine what is absolutely good or absolutely evil, but it may be possible to determine whether this kind of action is better than another on the basis of its greater, i.e., more creative possibilities.

Perhaps this appears to be a disguised form of utilitarianism. But I do not think it is because (1) there is no reference in it to the results of an action, only to the creation of new possibilities, and (2) there is no reference to the principle of pleasure. Creativity and pleasure are not necessarily correlative notions.

In summary, an attempt was made to show that the confusion in the ethical consciousness of our age stems from the rupture of the connection which has existed within our Western culture between the physics of Aristotle and a certain understanding of man's moral experience. I also tried to suggest that even though it is not possible to deduce a new ethics from a new physical science, it might be possible to learn something from the attitude inherent in the scientific methodology.[40]

Ultimately, the possibility of our being human depends, not from the mere fact that we have power, but from the knowledge we have of the direction in which we want to use that power. The tragedy of the modern idiot lies perhaps in the illusion that he can read God's book, even though he denies the existence of this God. Now he too must learn to become man.

[40]This does not mean, however, that scientific methodology can yield a new ethics, as was suggested by John Dewey when he spoke of the supremacy of the method.

THE DOMAIN AND DEVELOPMENT OF MORAL JUDGMENT: A THEORY AND A METHOD OF ASSESSMENT*

John Gibbs, Lawrence Kohlberg, Anne Colby, Betsy Speicher-Dubin
Graduate School of Education: Center for Moral Education
Harvard University

I. Introduction

The starting point of the study of moral judgment is the recognition that moral judgment refers to a mode of prescriptive valuing of the socially good and right. Other modes of judgment may pertain to prescriptive evaluation of truth or esthetics, description or analysis of naturally occurring phenomena, or pragmatic calculation of consequences (see Table 1). It is quite possible, of course, to engage in a psychological and philosophical study of one of the latter modes of judgment. The development of judgments of logico-mathematical and physical knowledge is Piaget's primary field of study. The development of the descriptive judgments in relation to social behavior and institutions is represented in the studies of levels of social cognition or role-taking (Selman, 1976) and social-cognitive epistemology (Broughton, 1976b). It is only when social cognition is extended into prescriptive judgments as to what is right or good that we can identify a moral judgment. When someone is asked, "What is a constitutional government?" or "What is a husband-wife relationship?" a level of social cognition can be inferred in the answer; it is when the person is asked, "Should you always obey a constitutional government?" or "Should you break a husband-wife relationship by divorce?" that his answer is likely to contain not only a social-cognitive judgment but, beyond that, a judgment of prescriptive valuing.

TABLE 1

MODES OF JUDGMENT OF VALUE AND TRUTH

I. **Socially Prescriptive Mode of Judgment**
   A. Ends of Welfare Orientation
   B. Character and Sanctions Orientation
   C. Normative Order Orientation
   D. Commutative Justice Orientation
   E. Justice as Fairness Orientation

II. **Practical Mode of Judgment**
   (Judgments of social choice and value based on considerations of what are the characteristics of the actor and the situation rather than what ought to be.)

*Adapted from material preparatory to the forthcoming book by L. Kohlberg, *et al.*, *Assessing Moral Judgment Stages: A Manual* (Humanitas Press).

    A. Psychological Orientation. (Judgments of what the self or actor would do, not what he should do, in terms of orientating to needs or motives, mental health, etc.)

    B. Pragmatic Orientation. (Judgments of should or would of social choice based on efficiency of means, probability of success or cost/benefits without reference to moral standards or ends.)

III. **Theoretical or Non-Practical Mode Judgment**

    A. Truth Orientation. (Judgment of the better or worse as the more true or as leading to the pure truth.)

    B. Aesthetic Orientation. (Judgment of the better or worse as the more beautiful.)

    C. Ontological or Religious Orientation. (Judgment of the better or worse as the more ultimately real or as coming from or leading to the ultimately real.)

IV. **Cognitive or Descriptive-Analytic Mode Judgment**

    A. Descriptive or Metaethical Statements. (Statements about the facts of human morality and moral decisions.)

    B. Descriptions of Social Practices or Behavior. (Statements about the facts of human psychology and human institutions which enter into social decisions.)

    C. Psychological Description

    D. Description of Physical-Biological Events

The *development* of moral judgment has been studied by Kohlberg and colleagues for nearly twenty years. To understand Kohlberg's work on moral development is to understand the work of any structural-developmental theorist. At the heart of this approach is the distinction between *quality* and *quantity*, and between *form* and *content*, in age-related change. Most age-related changes are changes in quantitative rather than qualitative aspects of responses, and do not involve transformations describable in formal terms. For example, as the child matures, there is an increment in speed and efficiency of immediate memory and information processing. Such a change involves differences in elements in information, but is not qualitatively new and does not involve a difference in form or organization.

A qualitatively, formally new kind of age-related change is called a "stage." Structural-developmental psychologists define the stage construct in terms of the following characteristics (Piaget, 1967/1971):

1. The particular modes of thought significant for a given stage constitute a "structured whole." As noted, a given stage-response on a task does not just represent a specific response; rather, it represents an underlying thought-organization.

2. The stages form an invariant sequence, order or succession in individual development.

3. Stages form an order of increasing differentiation and integration. Higher stages displace (and in another sense, reintegrate) the structures found at lower stages. There is a hierarchical preference within the individual, that is, a disposition to prefer a solution of a problem at the highest level available to him.

Theory and research on the characteristics of stage development have been discussed in recent psychological literature (e.g., Broughton, 1976a; Flavell, 1971; Gibbs, 1975).

To introduce Kohlberg's work, we will first discuss three fundamental *levels* in the development of moral judgment. The stages comprising these levels will be discussed subsequently. The levels of moral judgment are defined as: (a) general ways of defining what is right or valuable, and (b) reasons for upholding the right (see Table 2). The preconventional moral level is the level of most children under ten, some adolescents, and a few adults. The conventional level is the level of most adolescents and adults in our society and in other societies. The postconventional level is reached by a minority of adults, usually after the age of 20 to 25. The term "conventional" refers to judgments which uphold rules and expectations because of their function given dyadic groups or society as a whole. The preconventional level is so-called because an understanding and appreciation of conventional or societal rules and authority is not yet evident. The subject at the postconventional level understands society's rules and goes beyond them. Of most concern to us within the level of postconventional thinking is *principled* thinking; the principled individual basically accepts his particular society's rules insofar as his appreciation of them can be based upon general moral principles or values he has constructed, principles which ought to underly and guide any society's rules. When a society's rules or practices come into conflict with these principles, an individual at this level judges by principle.

TABLE 2

THREE LEVELS OF MORAL JUDGMENT

A. Preconventional Level

1. *What is right?* Right is usually following the rules. The rules, however, are literal. They are not understood in terms of the expectations of a society or of a notion of a good person. Bad is a label applied to an act without considering a person's motive. What is right is limited to following concrete rules or orders with power and punishment behind them; it is not defined in terms of the expectations and welfare of others. Where right is not a matter of obeying concrete rules or commands, it is a matter of serving interests of the self or those close to the self.
2. *Reasons for upholding right:* Reasons include self-interest, avoidance of punishment, deference to power, avoiding physical harm to others, and exchange of favors.
3. *Social perspective:* Right and good are seen from the point of view of one individual looking at other individuals or at the physical dimensions and consequences of rules and actions.

B. Conventional Level

1. *What is right?* Right means conforming to and upholding the rules, roles, and expectations of society at large, or conforming to the rules and expectations of a smaller group, like one's religious or political denomination. "Conforming to and upholding" rules and roles means more than just obedience, it means the inner motivation corresponding to the rules.
2. *Reasons for upholding right:* Reasons include approval and general social opinion, loyalty to persons and groups, the welfare of others and of society.

3. *Social perspective:* Right and good are seen from the point of view of a member of society or of a smaller group. The point of view is consciously shared with others. Individual or egoistic points of view are subordinated to the shared point of view.

C. Post-Conventional or Principled Level

1. *What is right?* Right is defined by general or universal human rights, values or principles which society and the individual should uphold. While it is usually right to uphold the law because the law does protect human rights, violations of the law are justified where the law is not protecting human rights.
2. *Reasons for upholding right:* Reasons are essentially defined by a "social contract," by the notion that by living in society you have made a generalized commitment to respect and uphold the rights of others (and the laws this entails) or by "principle," by commitment to moral principles which it is believed any moral person would perceive as rationally valid.
3. *Social perspective:* The perspective is *prior to society.* It is that of a rational individual defining values and principles prior to society or as a basis for defining a good society and committing himself to society.

One way of understanding the three levels is to think of them as three different types of relationship between the self and society's rules and expectations. From this point of view, a person at the preconventional level is one for whom rules and social expectations are something external to the self. A conventional person has achieved a socially normative appreciation of the rules and expectations of others, especially authorities, and identifies the self with the occupants of social or societal role relationships. The principled person has differentiated self from normative roles and defines values in terms of self-constructed reflective principles.

To illustrate intuitively these levels as they appear in our interviews, we can cite three different responses to a dilemma regarding whether or not to tell one's father about a brother's disobedience after the brother has confided in you. Here is the response of Danny (a subject in our longitudinal study) at the preconventional level.

> In one way it would be right to tell because his father might beat him up. In another way it's wrong because his brother will beat him up if he tells.

We can infer that others' rules and expectations for Danny are outside the self. The self's moral judgment predicts or describes them; it does not identify with them.

Here is an excerpt from an interview with another longitudinal subject, Andy:

> He should think of his brother but it's more important to be a good son. Your father has done so much for you. I'd have a conscience if I didn't tell, more than to my brother, because my father couldn't trust me. My brother would understand, our father has done so much for him, too.

Andy's response seems to be based not on what others will do, but on the internal concerns or expectations of others; Andy identifies with the "good son" in a normative family relationship. We judge that Andy is entering the conventional level in moral development.

Here is a response given by Ken (a third longitudinal subject) to the dilemma:

> Well, it's not really a matter of a brother and son decision, it's a matter of a right or wrong decision. Is the father right or is the son right? The father's act in the first place wasn't justified. Because of the original lack of good faith on the father's part, I don't think the brother has any obligation to tell. If the father's position had been justified, then I think Joe's lying would be unjustified. As it is, the brother has an obligation to keep quiet; his brother confided in him and trusted him.

Note that in Ken's response, the self's moral judgment is differentiated from the rules and expectations of others. What others expect is one thing, what is right is another. Moreover, although what others expect may coincide with what is right, the right is essentially based on principled consideration. For Ken the focus is not on specific rules or role expectations, but on the question of whether conditions which may justify an obligation are or are not present. Suggested by Ken's response is a principled level of moral judgment.

Having briefly described and illustrated each of these three levels, we can now ask what underlies and structures these levels, what gives them coherence. This question has many answers, but the most immediate one has to do with the *social perspective* of each level. Let us consider the conventional level first. We said earlier that the conventional level, the self is "identified" with society and its rules. We need now to clarify the concept of identification in terms of the conventional social perspective, that of the "member of society." The term identification is ambiguous; it supposes we are standing outside of Andy, our conventional subject, and judging the relation of his "self" to society, i.e., that he identifies with its expectations. We need to translate this notion into Andy's perspective, since he will not say "I am conventional, I judge in terms of what others expect of me," etc. The conventional social perspective, that of identification with societal rules and expectations, is the "we perspective" of a member of society who speaks as a member of society. The social perspective is that of a member of society (of the "average" person in society who recognizes he belongs to groups and institutions) who judges from a point of view which he believes is shared with other "average members of society." The ends, values, or needs of the single individual are subordinated to the ends and needs of the group (or of both parties in a shared relationship) or of the majority. To illustrate the conventional social perspective we cite Joe's (age 17) response to the question, "Why shouldn't you steal from a store?"

> It's a matter of law. It's one of our rules that we're trying to help protect everyone, protect property, not just to protect a store. It's something that's needed in our society. If we didn't have these laws, people would steal, they wouldn't have to work for a living and our whole society would get out of kilter.

Clearly, Joe is speaking as a member of society. "It's one of *our* rules that *we're* making to protect everyone in *our* society." Not only does he refer to the needs of society, but it is from the standpoint of *us*, members of society. The thing Joe is concerned about is *keeping the law.* His reason for being concerned is the *good of society as a whole.* This concern for the good of society arises from his taking the point of view of "us, members of society." The object of his concern, the good of society, in turn derives from a point of view, that of a "member of society."

Let us contrast this conventional member of society perspective with the perspective of the *preconventional concrete individual.* This point of view is that of the individual actor in the situation thinking about his interests and those of other individuals he may care about. Joe, whose conventional level response was just quoted, is one of the subjects whom we followed over a 15-year period. He was first interviewed at age 10, at which point he illustrated the preconventional individual perspective in response to the same question:

> It's not good to steal from the store. It's against the law. Someone could see you and call the police.

The reason for not stealing and for obeying the law, in other words, is punishment. The perspective here is preconventional, i.e., that of an individual considering right and wrong in terms of external consequences to the self. Joe at age 17 also considers that stealing is "against the law," but "law" in his thinking at that point is "something that's needed in our society." "Being against the law," then, seems something very different at the preconventional as opposed to conventional levels.

Let us now consider the perspective of the postconventional level. It is in one sense like the preconventional perspective in that it returns to the standpoint of the individual rather than taking the point of view of "us, the members of society." The individual point of view at the postconventional level, however, is one which can be universal for *all* individuals; it is that of any rational moral individual. The postconventional person questions and redefines the "member of society" perspective from an individual moral perspective so that social obligations are defined in ways which can be justified to any moral individual. An individual's commitment to basic morality or moral principles is seen as prior to, or necessary for, taking society's perspective or accepting society's laws and values. Society's laws and values, in turn, should be ones to which any reasonable person could commit himself, whatever his place in society and to whatever society he belongs. The postconventional perspective, then, is *prior to society,* it is the perspective of an *individual who has made the moral commitments or holds the standards on which a good or just society must be based.* This is a perspective by which: (a) a particular society or set of social practices may be judged, and (b) persons may rationally commit themselves to society.

Again, we will use Joe as an example. Joe was preconventional at age 10, conventional at age 17. Here is his postconventional response at age 24:

WHY SHOULDN'T SOMEONE STEAL FROM A STORE?
It's violating another person's rights, in this case to property.

DOES THE LAW ENTER IN?
Well, the law in most cases is based on what is morally right so it's not a separate subject, it's a consideration.

WHAT DOES MORALITY OR MORALLY RIGHT MEAN TO YOU?
Recognizing the rights of other individuals, first to life and then to do as he pleases as long as it doesn't interfere with somebody else's rights.

The wrongness of stealing is that it violates moral rights of individuals, which come prior to law and society. Property rights derive from more universal human rights (freedoms or rights which do not interfere with the like freedom of others). The demands of law and society derive from universal moral rights, rather than vice versa.

It should be noted that, in itself, reference to the words "rights" or "morally right" or "conscience" does not distinguish conventional from post-conventional morality. Orienting to the "morally right" thing or "following conscience" as against following the law need not imply the postconventional perspective of the rational moral individual. The terms "morality" and "con-science" may be used to refer to group rules and values which conflict with laws, or with the rules of the majority group. A Jehovah's Witness will go to jail for "conscience," but conscience may only mean God's law as interpreted by one's society or group; it does not necessarily mean the standpoint of any individual oriented to universal moral principles or values. To count as postconventional, such ideas or terms must be used in such a way that it is clear that they have a foundation for a rational or moral individual whose commitment to a group or society is based on prior principles. As an example, "trust" is a basic value at both the conventional and the postconventional levels. At the conventional level, trustworthiness is something you expect of others in your society. Joe expresses this as follows at age 17 in Story I:

WHY SHOULD A PROMISE BE KEPT, ANYWAY?
Friendship is based on trust. If you can't trust a person, there's little ground to deal with him. You should try to be as reliable as possible because people remember you by this, you're more respected if you can be depended upon.

At this conventional level Joe sees trust from the perspective of a truster as well as from that of someone who could break a trust. He sees that not only does the individual need to be trusted to have social relationships with others and for respect but that this is true because, as a member of society, he expects it of others in general.

At the postconventional level, the individual takes a further step. He does not assume that he is automatically in a society in which he needs the friendship and respect of other individuals. As principled thinking emerges, the subject answers from the point of view of why having any society or social relationships presupposes trust. He recognizes that if the individual is to contract into society, he must be trustworthy. As an example, Joe at 24 answers:

I think human relationships in general are based on trust, on believing in other individuals. If you have no way of believing in someone else, you can't deal with anyone else and it becomes every man for himself. Everything you do in a day's time is related to somebody else and if you can't deal on a fair basis, you have chaos.

In situations of moral conflict, the principled individual is aware of "the moral point of view," a point of view which each individual in the situation ought to adopt and act on. When obligations defined by fixed legal-social norms conflict with those established from the moral point of view, the latter obligations are usually given priority. At age 24 Joe is beginning to reflect "the moral point of view" as a decision-making perspective in his response to Story III:

> SHOULD HEINZ STEAL THE DRUG?
> Yes. It is the husband's duty to save his wife. The fact that her life is in danger transcends every other standard you might use to judge his action. Life is more important than property.
>
> SUPPOSE IT WERE A FRIEND, NOT HIS WIFE?
> I don't think that would be much different from a moral point of view. It's still a human being in danger.
>
> SUPPOSE IT WERE A STRANGER?
> To be consistent, yes, from a moral standpoint.
>
> WHAT IS THIS MORAL STANDPOINT?
> I think every individual has a right to live and if there is a way of saving an individual, he should be saved.
>
> SHOULD THE JUDGE PUNISH THE HUSBAND?
> Usually the moral and legal standpoints coincide. Here they conflict. The judge should weigh the moral standpoint more heavily but preserve the legal law in punishing Heinz lightly.

II. The Domain of Moral Judgment

Moral judgment is a philosophical as well as psychological domain, and can be philosophically conceptualized as a family of particular valuing orientations. Many particular moral orientations have been emphasized by various thinkers throughout philosophical history. For John Stuart Mill, the primary moral orientation was to ultimate ends and consequences, and to the maximization of human welfare or happiness. Aristotle saw morality as an orientation to one's highest personal and social perfection. For Kant, the primary moral orientation was to the concept of obligation to universal moral law (the "categorical imperative"). More recent moral philosophers have centered their ethical writings upon concepts like harmony or harmonious happiness (R. B. Perry) or fairness or justice (J. Rawls). In Tables 1 and 3 we list five basic orientations within the philosophical domain of moral judgment.

TABLE 3

MORAL ORIENTATIONS AND CONCERNS

A. **Ends of Welfare Orientation**
  1. Personal Prudence Concern

    2. Altruism Concern
    3. Group Welfare Concern

B. Character and Sanctions Orientation
    1. Character Concern
    2. Sanctions Concern

C. Normative Order Orientation
    1. Rulefulness Concern
    2. Role Norms and Obligations Concern

D. Commutative Justice Orientation
    1. Negative Reciprocity Concern
    2. Positive Reciprocity Concern
    3. Contractual Agreement and Trust Concern

E. Justice as Fairness Orientation
    1. Liberty and Autonomy Concern
    2. Respecting and Balancing Perspectives Concern
    3. Equality or Equity Concern

A. Moral Concerns

Nested within each moral orientation are two or three fundamental *moral concerns*. We define "moral concerns" as attitudes and concepts constructed by the individual which endow objects and events with moral value. Comprising the Ends of Welfare orientation, for example, are a Personal Prudence concern, an Altruism concern, and a Group Welfare concern; the Normative Order orientation breaks down into a concern for Rulefulness and a concern for Role Obligations; and so on. We believe these Concerns (see Table 3) approximate functionally universal moral valuing considerations.

B. Moral Issues

A moral concern becomes a moral judgment when applied to some referent, specifically some valued external object, event, or institution which we call an issue. Issues, in other words, are the conceptual objects of moral concern. For example, when we ask the question, "Should someone who steals out of extreme need be punished for breaking the law?" the focal issue is punishment. A hypothetical subject's moral judgment on this issue could indicate numerous concerns (e.g., Character, Rulefulness, Negative Reciprocity). It may be helpful to note some contrasts between Concerns and Issues:

    1. Concerns are general across Issues and situations; Issues are only relevant to some situations. While the Concern for character is evidenced in diverse situations, the Punishment and Blame Issue arises only in some contexts.

    2. Concerns are terminal values; Issues are usually instrumental values. Punishment (an Issue) is a good because it is instrumental to maintaining some Concern (Character, Rulefulness, Negative Reciprocity, Equality, etc.). Someone prescribing the "just due" of the Negative Reciprocity Concern is espousing a terminal value, a good in itself.

    3. Concerns are inherently normative; Issues need not be. General "is"

questions about Issues ("What is property, law, life, etc.?"), call for sheer social scientific description of the social institutions and motives involved. These descriptions do not necessarily include judgments. General "is" questions about Concerns ("What is justice, altruistic love, conscience, etc.?") ask not only for what a neutral observer would find them to be, but also what they ought to be.

4. Concerns are unitary concepts; issues are usually complexes of ideas. For example, Rulefulness is the concern for maintaining social standards, whereas law is an Issue referring to a complex institution involving the legal profession, the judiciary, the legislature, etc.

To say that a Concern is general, terminal, moral, and unitary, is to say, broadly, that it is *internal*—it is something "in" the person, something he "carries around with him" that defines or conceptualizes, for *him*, the value of objects or situations. Issues always involve something "out there," which are social objects and events rather than values and norms of individuals. Ten fundamental Moral Issues are listed in Table 4.

TABLE 4
THE TEN MORAL ISSUES

I. **Punishment and Blame**
Should someone be punished or not? Why?
What is fair punishment?

II. **Property**
Should someone give, take or exchange property or not? Why?
What are property rights?

III. **Affiliation Roles**
Should someone help another or maintain the other's expectations in a personal relationship? Why?
What are the motives and obligations of a good family member or friend?

IV. **Law**
Should someone obey or maintain a law? Why?
What are the characteristics of a good law?

V. **Life**
Should someone save a life or not? Why?
What makes life valuable?

VI. **Truth**
Should someone tell the truth or allow the truth to be disclosed or not? Why?
What defines truth-telling and why is it valuable?

VII. **Governance**
Should someone obey or accept the authority of another person or of a government or rule-making group? Why?
What are the characteristics of a good governor and a good citizen?

VIII. **Civil Rights and Social Justice**
Should someone violate or uphold the political, economic, and social rights of another person or group? Why?
What are the basic political, economic and social rights?

IX. **Sex or Eroticism**
Should one have a sexual relationship or not? Why?
What is the nature of a good erotic relationship and why is it valuable?

X.   Morality and Mores
Should one follow one's moral opinion or conscience when it conflicts with law, love or self-interest? Why?
What is the nature of morality and what is the basis of its validity?

The "externality" of the Moral Issues is indicated by the fact that the issues can also be conceptualized as moral institutions (where "institution" is a complex of rules and roles defining rights and obligations and centering on some overall purpose or value; cf. Rawls, 1971). Punishment, for example, is a part institution within the legal institution or criminal justice system which involves judge, police, lawyer, defendent, legislatory, defines specific rights and duties, and has an overall value or purpose (civil order, justice).

The Moral Issues refer only to institutions which can be pertinent to moral discourse. They do *not* extend to institutions related to non-moral modes of judgment (see Table 1). Examples of non-moral institutions are: (1) the institution of science and its value objects, publications of truth; (2) the institution of religion and its value object, faith; (3) the institution of education and its value object, human development; (4) the institution of "culture" and its value object, art; and (5) the institutions of engineering and technology and their value object, production. One clear way in which the moral issues and institutions differ from the non-moral institutions is that violation of the norms of the moral institutions are often criminal offenses, i.e., deviations not only forbidden by law but requiring punitive sanctions (as opposed to the restitutive sanctions of civil law). A second related distinction between the ten moral issues and other institutions or value objects is that each of the moral issues define certain basic or universal rights. All citizens have rights to (1) freedom from arbitrary punishment, (2) property, (3) to enter into affiliative or family contracts and relations, (4) political rights to a say in the government, (5) legal rights, (6) a right to life, (7) certain civil rights, (8) a right to access to information, (9) a right to sexual liaison and privacy, and (10) a right to moral respect or dignity. It would seem strange in contrast to see that there are fixed rights to scientific knowledge, to artistic experience, religious revelation or faith, etc.

III. The Development of Moral Judgment

In this section we will refine and elaborate upon our introductory discussion of moral judgment development as the sequential growth of levels in social perspective taking and prescriptive valuing.

A. Stages

A fuller understanding of the moral judgment levels requires an appreciation of moral judgment *stages.* An indication of the six moral stages is provided in Table 5.

TABLE 5

SIX STAGES OF MORAL THOUGHT

Level A: Preconventional Level

Stage 1: The Heteronomous Stage
Content of Stage:
> *Right is blind obedience to rules and authority, avoiding punishment, and not doing physical harm.*
>
> a) *What is right* is to avoid breaking rules backed by punishment, obedience for its own sake, and avoiding physical damage to persons and property.
> b) *The reasons for doing right* are avoidance of punishment and the superior power of authorities.

Social Perspective of Stage:
> *Egocentric point of view.* Doesn't consider the interests of others or recognize they differ from actor's. Doesn't relate two points of view. Actions are considered physically rather than in terms of psychological interests of others. Confusion of authority's perspective with one's own.

Stage 2: The Stage of Individualism and Instrumental Purpose and Exchange
Content of Stage:
> *Right is serving one's own or other's needs and making fair deals in terms of concrete exchange.*
>
> a) *What is right* is following rules but when it is to someone's immediate interest. Right is acting to meet one's own interests and needs and letting others do the same. Right is also what is fair, that is, what is an equal exchange, a deal, an agreement.
> b) *The reason for doing right* is to serve one's own needs or interests in a world where you have to recognize that other people have their interests, too.

Social Perspective of Stage:
> *Concrete individualistic perspective.* Separates own interests and points of view from those of authorities and others. Aware everybody has their own interest to pursue and these conflict, so that right is relative (in the concrete individualistic sense). Integrates or relates conflicting individual interests to one another through instrumental exchange of services, through instrumental need for the other and the other's good will, or through fairness as treating each individual's interest as equal.

Level B: Conventional Level

Stage 3: The Stage of Mutual Interpersonal Expectations, Relationships, and Interpersonal Conformity
Content of Stage:
> *The right is playing a good (nice) role, being concerned about other people and their feelings, keeping loyalty and trust with partners, and being motivated to follow rules and expectations.*
>
> a) *What is right* is living up to what is expected by people close to you or what people generally expect of people in your role as son, sister, friend, etc. "Being good" is important and means having good motives, the showing of concern about others. It also means keeping mutual relationships, maintaining trust, loyalty, respect, and gratitude.
> b) *Reasons for doing right* are: 1) the need to be good in your own eyes and those of others, 2) your caring for others, and 3) because if you put yourself in the other guy's place you would want good behavior from the self (Golden Rule).

Social Perspective of Stage:
> *Perspective of the individual in relationship to other individuals.* Aware of shared feelings, agreements, and expectations which take primacy over individual interests. Relates points of view through the "concrete Golden Rule," putting yourself in the other person's shoes. Does not consider generalized "system" perspective.

Stage 4: The Social System and Conscience Stage
Content of Stage:
> The right is doing one's duty in society, upholding the social order, and the welfare of society or the group.

- a) *What is right* is fulfilling the actual duties to which you have agreed. Laws are to be upheld except in extreme cases where they conflict with other fixed social duties. Right is also contributing to society, the group, or institution.
- b) *The reasons for doing right* are to keep the institution going as a whole, "what if everyone did it," or self-respect or conscience as meeting one's defined obligations.

Social Perspective of Stage:
> Differentiates societal point of view from interpersonal agreement or motives. Takes the point of view of the system which defines roles and rules. Considers individual relations in terms of place in the system.

B/C Transitional Level
> This level is postconventional but not yet principled.

Content of Transitional Stage(s):
> 4(5) *Obligation to our conscience orientation.* Aware of relativity of different social standards, so orients to personal moral values or conscience. "Conscience," however, is the internalized social standards of Stage 4. One has a duty to follow one's conscience. There may be an objective external moral law expressing the essence of social morality.

> 4-1/2 *Choice is personal and subjective.* It is based on emotions and hedonism rather than conscience, since conscience is seen as arbitrary and relative, as are terms like "duty," "morally right," etc.

> 5(4) *Decision is personal and subjective unless it impinges on rights of others.* Morality is arbitrary and relative because one has the right to free choice. Rights, however, are bounded by the like rights of others.

Transitional Social Perspective
> Subjective and "outside of society." The perspective is that of an individual standing outside of his own society and considering himself as an individual making decisions without a generalized commitment or contract with society. One can pick and choose obligations which are defined by particular societies, but one has no principles for such choice.

C. Postconventional and Principled Level

Such decisions are generated from rights, values, or principles which are (or could be) agreeable to all individuals composing or creating a society that *would* have fair and beneficial practices.

Stage 5: The Stage of Social Contract or Utility and of Individual rights
Content of Stage:
> The right is upholding the basic rights, values, and legal contracts of a society, even when they conflict with the concrete rules and laws of the group.

- a) *What is right* is being aware of the fact that people hold a variety of values and opinions, that most values and rules are relative to your group. These "relative" rules should usually be upheld, however, in the interest of impartiality and because they are the social contract. Some non-relative values and rights like *life* and *liberty*, however, must be upheld in any society and regardless of majority opinion.
- b) *Reasons for doing right* are, in general, that Stage 5 individuals feel obligated to obey the law because they have made a social contract to make and abide by laws for the good of all and to protect their own rights and the rights of others. They feel that family, friendship, trust, and work obligations are also commitments or contracts they have freely entered into and entail respect for the rights of others. They are concerned that laws and duties be based on rational calculation of overall utility, "the greatest good for the greatest number."

Social Perspective of Stage:
> *Prior to society perspective.* Perspective of a rational individual aware of values and rights prior to social attachments and contracts. Integrates perspectives by formal mechanisms of agreement, contract, objective impartiality and due process. Considers "moral point of view," "legal point of view," recognizes they conflict and finds it difficult to integrate them.

Stage 6: The Stage of Universal Ethical Principles
Content of Stage:
  Guidance by universal ethical principles which all humanity should follow.
  a) *What is right:* Stage 6 is guided by self-chosen ethical principles. Particular laws or
     social agreements are usually valid because they rest on such principles. When laws
     violate these principles, one acts in accordance with the principle. Principles are
     universal principles of justice: the equality of human rights and respect for the
     dignity of human beings as individual persons. These are not merely values which
     are recognized, they are principles used to generate particular decisions.
  b) *The reason for doing right* is that, as a rational person, the Stage 6 individual has
     seen the validity of principles and has become committed to them.
Social Perspective of Stage:
  Perspective of a "moral point of view" from which social arrangements derive or on
which they are grounded. The perspective is that of any rational individual recognizing the
nature of morality or the basic moral premise of respect for other persons as ends, not
means.

Perhaps the best way of getting a handle on the moral judgment stages is
through a description of their underlying social perspectives. We will start our
discussion with the preconventional stages, stages 1 and 2. Recall the dilemma,
described earlier, on whether an older brother should tell his father about his
younger brother's misdeed, revealed in confidence. We quoted ten-year-old
Danny's reply:

> In one way it was right to tell because his father might beat him up. In another way
> it's wrong because his brother will beat him up if he tells.

At age 13, asked about the same dilemma, Danny replies:

> The brother should not tell or he'll get his brother in trouble. If he wants his brother
> to keep quiet for him sometime, he'd better not squeal now.

Even in Danny's reply at 13, there is no evidence that social expectations are
appreciated in a normative sense. In both cases Danny's moral judgment is
preconventional.

It will be worth our while to consider the two cases more closely. In
Danny's reply at age 10, right and wrong are scarcely distinguished from physical
consequences. This is Stage 1. Underlying this Stage is a social perspective centering on physical consequences to the self. Danny's second reply is a bit different. There is now an awareness of the reciprocal points of view of individuals
with a more psychological understanding of their pragmatic interests. Specifically, Danny's judgment now reflects concern about the welfare of his brother on
the basis of his own interests as they feed into the interests of the brother
through exchange. This more psychological, pragmatic perspective is that of
Stage 2, the "instrumental exchange" stage of moral judgment.

The conventional level, comprising Stages 3 and 4, is perhaps the easiest
level to explain in terms of social perspectives. Again, let us consider two examples (both quoted previously). Here is Andy's response:

He should think of his brother but it's more important to be a good son. Your father has done so much for you. I'd have a conscience if I didn't tell, more than to my brother, because my father couldn't trust me. My brother would understand, our father has done so much for him, too.

Here is Joe's response:

WHY SHOULDN'T YOU STEAL FROM A STORE?
It's a matter of law. It's one of our rules that we're trying to help protect everyone, protect property, not just to protect a store. It's something that's needed in our society. If we didn't have these laws, people would steal, they wouldn't have to work for a living and our whole society would get out of kilter.

The self implicit in both responses is identifiable as that of a "member of society" or social group (a good son, a good citizen). Again, however, a distinction can be made. In the case of Andy's judgment, the "member of society" is an occupant of a role in a dyadic relationship (Andy as son to father, brother to sibling). Andy's moral decision is based on how best to be a "good" (trustworthy, grateful) role occupant, a kind of decision-making which is the hallmark of Stage 3. Evident in Joe's reply, on the other hand, is a full-fledged member-of-society perspective, the perspective of someone taking the point of view of a social *system*. Joe is concerned with social institutions and practices (property, law) and appreciates their value in terms of maintaining society. The social-system perspective underlies Stage 4.

Turning to the postconventional level, a typical Stage 5 orientation distinguishes between a moral point of view and a legal-institutional point of view and understands, at least to some extent, the priority of the moral point of view to that of the social system. The following response with respect to Dilemma III (see Appendix, Form A) suggests Stage 5:

SHOULD HEINZ STEAL THE DRUG?
It's worth it in a sense. It's all well and good to talk about property rights but they don't mean much in a society that doesn't value human life higher.

At Stage 6, obligation is clearly defined in terms of universal ethical principles of justice from which basic legal arrangements may be derived. An example of a Stage 6 response to Dilemma III is as follows:

It is wrong legally but right morally. Systems of law are valid only insofar as they reflect the sort of moral law all rational humans can accept. The existence of an implicit social contract and the violation of the conditions of the contract is always something that must be considered. If one goes this far, one must consider the personal justice involved, which is the root of the social contract. The ground on which society should be created is individual justice, the right of every person to an equal consideration of his claims in every situation, not just those which can be codified in law. Personal justice means, "treat each person as an end, not a means."

Indicated by this response is a very clear awareness of the principle, "Treat every individual as an end, not a means," which is more basic than, and which generates, the socio-legal point of view.

B. Specific Patterns of Stage Growth

Our concern in this subsection is with specific patterns of growth in moral thinking. We speculate that our Issue system (see Section II) provides a useful framework for understanding patterns of growth in moral judgment stage development. Specifically, a given issue may be a *point of entry* to a given stage. Reasoning at a higher stage seems first to appear with regard to a particular issue, then generalize or "spread" to other issues (much in Piaget's sense of "horizontal decalage"). For example, a child first moves to instrumental exchanges (Stage 2) in terms of the Property Issue. Later he generalizes instrumental exchanges from Property relations to affiliation and authority in the family. Another example is the change from Stage 2 into the ideal-reciprocity or Stage 3 "entry point," affiliative relations thinking. This transformation is especially dramatic; subsequent stage development on the Affiliations issue involves further structurings related to social systems and fundamental human rights, but the innovation of ideal reciprocity retains its central meaning. In general, the most dramatic or qualitative structural differences on an issue are found at the stage for which that issue serves as an entry point.

Since the institution of property and economy is concrete, instrumental, and a system of exchange, it is understandable that property is the entry point to Stage 2. The notion that the child enters Stage 2 in terms of the economic system is made plausible by the fact that children do become concerned about property and contractual exchange in the concrete operational period (age 7-10; Piaget, 1932/1965).

The emergence of Stage 3 means that the child enters the family affiliative system, which, like the economic institution, is definable as a dyadic institution. Added to physical exchanges by the affiliative system are emotional or expressive interactions, i.e., the giving and receiving of love or concern for the welfare of the other. While family relations do include the exchange of valued goods, their central focus is upon affection, care, and intimacy. The family affiliative system is a system of normatively regulated exchanges of emotion, oriented to mutual loyalty.

Underlying the emergence in the older child of normative concerns for caring and mutual loyalty are qualitatively new or innovative developmental events. Of course, from an early age the child has been engaged in exchanges of affection and emotional expression. Affiliative values cannot become ideally normative values, however, until they are structured by a simultaneous and mutual or "third-person," social perspective-taking (Selman, 1976). The child's construction of this social role-taking perspective means that he achieves an appreciation that both individuals in a dyadic relationship are co-conscious or are sharing an attitude or value because they are oriented to one another. The child's third-person or "ideal" appreciation of sharing and mutual loyalty relates, in turn, to the general discovery at Stage 3 of the *intrinsic values of relationships* as opposed to the values and exchanges of the individuals (and their separate interests) involved.

The next "entry" institution is the Political or Governance order and the related institution of Law. Governance is closely related to "authority" because the central concerns of political relations as such are relations of power as authority. The forms of government, e.g., monarchy, democracy, dictatorship, and autocracy, describe various patterns of distribution of authority where authority is considered *legitimated* power. In order to orient to authority systems as "intrinsically valuable," the child must see that all subsets of relations are themselves logically ordered in relation to one another and so become "immoral" or "chaotic" if they do not have a third ordering principle, an orientation to common rules or to a common authority. What is central to Stage 4, then, is the notion that each actor is self-consciously oriented to the *system* in which he has a role, and sees the need of that system. The system is not only made up of common members (Stage 3), but of roles orienting to one another in an over-arching structure.

Entry points to Stage 5 are Civil Rights, Social Justice, and Life. Stage 5 is centrally oriented to establishing social justice and civil rights. At Stage 4 justice and order (derived from the authority of the governance system) tend to be contiguous with or subordinate to society's will. The only alternative conception to the social order, to society, is a "state of nature" conceived as chaoe, violence, and the lack of "civilization." In contrast, Stage 5 considers (at least implicitly) a hypothetical State of Nature in which men rationally and nondestructively pursue self-interest and have rights. This implies that there are many possible systems of social order, and that one searches for a universal legal-moral basis (as embodied in, e.g., a Constitution, Bill of Rights) valid for any particular order. Legal justice itself is seen as involving, first, formal or procedural justice, the impartial or objective definition and application of law, and, second, substantive justice, the maintenance of equal liberty and opportunity for individuals and groups. Life becomes a central issue at Stage 5 in that it becomes a universal intrinsic right.

The "entry point" from Stage 5 into Stage 6 has been difficult to determine because of the rarity of Stage 6 data, and we regard the matter as one requiring further research before grounded speculation can be offered.

IV. Assessment of Moral Judgment Stages

The question we now address is a practical one: assuming our theory of the domain and development of moral judgment is accepted as true, how does the researcher collect appropriate data and proceed to identify, validly and reliably, moral judgment stages? The question is of course crucial, for if the stage constructs cannot be reliably and validly scored, then their empirical significance is problematical.

The bridge we use to span the gap between theory and data—that is, our research instrument—has three parts: a standard moral interview format, "structural" interviewing techniques, and a standard-form scoring manual.

A. The Moral Interview Format

The dilemmas used in our standard moral interview are included in the Appendix. These dilemmas were selected and constructed with the following criteria in mind:

1. The dilemmas should be basically comprehensible to—and represent moral conflicts for—preadolescents, adolescents, and adults in all cultures. Conflicts uniquely relevant to particular age, sex, and cultural groups were avoided. As an example of success in meeting this criterion, Turiel (1973) found that sex of subject, sex of agent in the dilemma, and sex of interviewer did not affect stage of moral reasoning on the dilemma. The fact that the dilemmas represent moral conflict to all age and cultural groups is indicated by the fact that there are substantial splits in decision-choice on each dilemma in any age or cultural group.

2. The dilemmas should sample the basic *Moral Issues* (see Section II) about which adolescents and adults are concerned in every culture. Basically, the Moral Issue is the general thing being solved, judged, or reasoned about in the particular dilemma. Moral Issues define an action or choice (obey the *law*, don't obey the *law*) and a "value" (Is the *law* always good or not?). A moral dilemma involves a choice between conflicting values. As an example, take Dilemmas III or IV. At higher stages (and to some extent at all stages) the central choice is between *Life* and *Law*. Dilemmas III' and IV' (sequels to III and IV) involve the issues of Punishment and of Conscience/Morality. In general, a set of moral issues can define the nature of moral conflict situations. The moral issues represented in the two forms of the Moral Judgment Interview (Forms A and B), by dilemma, are as follows:

Form A
Story III: Life (and Affiliation);
             Law (and Property)
Story III':   Punishment and Blame (and
             Governance);
             Conscience/Morality
Story I: Property;
             Affiliation

Form B
Story IV: Life (and Civil Rights);
             Law
Story IV':   (same as for Story III')
Story II: (same as for Story I)

The standard interview is designed to "push" for the respondent's highest level of thinking on each issue. The standard scoring manual allows a clear distinction between high sounding verbalizations elicited by "high probes" and genuine higher stage thinking.

B. "Structural" Interviewing

"Structural" interviewing, considered somewhat whimsically, is the art of asking a subject "why" enough times to find out how he gets profound, but not enough times to find out how he gets angry. The goal of moral judgment interviewing, in other words, is to penetrate beyond a subject's opinions, attitudes, or beliefs, to the reasoning or justification which directs them. Many of the probe questions we have found most useful over the years are incorporated into the standard interview format (see Appendix), and for this reason the interviewing forms can in many cases be distributed for written responses without any individual interviewing. In general, however, scoring validity and reliability are promoted by individual verbal administration of the interview, preferably by interviewers who are experienced in stage-scoring and in the techniques of "structural" interviewing.

Discussion of specific interviewing techniques would require considerable space. Briefly, good or "structural" interviewing means fulfilling the needs to: (1) explain to the subject the interview goal of trying to understand and bring out his or her underlying thinking on moral dilemmas; (2) ascertain that the subject fully understands a given dilemma before proceeding with questions on it; (3) encourage the subject to answer prescriptively rather than descriptively (e.g., "So that's why you think Heinz would steal the drug. Do you think Heinz *should* steal the drug?"); and (4) enable the subject to reflect on his moral suppositions through probing ("What do you mean by justice?"; "Why is keeping good relationships important?"; etc.).

C. The Standard Form Scoring Manual

The assessment of moral interview data is done by reference to a standard scoring manual. The system of scoring in the newest manual is now under construction (we are grateful to the National Institute of Health for support of this work). In using the Standard Scoring Manual, the scorer's first concern must be not with scoring but with *coding* information. Coding for Issue is rather straightforward, since the dilemmas and dilemma questions are quite directive as to issue. The scorer must also code for concern, an effort which of course requires familiarity with the Moral Concerns system (Section II). Probably the best basis for both Issue and Concern coding is a thorough familiarity with the standard manual units which incorporate both constructs: namely, the "Criterion Concepts."

A nutshell description of the relation of Criterion Concepts to Issues, Concerns, and Stages, is as follows. An *Issue* defines an "object" of value in a moral interview; a *Concern* defines *why* that object is valued; a *Stage* defines *how* or the *way* in which the object is valued. Encompassing all of these terms is the *Criterion Concept*, which is a particular point within the stage at which a subject addresses a concern to an issue in the interview.

To demonstrate how the scoring system works, we will consider several examples of moral judgment data one might come across from interviews with adults. Recall some previously cited (p. 33) data:

SHOULD HEINZ HAVE DONE THAT?
If he has exhausted every alternative. It's worth it in the sense of the value of human life because it's all well and good to talk about property rights but I don't think they mean much in a society that doesn't value human life higher.

Similar justifications for Heinz's stealing the drug from other data are:

(1) ". . . the value of human life is logically prior to the value of property. That is, property can have no value unless human life is valued."

(2) ". . . material possessions supplement life, if there is no value placed on life, material possessions become worthless."

(3) "You can't escape the logical thing underneath, the whole idea of life, your life or another person's. People feel that it is best for all in the structure of society to live in such a way as to preserve first life and then property. It doesn't matter whose life or whose property when there is a conflict."

The first step in assessing any of these cases is to code the "what" of the passage. Clearly, the Issue to which all subjects are addressing themselves is Life, and the Concern is for the welfare of others (Altruism). So such a passage is "about" altruism as applied to life.

The second step is to stage-score the way in which the subject is thinking about altruism as applied to life. In the standard scoring manual are a number of "altruism-applied-to-life" points or Criterion Concepts, and the one at Stage 5 is especially pertinent:

Stealing to save the life is justified because of the moral or logical priority of the right to life (or value of life), in general, to the right to property (or value of property).

This Criterion Concept seems to be the skeleton for any of the data passages cited. Beneath the Criterion Concept in the manual is an "explication" of why such a statement is interpreted as indicative of Stage 5:

The justification for stealing to save the life reflects a logical or rational appreciation that life is primary and that the value of property presupposes and derives from the value of life; that is, property serves to enhance life whereas life cannot rationally be viewed as serving to enhance property. This logical priority of life to property is established by the Stage 5 universalizing to all socio-moral agents from the recognition that any individual would rationally identify his life as more fundamental than his property.

Once one has completed all coding and scoring, one's final step is to compute, across all issues in the interview, the overall stage score for the given subject.

V. Conclusion

We would like to conclude by reflecting on a number of matters: on the presuppositions of our approach, on the significance of judgment for moral action, and on the implications which we feel the practice of moral stage scoring ought, and ought not, to have.

A. Our Approach

Our approach (derived mainly from developmental structuralism as propounded in this century by Piaget and Dewey) has as its central feature the thesis that the human subject is a *creator*, not just a creature, *of meaning*. Stages in the human construction of meaning may in part be convenient fictions of the theorist, but ultimately reflect efforts to represent *human epistemological, psycho-social, and socio-moral realities.* As Piaget (1965/1971) writes:

> . . . the human subject in general . . . uses norms of every kind, cognitive, ethical, etc. He is engaged in the world and attributes to everything a 'meaning' from vital, social, or personal, as well as epistemological points of view. . . . What needs to be strongly emphasized is that it is the subject himself in his interpersonal relationships and in his own spontaneity who is the origin of these 'meanings,' not the philosopher or the psychologist. (p. 225)

There are, in other words, two presuppositions to our theory. The first is that the researcher is capable of seeing things from the viewpoint of subjects, of understanding what they are saying or thinking in their own terms. Insofar as each of us has been through the stages and has heard the viewpoint of each stage, we should be able to put ourselves in the framework of a subject at a given stage. As William James once remarked in another context: "Building up an author's meaning out of separate texts means nothing, unless you have first grasped the center of his vision by an act of imagination." If one understands the subject's perspective in terms of the meanings he finds in the world, one can then adequately describe a given stage, although any brief description of a stage is bound to be stated from the external rather than phenomenological frame of reference.

The second presupposition of our theory is that there is a pattern of connections within the subject's meaning, that is, a structure or set of relations and transformations. In this sense, the task of the definer of stages is like that of the literary critic or humanist trying to analyze the pattern of ideas involved in the work of Aristotle or Shakespeare. The developmental psychologist's interviews are like the humanist's texts. The test of accuracy of interpretation is that if it is claimed that certain ideas are related in certain ways in the text, this relationship makes sense in other places in the text or in the text as a whole. Acceptance of a humanistic analysis of the structure of Aristotle's thought does not depend upon acceptance of a theory of the psychology of Aristotle's personality. Similarly, acceptance of a structural analysis of the child's thought does not imply a commitment to a theory of the child personality.

There is a step of generalization made by the stage-psychologist not made by the literary critic. The critic analyzes the pattern of one person's mind; the stage-psychologist analyzes the pattern common to *all* children at a certain level of development. Developmental-structural theory is a theory about *all individuals*, not about groups or averages for children. We are interested, to quote Jean Flavell (1970), in "the Development of Man, as contrasted with the developments of men" (p. 253). As noted earlier, making a stage-developmental generalization requires distinguishing between culturally or individually varying *content* in the child's thought and the reasoning pattern or *structure* of his thought. Correctly distinguishing between "structure" and "content" in stage description can be a problematic endeavor. If you take out too much as "content," you have stages without meat from the understanding of the individual child and his development. If you leave in too much as content, you have a picture of the stage true for some but not all individuals assigned to that stage rather than universal structural patterns.

B. Relation of Moral Judgment to Moral Action

A question which has probably confronted every psychologist in this approach at one time or another is a version of the popular "relevance" question. It is asked of us by laymen as well as professional colleagues of other persuasions. In the context of moral development research it goes something like this: "I suppose it's all right for you to talk about 'stages' in people's verbal judgments on moral questions, but wouldn't you really rather study something that matters, like how people actually *behave* in real life?" The relation of stages of moral judgment to maturity of moral behavior is admittedly an important question. Our answer starts by pointing out that moral judgment, too, is a "behavior." We are tempted to subscribe to Piaget's (1970/1971) elusive but profound definition of "behavior" as "simply the organization of life itself, applied or generalized to a wider range of exchanges with the environment . . . extending the scope of the organic forms" (p. 364). Using the term behavior broadly, we define moral judgment as the behavior of *reasoning about or justifying prescriptive social valuings and meanings*, and moral "behavior" as the behavior of *situational socio-moral actions or conduct*.

In this sense, we speak of the psychology of human development as the study of *parallel behavioral areas of structural development.* There are, among others, the domains of logico-mathematical reasoning, of social perspective-taking, of moral judgment, and of socio-moral conduct. Social stage is only one component of moral stage, and moral stage is only one component determining the maturity of moral action. To act in a morally mature way requires a high stage of moral reasoning. One cannot follow moral principles if one does not understand or believe in moral principles. However, one can reason in terms of principles and not live up to these principles. A variety of factors determine whether a particular person will live up to his highest stages of moral reasoning in a particular situation. Partly it depends on the pressures and ambiguities of the situation; partly it depends upon the extent of the subject's tendency to slip into the egocentrism of immediate interests (or, to put it positively, upon the extent of the subject's general will or "ego strength" [Kohlberg, 1964]). The relation of moral judgment to moral conduct has recently been treated in a similar light by Brown and Herrnstein (1975, pp. 287-340).

The moral judgment stages, while related to moral actions, must be identified on the basis of moral reasoning and justifying alone. What makes a situational action "moral" or "immoral" is the prescriptive moral judgment of the act made by the actor or his culture. Our conception of the moral is grounded on universal features of moral judgment, not on particular cultural definitions of moral judgment or conduct.

C. Ethics of Moral Judgment Stage Research

It should be clear by this point that the stages represent "ways of moral thinking," not kinds of personality. Yet the extent to which the moral stage descriptions have been used as "diagnostic"—i.e., pejorative—labels on people is dismaying. It cannot be over-emphasized that stages are types of thinking or functioning, not types of persons. Knowing that someone's thinking is moral Stage 2 is not to say that that person does not think or act morally; it is to recognize his sense of right and fairness as Stage 2. To understand a person's Stage 2 reasoning helps us to understand his point of view, to put ourselves in that person's place and see the world through his eyes. We sometimes label the Stage 2 way of thinking "instrumental egoism," but this does not mean that Stage 2 individuals care nothing for other people or have no sense of fairness. It means, rather, that their concern for others is limited by the notion that people basically have to look out for themselves in this world, so that good relations are based on trade-offs.

One can recognize an ethical abuse in the practice of moral stage research when the characteristic tone of the stage descriptions is condemnatory, e.g., "Stage 2 thinks only of himself, can't see things from anyone else's perspective," etc. A correct statement would be, "Stage 2 thinks everyone should consider consequences to himself, expects one's own perspective to be the final one," etc. A good moral judgment researcher, like a good counselor, must see through the interviewee's eyes. As we strive to foster desperately needed moral maturity in judgment and action, our stance toward the human individual must remain one of affirmation and respect.

Appendix

Moral Judgment Interview

Form A

Story III. In Europe, a woman was near death from a special kind of cancer. There was one
drug that the doctors thought might save her. It was a form of radium that a
druggist in the same town had recently discovered. The drug was expensive to
make, but the druggist was charging ten times what the drug cost him to make. He
paid $200 for the radium and charged $2,000 for a small dose of the drug. The
sick woman's husband, Heinz, went to everyone he knew to borrow the money,
but he could only get together about $1,000, which is half of what it cost. He told
the druggist that his wife was dying, and asked him to sell it cheaper or let him
pay later. But the druggist said, "No. I discovered the drug and I'm going to make
money from it." So Heinz gets desperate and considers breaking into the man's
store to steal the drug for his wife.

1. Should Heinz steal the drug? Why or why not?
2. If Heinz doesn't love his wife, should he steal the drug for her? Why or why not?
3. Suppose the person dying is not his wife but a stranger. Should Heinz steal the drug for
   the stranger? Why or why not?
4. What's to be said for obeying the law in this situation or in general?
5. Heinz might think it's important to obey the law and to save his wife, but he can't do
   both. Is there a way to resolve the conflict between law and life, taking the best
   arguments for both into account? How or why not?

Story III'. Heinz did break into the store and got the drug. Watching from a distance was an
off-duty police officer, Mr. Brown, who lived in the same town as Heinz and
knew the situation Heinz was in. Mr. Brown ran over to try to stop Heinz, but
Heinz was gone by the time Mr. Brown reached the store. Mr. Brown wonders
whether he should look for Heinz and arrest him.

1. Should Mr. Brown, the off-duty policeman, arrest Heinz? Why or why not?
2. Mr. Brown finds and arrests Heinz. Heinz is brought to court and found guilty. Should
   the judge sentence Heinz or let him go free? why?
3. The judge has to think about society. Thinking in terms of society, what is the best
   reason for the judge to give Heinz a sentence?
3a. If you disagree with this reason, why?
4. Why is it important generally to punish people who break the law?
5. Heinz thinks that his stealing was the right thing to do, but knows that it was against
   the law. How should a person decide when he has to choose between following his own
   judgment and upholding the law?
6. Should your conscience bother you if you were in Heinz's situation and you stole the
   drug? Why or why not?
7. Should your conscience bother you if you were in Mr. Brown's situation and arrested
   Heinz?
8. What does the word conscience mean to you? What does "morality" mean to you?
9. Some people think that Heinz should steal the drug; some think he should not. Would
   you say that there is a morally right action or answer as to whether Heinz should steal
   the drug or is it each person's personal subjective opinion? Could somebody disagree
   with what you think is right and be just as right? Is the morally right usually a matter of
   personal opinion or is there some ultimate truth or guide in morality?

Story I. Joe is a fourteen-year-old boy who wanted to go to camp very much. His father
promised him he could go if he saved up the money for it himself. So Joe worked
hard at his paper route and saved up the $40 it cost to go to camp and a little more
besides. But just before camp was going to start, his father changed his mind. Some

of his friends decided to go on a special fishing trip, and Joe's father was short of the money it would cost. So he told Joe to give him the money he had saved from the paper route. Joe didn't want to give up going to camp, so he thinks of refusing to give his father the money.

1. Should Joe refuse to give his father the money? Why or why not?
2. Is the fact that Joe earned the money himself an important consideration here? Why or why not?
3. Joe might consider the money something he earned and that he has property rights in this case. Is it important for a father to respect his son's property? Why or why not?
4. What is the basic value or importance of property rights in general?
5. Not only did Joe earn the money, but his father made a promise. Is that an important consideration here? Why or why not?
6. Why should a promise be kept?
7. Is it important to keep a promise to someone you don't know well or are not close to? Why or why not?
8. What do you think is the most important thing for a son to consider about his relationship to his father in this or other situations?
8a. Why is that important?
9. What do you think is the most important thing for a father to consider about his relationship to his son in this or other situations?
9a. Why is that important?

Form B

Story IV. There was a woman who had very bad cancer, and there was no treatment known to medicine that could save her. Her doctor, Dr. Jefferson, knew that she had only about six months to live. She was in terrible pain, but she was so weak that a good dose of a pain-killer like ether or morphine would make her die sooner. She was delirious and almost crazy with pain, and in her calm periods she would ask Dr. Jefferson to give her enough ether to kill her. She said she couldn't stand the pain and she was going to die in a few months anyway. Although he knows that mercy-killing is against the law, the doctor thinks about granting her request.

1. Should the doctor give her the drug that would make her die? Why or why not?
2. Should the woman have the right to make the final decision? Why or why not?
3. Is there any sense in which a person has a duty or obligation to live when he or she does not want to, when the person wants to commit suicide? Why or why not?
4. How does the fact that mercy-killing humans is against the law affect your decision as to whether it is right or wrong for the doctor to give her the drug? Why?
5. What's to be said for obeying the law in this situation or in general?

Story IV'. Dr. Jefferson did perform the mercy-killing by giving the woman the drug. Passing by at the time was another doctor, Dr. Rogers, who knew the situation Dr. Jefferson was in. Dr. Rogers thought of trying to stop Dr. Jefferson, but the drug was already administered. Dr. Rogers wonders whether he should report Dr. Jefferson.

1. Should Dr. Rogers report Dr. Jefferson? Why or why not?
2. The doctor does report Dr. Jefferson. Dr. Jefferson is brought to court and found guilty. Should the judge sentence Dr. Jefferson or let him go free? Why?
3. The judge has to think about society. Thinking in terms of society, what is the best reason for the judge to give the doctor a sentence?
3a. If you disagree with this reason, why?
4. Why is it important generally to punish people who break the law?
5. Dr. Jefferson thinks that his performing the mercy-killing was the right thing to do, but knows that it was against the law. How should a person decide when he has to choose between following his own judgment and upholding the law?

6. Should your conscience bother you if you were in Dr. Jefferson's situation and you gave the drug? Why or why not?
7. Should your conscience bother you if you were in Dr. Rogers' situation and you reported Dr. Jefferson? Why or why not?
8. What does the word conscience mean to you? What does "morality" mean to you?
9. Some people think that the doctor should kill the woman; some think he should not. Would you say that there is a morally right action or answer as to whether the doctor should kill the woman or is it each person's personal subjective opinion? Could somebody disagree with what you think is right and be just as right? Is the morally right usually a matter of personal opinion or is there some ultimate truth or guide in morality?

Story II. Judy was a twelve-year-old girl. Her mother promised her that she could go to a special rock concert coming to their town if she saved up from babysitting and lunch money for a long time so she would have enough money to buy a ticket to the concert. She managed to save up the $5 the ticket cost plus another $3. But then her mother changed her mind and told Judy that she had to spend the money on new clothes for school. Judy was disappointed and decided to go to the concert anyway. She bought a ticket and told her mother that she had only been able to save $3. That Saturday she went to the performance and told her mother that she was spending the day with a friend. A week passed without her mother finding out. Judy then told her older sister, Louise, that she had gone to the performance and had lied to her mother about it. Louise wonders whether to tell their mother what Judy did.

1. Should Louise, the older sister, tell her mother that Judy had lied about the money or should she keep quiet? Why?
2. In wondering whether to tell, Louise thinks of the fact that Judy is her sister. Should that make a difference in Louise's decision?
3. Is the fact that Judy earned the money herself an important consideration here? Why or why not?
4. Judy might feel that since she earned the money, it is her property. What is the basic value or importance of property rights here and in general?
5. Do you think that it's especially important for a mother to respect her daughter's property? Why or why not?
6. Not only did Judy earn the money, but her mother made a promise. Is that an important consideration here? Why or why not?
7. Why should a promise be kept?
8. Is it important to keep a promise to someone you don't know well or are not close to? Why or why not?
9. What do you think is the most important thing for a daughter to consider about her relationship to her mother in this or other situations?
9a. Why is that important?
10. What do you think is the most important thing for a mother to consider about her relationship to her daughter in this or other situations?
10a. Why is that important?

References

Broughton, J. "The Cognitive-Developmental Approach to Morality: A Reply to Kurtines and Greif." Paper submitted for publication, 1976(a).

————————. "The Development of Cognitive Epistemology: Concepts of the Subject/Object Relation from Childhood to Adulthood." Paper submitted for publication, 1976(b).

Brown, R. & Herrnstein, R. J. *Psychology.* Boston: Little, Brown, & Co., 1975.

Flavell, J. H. "Stage-Related Properties of Cognitive Development." *Cognitive Psychology* 2 (1971):421-453.

————————. "Cognitive Change in Adulthood." In L. R. Goulet & P. B. Baltos (eds.), *Life-Span Developmental Psychology: Research and Theory.* New York: Academic Press, 1970. Pp. 247-253.

Gibbs, J. C. "The Piagetian Approach to Moral Development: An Overview." In Meyer, J.; Burnham, B.; & Cholvat, J. (eds.), *Values Education: Theory, Practice, Problems, Prospects.* Waterloo, Ont.: Wilfrid Laurier Press, 1975. Pp. 51-64.

Kohlberg, L. "Development of Moral Character and Moral Ideology." In M. L. Hoffman (ed.), *Review of Child Development Research* (Vol. 1). New York: Russell Sage Foundation, 1964.

Piaget, J. *The Moral Judgment of the Child.* New York: The Free Press, 1965. (Originally published 1932.)

————————. *Biology and Knowledge: An Essay on the Relations Between Organic Regulations and Cognitive Processes.* Chicago: University of Chicago Press, 1971. (Originally published 1967.)

————————. *Insights and Illusions of Philosophy.* New York: World Publishing Company, 1971. (Originally published 1965.)

Rawls, J. *A Theory of Justice.* Cambridge, Mass.: Harvard University Press, 1971.

Selman, R. "A Structural Approach to the Study of Developing Interpersonal Relationships Concepts: Research with Normal and Disturbed Preadolescent Boys." In A. Pick (ed.), *Annual Minnesota Symposia on Child Psychology.* Minneapolis: University of Minnesota Press, 1976 (in press).

Turiel, E. "Sex Differences in Moral Judgment Development." Unpublished paper, Harvard University, 1973.

MORAL EDUCATION AND ITS CURE

Bill Puka
Department of Philosophy
Trinity College, Connecticut

> If we do not know what morality is we cannot teach it. In crucial ways we do not
> know what morality is. Yet we must teach it because it is of prime importance and
> must be learned. Moreover, teaching must not be brainwashing; it must be moral.

The following essay consists of four major sections which combine to make one
argument addressed to the above dilemma, but which may be read separately.
The first section discusses the issue of ethical objectivism and relativism in
philosophy and psychology. The second (p. 53) analyzes Kohlberg's theory of
moral development in relation to the limits of a justice ethic as compared to a
perfectionism or love ethic. The third section offers a highly speculative and
debatable, though perhaps stimulating, alternative model on which to view
moral-social consciousness development (p. 63). The final section (p. 75) provides suggestions for moral-political educational reform. It maintains that truly
free education must involve not only the stimulation of cognitive development,
but training in conative and interpersonal skills as well as techniques for politi-
cal-social analysis and consciousness-raising. The actualization of the proposed
educational approach is evaluated as a model for ethical justification.

I. Objectivism vs. Relativism

An objectivist (as opposed to a relativist) holds that morality is a matter of truth
(and falsity). Indeed, what if this were not the case? Could we imprison or
execute people, die for our country, forego incredible pleasures and interpersonal shortcuts on the basis of mere biases we or some other people hold? There
must be some bedrock somewhere, some unshakable foundation upon which to
structure the course of ultimate human affairs. Truth and justice are seen as that
bedrock. Both are alleged to make us free—truly and fairly free.

   If morality is true, what is it true of? Either it is true of some ethereal
realm (Idealism, Natural Law Theory), or of the world (naturalism). Since our
problem is to find bedrock, we'll leave ethereal realms up in the air, at least for
the present. Naturalists in ethics divide into two categories—those who believe
that ethical statements are true of the external world, and those who believe that
such statements are true of our moral attitudes or belief systems. Objectivist
members of both camps argue that prescriptive utterances are true in the same
way that scientific or factual statements are. Some of us may wonder immediately whether we have not already lost the sort of bedrock we are looking for
when we equate ethical with scientific-factual truth.

Are ethical truths of these natural sorts facts about the world primarily, or facts about us, i.e., commitments we hold? We may ask the same question as regards non-moral facts. One answer is that these facts are true of both the world and us (of our commitments), but that the commitment aspect of them is not troublesome for our truth and objectivity requirements. If we can agree on the stipulation of certain criteria as valid for observing, describing and explaining the world, then the data we gather is indeed true relative to those criteria agreed upon. We agree on these criteria as a function of further commitments we share regarding the goals of empirical knowledge, e.g., to enable us to predict and control the world.

What we call facts or truths are selective ways of conceptualizing the world which assume the effect of our interaction with it in that conceptualization. The selectivity of our theories toward data is a function of our purposes and commitments in devising theories. For example, believing a trolley car is what we call solid and moving will help to keep us from getting run over. Almost no way of thinking about the trolley will allow us to disrupt its registering on our senses as painful and debilitating in drastic ways when it, as we say, collides with our body. Of course some see this event as death, others as rebirth. Some could say we were hit by the trolley (or thought we were) only because we believed in it. We ignore people with these latter sorts of commitments, theories of reality, and conventions regarding valid evidence. Part of the reason we feel justified in doing so has to do with views we hold on probability and justified belief. We feel that the best explanation for so many of us interpreting the trolley car case as a serious accident rather than a dream, and our consequent ability to function competently in the world, is that the world *is* the way we *think* it is. In this sense, although our vision of reality is relative to us and our commitments, it is a picture of *reality* nonetheless. Here we find a path to de-relativization. Reality is there, and ours is but one picture of it. Why one picture is termed better or truer than another may not depend totally on the degree to which it fits reality, but the degree to which it fits our practical purposes. Still, each picture (theory) may be in its own way an accurate rendering of one unitary, enduring reality. Its objective, rather than its pragmatic truth, depends on its ability to capture that reality as it is.

It may be possible to formulate a distinction which exposes an incommensurateness between objectivism in the moral and non-moral realms as follows. With regard to non-moral facts it is *external reality* that is taken as the standard of our agreement in interacting with the world. On the other hand, moral statements if true, are held true of our interaction with the world, assuming our psycholophysiology as standard. It's something more about *us* than about the world, that makes something good or bad. If our pain receptors and emotional or conceptual sets were altered, good and bad would to some extent change. This change would occur not only in their application to the world, but in fact. That is, good and bad would have changed, though the situations to which they now would be applied differently, would have undergone no alteration. Though like anatomical, conative, and cognitive changes might effect our *view* of the physical world as empirical observers, the "truth" of the world versus our description of it, would not change thereby.

In science disagreement between us over factual judgments is explained by measurement error and/or individual differences in observational abilities. We attempt to eliminate such variance through technical measuring devices and statistical controls. In ethics, such individual differences or commonalities can be seen as the reality itself, or are at least the crucial side of that interaction which makes up reality. If facts of our psychology and physiology determine ultimate moral reality in this way, then individual differences between us in that psychology could make our moral reality non-unitary, i.e., ultimately pluralistic or relative.

Some naturalist objectivists would claim that my reliance on psychophysical[1] differences does not do justice to their view. This is because the reliance of these theorists on psychology is not as purely empirical, but it is rather more normative and metaphysical. The problem in ethics, as these theorists see it, is to specify a *standard* psychology; a theory of the correct moral judge, self-actualized exemplar, wise man (person), or ideal observer. Here we may draw a parallel between the standard observer used by science to eliminate the problematic quality of subjective observational differences, and the ethical judge par excellence. From such a perspective one can judge certain psychologies or conceptual schemes inadequate or morally objectionable, given the judgments they yield. Earliest versions of such a theory termed people morally blind who lacked the intuitive capacity of moral insight. Yet how does one decide who possesses clear or fuzzy moral vision without direct reference to moral facts in the external world? What is it about one person that makes her (him) a better moral judge than another? And what would constitute an ability to judge in the moral case which would parallel the scientific one involving observation of environmental events? One possible recourse for the naturalist might involve reference to other parts of our psychology. That is, we might judge one person's moral judgments insightful because they demonstrate the ability to make judgments which tend to satisfy our psychophysical needs, e.g., for pleasure and the avoidance of pain, self-esteem, survival of the species, ability to cope with and function in new social environments efficiently, and the like. We need not hold that judgments of the moral sage demonstrate moral insight for this reason (i.e., their utilitarian effects). Rather we may note that correct moral judgments tend to have these utilitarian consequences and so that the sage who makes such judgments is likely to possess clear moral vision. Such a view could be shored up with auxiliary considerations about the preferability of a psychology (a degree of cognitive development) which would lead to the enhancement of an individual's well-being, and that of those interacting with that individual. Another approach to

---

[1]By psychophysical I mean the combination of psychological and physiological properties which combine to make up personality or personality types.

the problem is to limit the realm of legitimate or relevant psychology *so as to stipulate* common elements of persons in judgment, action, and treatment. Such theories of moral personhood and the complementary notions of respect for persons to which they give rise will be discussed in a moment.

Most forms of psychological and educational theory related to moral development as well as most moral philosophical theories, assume and build upon the conventional morality of the culture or subculture in which they occur; both in form and content. Relativists do not see this as a problem. Others who happen to be worried about indoctrination in education as well as ideological or cultural bias in research or theory, seek to demonstrate the intercultural universality and the logical generalizability of these moral conventions.

In psychology this rationale takes the following form: If basic similarities can be found in at least the structure of moral views, interculturally, the most likely explanation of this similarity would be that it is based on something universal in the interaction of our psychophysiology with the world.

We may question, however, whether the finding of widespread similarities in moral views through cross-cultural research, would solve crucial problems for the objectivist. Why is this so? Firstly, in looking to aspects of our cognitive faculties for the moral foundation of universality in values, principles, judgments and the like, we may be finding a basis in aspects of other faculties, e.g., fear, greed, cruelty, and aggression, which these cognitions accompany or reflect. Findings may also reflect transcultural spread of biases which become no less arbitrary for being widely held, especially if explanations for their spread which do not refer to their justifiability can be provided. Thirdly, morality is an "ought" rather than an "is" enterprise, though we must be careful in specifying what this implies. Morality is "willing," if not *designed*, to pose a crucial trade-off between what is natural (factual) versus what may be unnatural but *preferable* (ideal) in a variety of non-factually determined ways. *Facts limit but do not determine the forms of imagination which are the source of ideals.*

In philosophy, a typical objectivist strategy involves specifying logical criteria which any adequate moral view must fulfill. Typical criteria are universality, reciprocity, publicity, finality, perhaps supremacy, prescriptivity. The validity of these criteria, unfortunately, to a large extent depends on previous assumptions as to which moral view is true or most adequate. In fact these criteria often appear to have been devised in order to account for or make explicit what some people found acceptable in certain views for other reasons. Certain other people, especially non-rationalists, non-deontologists, social perfectionists and the like, merely reject these logical criteria because their theories do not satisfy them. Where there is lack of agreement regarding foundation assumptions—fundamental criteria stipulating how even the form of an adequate moral theory should look—the objectivist is in trouble. An obvious bridge over such waters could be built via the vindication of the person, or the thinking of the person who holds these beliefs the objectivist supports. Wise man (person) and ideal observer theories actually represent forms of this project, constructed without "getting into personalities." Looking at modern philosophy one would think that there is not much disagreement or disparity of this sort, except from what seems a lunatic fringe: Nietzsche, C. L. Stevenson, D. H. Lawrence, Sartre, Marx. But is this due to the superior reasoning ability of the philosophical establishment, or its tendency to hire colleagues of certain sorts, while not hiring others?

In psychology, Lawrence Kohlberg's theory of moral development attempts to take both of these routes to objectivism, i.e., (1) the empirical search for psychological universals in moral thinking, and (2) the philosophical justification of these universals as more and less adequate on the basis of the form of thinking they typically express.[2] Kohlberg in fact buttresses these two enterprises against each other for their mutual support. He claims to have found data confirming the existence of six formal levels of moral thinking which all people as they develop (would) go through in sequence (if allowed to develop optimally). These are psychological stages which occur in persons, regardless of their cultural training.

Kohlberg claims, moreover, that the explanation for why people do develop in this way is the same as the philosophical justification for why they *should.* Cognitive development represents our active interactions with the environment to attain competence in dealing with it. In moral development the competence problem is to resolve conflicts of interest between yourself and others (and later between all persons equally) in as fair a way as possible. The most adequate (complexly accurate) intellectual form such fair resolutions can take from the philosophical point of view, is embodied by a particular form of justice theory; justice at the Stage 6 level. In psychological terms, fairness is the resolution of interests in a conflict situation which anyone would find acceptable from the position of any interested party to the conflict, if (s)he were not stubborn, close-minded, or thinking confusedly. As a decision-procedure, Kohlberg terms this Ideal Role-taking. Kohlberg claims that although these forms (stages) of thought are developed via intellectual grappling with the *content* of conventional morality, they do not depend on it nor build it into their *structure.* Stage 6 represents the highest or most adequate form of moral thought (conflict resolution) *possible.*

Were Kohlberg's claims true, they would speak against the fundamental relativity or lack of uniqueness of moral truth as regards ultimate individual differences in our psychology. Secondly, Kohlberg's claims would give some independent and powerful justification to the objectivist choice of philosophical criteria for adequacy in moral theory, e.g., universality, reciprocity. This is so because higher stage thinking is more demonstrative of such qualities. Thirdly, these claims would function so as to circumscribe the role of ideology, commit-

[2]Kohlberg is actually not a naturalistic objectivist in important ways. His search is for intersubjective agreement between people whose cognitive structures are fully developed. Such agreement, although resting on these psychological structures is not true of them, in a sense. Metaethically, Kohlberg is a prescriptivist and a Platonist in many ways. For present purposes, these details are not amply crucial to merit extensive discussion.

ments, and politics (and so of academia, the Church, big business and government) in determining the views of morality we are likely to hold. According to
Kohlberg, our acceptance of the conventional moral view (false ideology) of our
society represents merely a stage (stage 4, to be exact), we may and likely will
transcend as we grow and develop.

We may yet ask whether Kohlberg's theory is true of psychology and
morality per se, or perhaps itself the reflection of the progressive internalization
of a particular cultural ideology it is actually measuring. That is, is Kohlberg
measuring a culturally based form of moral thinking which has merely been
spread to many parts of the world through the ideological imperialism of mis-
sionaries and propaganda? Is the very content of this ideology and moral structure, e.g., that all men should accept universal moral principles, what caused this
spread? Note that Kohlberg need not deny the partial influence of ideology on
the *content* of our moral views. It is the level of logical sophistication and the
degree to which this form determines different contents (as it does), that concerns him most. Yet the purported content of this *form*, of these *levels* of
sophistication (e.g., that a higher level is based on principles that apply to all
people equally and features a greater correlativity of rights with duties), may
itself represent an ideological *bias.*

When I speak of ideological bias in the Kohlberg case, I mean to denote
influences in the description of the stages which do not reflect either or both
psychological findings regarding universal features of our cognitive faculties and
the logic of morality alone, but rather additional features which are culturally
relative and objectionable on a variety of bases. In a moment I will present a
critique which rests more squarely on the notion of false ideology. A false
ideology is a discription of moral beliefs or the beliefs about morality themselves
which actually do not reflect moral facts but rather, e.g., the disguised economic
interests of a particular socio-economic class, or untested and perhaps untestable
(if not false) assumptions about human nature and the logic of morality. The
"false" in false ideology is difficult to define, measure, and justify. It seems
always to rest partially upon a normative dispute rather than just upon facts.
Insofar as it rests on facts alone, it does so by seeing facts and the fact-gathering
context together. The details of false ideology and how it is specified will have
to go undiscussed here.

The Kohlberg thesis is a vast one. Here it is claimed that every moral
system underlying every socio-cultural ethic or policy in the history of the world
can be ranked as more or less intellectually mature, and so as objectively better
or worse (more or less adequate). Moreover, such a ranking may be effected with
little reference to facts about the world except those regarding the unfolding
logic of our own active minds. This is a theoretical position worthy of careful
consideration.

II. Give Me That Old Time Justice

Kohlberg's theory and its applications represent a welcome contribution to moral psychology and moral education. This is so, most significantly, because Kohlberg's theory is in many ways inclusive of its rivals in both psychology and education, while surpassing them. Like Values Clarification (Raths, Harmin and Simon, 1966), Kohlberg's techniques yield clarity in value judgments. Like social learning theory or behavior modification, Kohlberg's system effects and measures moral learning. Kohlberg's theory is inclusive of its rivals in developmental theory also, i.e., Freudianism and Social Learning Theory. To put things somewhat crudely, when the child is most-undeveloped and rodent-like, most prone to Oedipal conflicts, power and fear most populate even her (his) *cognitive* processes (Kohlberg's Stage 1). As the child becomes less and less rodent-like, more of a social (genital stage) animal, motivations and cognitions become more complex. (S)he becomes reason-oriented, secondarily, tertiarily ("nthiarily") reinforced by social contingencies and the like (Kohlberg's Stages 3-5). I mean in no way to imply that these competing theories would accept competing explanations of moral learning and development data. The inclusiveness I point to involves the apparent ability of Kohlberg's theory to provide an evenly plausible explanation of the relevant data of development from early childhood to adult levels. Alternative theories, though plausible in their explanation of moral learning in childhood, seem compelled to stretch their conceptual systems especially in order to account for later-in-life learning or development.

Many people react with great hostility to Kohlberg's position, and will not accept the notion that people think at different levels or along a continuum of moral sophistication approximated by Kohlberg's stages. I would advise such skeptics to take to reality and extensively interview people as Kohlberg and others of us have done. It is important to keep in mind that Kohlberg's theory represents an interpretation of the data as he found it, not an attempt to squeeze people's moral beliefs into some a priori set of logical stages thought up beforehand.

Although many of Kohlberg's claims may be faulty, as one would expect of any scientific theory, I would like to concentrate mostly here on the limitations of Kohlberg's approach due to the philosophical foundations on which it stands (as one theory, indivisible), as well as how the virtues of this approach may be expanded. Kohlberg would be the first to agree that his theory is limited in its focus and use, and has not yet been fully worked out. This is especially true of his highest stages, Stages 5 and 6, and their relation to each other.

Kohlberg holds that justice is the center of morality. To render this belief plausible in my own mind, I interpret it as saying that justice is at the midpoint between bad and good; between worst and best. This is, to say the least, not an interpretation Kohlberg is friendly to. Justice on the whole is a political, not a moral concept. It defines what is morally permissible (i.e., what is not blameable, punishable, or wrong) rather than what is morally admirable or desirable in

a more positive sense. For this reason it seems fair to say that justice is nega-
tively oriented, within the moral point of view. It tells us in terms of duties and
obligations what things we can't avoid doing or must refrain from doing in order
to merely remain passably moral, i.e., not immoral. Yet it offers us little guidance in how to be better. As a characteristic in a moral person, being just may be
necessary as a minimal condition, though this is debatable, but is hardly a very
desirable trait as expressed in most social interaction situations. In morality,
which normally applies foremost to interpersonal rather than legal or govern-
mental interactions, we expect more than and perhaps something which does not
include mere justice or fairness from a fellow human being. Yet we expect *moral*
treatment. We expect consideration, civility, reasonableness, some degree of caring, kindness, willingness to do favors, a smile, and the like. Some of these
stances are consistent with fairness whereas some may often conflict with it.

Philosophers who see justice as central to morality are normally included
within the so-called deontological moral tradition. Those who see love, pleasure,
virtue, personal development, beauty or achievement as central are termed teleologists, consequentialists or perfectionists. Kohlberg is admittedly a deontologist. His Stage 6 admits of only deontological theories of justice, exemplified, for
example by John Rawls' theory of Justice as Fairness. Below this (at Stage 5)
Kohlberg places consequentialist or teleological theories such as rule-utilitarian-
ism. The teleologist defines right as what maximizes good. The deontologist
holds that right is to be defined somewhat independently of good and as prior to
good. The deontologist sees right *as defining* good. Simply put, this implies for
the deontologist, that ends do not justify means. Here is where respect for
persons becomes most important for the deontologist. We cannot justifiably
boost social welfare if it means violating the rights (to life, liberty, or property)
of individuals. We cannot commit wrongs to produce goods. We should not have
fun at a party by humiliating one of its guests. Deontology's view of morality as
a filtering device (taking out the wrong and okaying the rest) is part of the
liberal political tradition which sees enforcement of public morality (rights) as
government's only legitimate role. Government must leave all else, e.g., whether
people are more or less kind to each other, virtuous, and so forth, alone! These
fall within the province of private morality and involve a realm of conscience
(ego-ideal? taste? sensitivities?), to be left up to each individual.

As I will imply in a discussion of the "respect for persons" issue, the
proper realm of public morality, of what rights exist and should be enforced,
might also be seen as a varying matter of taste, as the forwarding of the ideal of
autonomous living. Libertarians might respect a person's property right
if it stood in the way of a starving horde who needed food to survive. The
communist would not respect a person's right to property nor perhaps even
liberty or life if s/he pushed such a property claim in opposition to this social
need. Such rights, i.e., rights which could oppose such social goods, would be
said not to exist. How we define individual rights depends upon the political
purposes morality may be made to serve. This is true of *politics*; of *enforcing*

claims. But *morality* need not be so hands-offish. Moral goodness need not be defined by the individual's ability to provide for her (his) own welfare, and others be damned. For this reason teleologists often deemphasize justice and accentuate happiness, human flourishing and social welfare. Moreover, they do not emphasize the obligation-supererogation split, i.e., the distinction between what one *must* do not to be horrible, versus what one *should* do so as to promote the greater good.

One characteristic of this obligation-supererogation split in the liberal philosophical tradition is that the line of obligation seems always to be drawn around those moral actions philosophers already perform. Supererogation is then characterized as what they need not do but do sometimes just to show how nice they are. Showing how nice one is in this way, might consist in sending the $10 you were about to spend on your tenth hat, to save the lives of three famine victims who would otherwise starve to death. Many justice-as-fairness theorists recognize some degrees of positive obligations to help those in need. Kohlberg's Stage 6 morality surely does. But still it is only willing to go so far. "Morality stops here!" But why? One sensible answer is that at this point the push of morality should stop. This is obligation. But being kind, loving, virtuous, this should involve the pull of morality. (Push is negative, pull is positive morality.) "Good shines in the distance and the good among us follow her." It is not an instance of kindness to perform a beneficial action out of obligation, fear of disapproval or punishment or perhaps, even self-interest. Yes indeed, this statement is both true and important. Yet we should note that it is also not just to act justly as a way of minipulating people, for fear of being arrested, or the like. Still we are willing to enforce and obligate justice. If people will not be kind, we may want to obligate it. If people will not be truly just, we may not want to obligate that. There is an alternative to both procedures. We may jointly undertake social policies (e.g., in education and in the media) which will help people develop into the type of people who will be just and kind without compulsion, i.e., for the right or best of reasons.

Justice defines its role as the resolution of conflicting claims. Kohlberg quite oddly defines morality itself on this justice model. "Most social situations are not moral because there is no conflict between the role-taking expectations of one person and another" (Kohlberg, 1971, p. 192). He ascertains people's stages of *moral* reasoning by observing and tabulating the cognitive strategies they use to resolve conflicts—moral dilemmas which he presents them. But is this the only function of morality? If two people or societies agree on how to resolve conflicting moral claims, is morality silent or satisfied? Even if these people are Hitler and Mussolini (Nazis and Fascists) and the resolution of conflict involves immolating Jews? No, of course not. For Kohlberg could pose a problem that could not be resolved at the level either of these "thinkers" display, of if it were resolved to their satisfaction, would not show moral adequacy, but stubbornness, erroneous factual beliefs, and a host of delusions. And what then? This of course demonstrates a clear difference between the justification of a moral judgment (stage) versus the decision-procedure people at that stage, or *using* that stage, might utilize. Kohlberg often blurs this distinction in dealing with the judgment-action problem and his Stage 6 ideal role-taking procedure (mentioned previously).

An essential deficiency of deontological justice morality is that it is to some degree neutral (a-moral) as regards people's interests or social goods. "Whatever the conflicting interests are, so long as they do not inherently involve the harming of others, justice will resolve them." It can make no preferential judgment between interests in producing or possessing more color TVs vs. interests in moral charities, social reform work, kindness to others, and one's personal improvement. In self-defense, justice notes that it is difficult to rank interests. Many people advance different rankings. Yet the fact that total agreement in this area has not been achieved does not mean that we should ignore the issue, or ignore its clear-cut areas of agreement. Were we to adopt such a policy in the negative areas of morality, robbery and killing could perhaps not be censured. We surely could have no extensive system by which to redistribute wealth in our society and provide extensive social services. One way to *achieve* agreement on rankings of interests and ideals would be to take this area as seriously and deal with it as systematically as we do areas of obligation; as demonstrated by the development and utilization of our huge judicial system. Even if morality cannot say, "You *must* be more kind or else!" (ideally it should never say that even about obligations) it might say, "You *should* be more kind." It is how this "obligation" to be better is *applied* that counts. We should not assume that this "obligation" does not exist just because it does not look like or cannot function as a club. Political theory deals with clubs. Morality need not follow suit.

Kohlberg has observed what he terms a hierarchy of values which develops with a child's cognitive sophistication. At earlier stages children seem to value possessions, pets and people somewhat equally. In time the value of human life, followed hopefully by animal life, takes precedence over material value. Such value-rankings take us a very short way. Might there be more extensive hierarchies of value regarding virtue and perhaps different types of moral exemplar as more or less exemplary? Kohlberg finds this an interesting area to research. Indeed, it *should* be researched. In the final section of this essay I offer a few suggestions as to how we might justify value rankings as a function of decision procedures.

The positive side of morality need not be seen as opposed to the negative, though I see them as often conflicting. I say "negative" advisedly, since guilt, blame, enforcing rights, threatening and obligating, are not good things, but bad. They are wielded by morality as purportedly necessary evils. A very redeeming feature of Kohlbergian justice is that it actually "cheats" on deontology a bit in squeezing out some of the less savory aspects of negative morality such as blame, at Stage 6. This is why Kohlberg emphasizes the fairness aspect of justice.

Put simply and inspirationally, the positive side of the moral perspective as we know it, might see "Better" as the center of morality. Its positive role is not to resolve conflicts of interest, regardless of what interests conflict, but to help people develop better interests, become better people, and become less likely to conflict or resolve conflict in ways that require justice. "Higher" morality is not founded on reciprocity in relationships—"I lend you goods as you lend them to me, but I'll be damned if I'm going to be a sucker." A deeply understanding and kind person *cannot* be a sucker; cannot be taken advantage of. This is so even though those who try to abuse her (him) should not do so. "True" morality transcends its lower forms and goes on from there. Stage 6 is half way to 12, and Stage 12 is just the beginning. (Actually, Kohlberg's Stage 5B may be both a bit beyond half way and a bit beyond Stage 6.) Morality is a consciousness-raising enterprise that is not so much a matter of right and wrong, good and bad, as it is a matter of better and better, i.e., a matter of *evolution.* What we should work toward in morality is not the validation and justification of where our moral consciousness is now, but the means to its transcendence—the transcendence of judgmentalism, obligation, duty, rights, blame, guilt, censure and even justifiable resentment.

Kohlberg terms the motivation of a Stage 6 to practice what (s)he preaches, as involving self-condemnation. "If I don't do what I know to be right, then I'm not the person I thought I was, I have not lived up to my self-ideal, I am less moral than I should be." In earlier stages motivations such as fear, guilt and shame filled this role. All of these motivations are negative and self-negating. Even action from a sense of obligation, duty or justice demonstrates the alien role of morality in our desire system. Positive moral development should be social development. It should help us become the kind of people who *want* to do what we now see as things we *should* do. It should make our ideals our interests. This is positive morality. Is it any less a function of false ideology than negative morality? Let us construct a non-Kohlbergian interpretation of Kohlberg's findings and theory; one which interprets Kohlberg's work as basically an expression of politically liberal rhetoric and consciousness, rather than a description of human psychology per se. In the spirit of such interpretations we shall call this the Anti-Kohlbergian Manifesto, and shall launch it as an attack.

Off the Stages

Kohlberg's theory represents a characterization of mainly authoritarian moral reasoning and social learning in Stages 1-3. Stages 4-6 represent increasing contamination of psychological factors with a certain type of political-legal ideology. In the first two stages children are shown to reason individualistically (egocentrically), conceiving of moral situations in terms of progressively broadening interpersonal units. Conception and resolution of dilemmas in terms of power relationships at these earliest stages, to some extent represents merely psychological features of our development, e.g., the perceived power, competence, and physical size of adults in relation to their children. At the same time there is likely to be contamination even here of cultural features having to do with the nuclear and extended family and/or with authoritarian adult-child hierarchies. Tribal children in less authoritarian cultures might show stronger tendencies earlier in their development to adopt full tribal (social) perspectives from which to view and resolve dilemmas. Moreover, their cognitive motivations might show more concern with community solidarity than fear or power at the earliest stages.

It should be noted that Kohlberg's cross-cultural work did not attain evidence of principled, "higher" stage, reasoning in foreign cultures. Is this due to lack of cognitive stimulation in these areas, or deficiency in the social programming related to the socio-economic interests of the governments there? The role-taking opportunities we in North America are provided with, lead to higher stage thinking within a particular economic and liberal democratic context which touches our mentality from the moment of our contact with the media, the national anthems and the beginning of native language and history lessons. New validation (in press) of Kohlbergian stages in children of a Kibbutz environment are therefore most interesting (Reimer, 1976). We should expect some of the private property based nuclear family influence to be mitigated here, demonstrating the more purely psychological nature of Kohlbergian stages. However, we must look more closely at the family structure and social models utilized in particular kibbutzim before we can dismiss the likelihood of extensive culture bias contamination. What would we find in a culture where children were raised by slightly older children and parents did not step in (as they do in large families where older children do child-rear) as the power figure? Is it necessary that adults play such a role? Can non-authoritarian childrearing and social cooperation work and be self-regulating?

Kohlberg terms Stage 4 morality conventional because it represents an acceptance of the social values held in that Stage 4 person's particular culture as valid, and valid basically as a function of that society's holding it. Most people who rise above Stage 4, which is not *most* people, see through the arbitrariness and often the hypocrisy of conventional values. What they soon come to see if thoughtful, however, is not that there are no valid moral rules, but that valid moral rules transcend this or that social system and apply to all people as people. This realization, self-creation, and self-legislation of truly principled and post-conventional morality represents Stage 5. (If one then goes to graduate school in philosophy and continues doing moral philosophy for years and years, one may arrive at the Stage 6 level.)

Kohlberg at the same time characterizes present-day Liberal democratic systems as founded upon Stage 5 principles. If this is so, then it would seem that by merely thinking harder about the conventional morality (Stage 5) one could progress from a Stage 4 to a Stage 5 understanding of it. On what grounds can we call a Stage 5 understanding of Stage 5 principles post-conventional? Look at the founding documents of Liberal ideology: "All men are created equal . . . are equal in the eyes of the law." The basic message of Christianity is that we are all equal in the eyes of God, brothers under the skin, and the like. Stage 6 also represents merely a further extrapolation and sophistication of the legalistic fair-play notions of conventional morality at Stages 4 and 5. What is kept constant in moving from Stage 4 through 6 is not only a merely factually erroneous content (false ideology) in one's views, but a brand or structure of moral conceptualization which is itself the reflection and universalization of a particular political-economic worldview.

The very notion of principles which apply to all persons as persons, to some extent independent of differential individual and social characteristics, not to mention socio-economic conditions, represents what may be termed a conventional morality which turns out to be a false one at that. Indeed it does not apply to one's nation-society per se. Yet it applies to and is characteristic of a type of consciousness, i.e., bourgeois or false consciousness, as opposed to others, e.g., radical leftist consciousness. It defines rights and duties in individualistic terms and thereby protects the property of the affluent against the needs of those less affluent. Moreover, it offers us a stagnant view of human nature and the relation of facts to moral issues and their solutions. In this sense structure as well as content may apparently remain somewhat constant from Kohlbergian conventional through post-conventional stages, when viewed from the perspective of an expanded notion of stage as consciousness. Stages 4-6 do not represent essential restructuring in logical form, but rather broadening of perceived range from a particular class ideology as it occurs in one's country to that same class ideology more internationally conceived. There is little significance in the fact that this might also include a refining of right-duty correlativity.[3]

At level 4½, as Kohlberg notes, we may indeed see through the hypocrisy and arbitrariness of our conventional morality (Liberal ideology), but why interpret movement to Stage 5 as coming to our senses as compared to rationalizing our inability to leave the fold? (By "rationalizing" I mean not only deceiving oneself, but also, with *bad* reasons.) Might Stage 5 not represent a high-level excuse for selling out to the establishment after seeing it for what it is? So what if this sell-out takes a more complex or extended form, given that the form is faulty? More complex lies are merely, perhaps, more dangerous lies.

It should be kept in mind that Kohlberg is gathering and interpreting data under the influence of a particular socialization, training, and ideology. The way he and others do psychology, the basic assumptions and methods of so-called empiricism are vulnerable to powerful political and psychological critique. We need not totally believe or adopt the ideologies of these critiques (and those "manifestoed" above) to feel that there may be good grounds for at least being suspicious as to the validity of the moral views or beliefs we adhere to. Similarly, we need not swallow all of Freudian theory to recognize that we sometimes do

---

[3]It should be noted that Kohlberg's substaging practices produce one substage between 5A and 6, namely, 5B, which runs counter to the criticism just lodged above. One might believe that this substage demonstrates, through its teleological form, the erroneousness of the criticism in question. A more plausible alternative is that 5B does not belong in Stage 5, but above what is now termed Stage 6.

things for reasons we often "hide from ourselves" or fail to recognize except in retrospect. Among unconscious influences on our choices and behavior are political and social influences of which we are not totally aware.

The rationalization problem is particularly acute in Kohlberg's area of research and educational intervention. Indeed, Kohlberg's data can in no way distinguish a justification from what might be seen as a rationalization. (Again it should be noted that in speaking of rationalization here, I mean to emphasize the use of self-deception through *faulty* thinking.) The judgment-action problem is the name given to instances in which people do not act as they judge they should. Yet, I would think that if there were *not* some gap between what people replied to the Kohlberg interview and what they would do in a real situation, we should then have cause to wonder. Morality and moral thought in our culture are exceedingly rationalistic at higher levels—witness our constitutions, legal codes, Church canons and the like. Those who are most talented at reasoning and arguing will be best at moral reasoning. This is because their talent will be the most useful of all talents to their cognitive development. At least this would be so if *role-taking* were not taken by Kohlberg as essential to moral reasoning development. But note, that role-taking is a *cognitive* skill. It is *not* empathy or role-playing and should not be confused with them. Role-taking is the ablity to know that someone else's perspective may be different from one's own and only to some degree exactly how it may be different. Role-taking is then a gedanken- or thought-experiment. Facility at such intellectual experimenting is crucial to the talent of a reasoner, in a way it is not to a so-called sensitive or perceptive person.

With great facility at argument and reason-giving, yet no necessary abundance of sensitivity, the growing rationalist child is in perfect shape to rationalize. Moreover, it is plausible to believe (though not statistically documented) that intellectual children as they develop, are likely to neglect interpersonal feeling-skills, lack emotional openness toward their own insides, and utilize intellectualization and rationalization as their major defense mechanisms against others and their own self-doubts or accusations. They so use it because it's what they're best at. My experience and that of those intellectuals and people who know (or treat) intellectuals confirms this stereotype. You may consult your own experience.

This noted, it becomes at least questionable whether one ought to stimulate the development of sophisticated moral reasoning in those most likely to develop farthest while at the same time lacking the emotional maturity to develop best. Why it is *better* to proceed up the stages intellectually becomes questionable, from the moral point of view. (Keep in mind that Kohlberg defines the "betterness" of each stage psycho-ethically). Rationalization is not most critical for Kohlberg theoretically when couched in terms of self-deception except as regards the judgement-action problem. For though reasons we present for holding a view may be self-deceptive (i.e., because they are actually *not* our reasons), they may be good reasons.

Rationalization is a crucial problem in another sense, that is, in that role-taking may be utilized either as a means to empathy toward, or manipulation of others. From the moral point of view in role-taking we must not only be able to recognize that others have a point of view, or even what that point of view is, but to assume that point of view fully. We must regard that person's welfare from *their* point of view with a degree of self-interest not uncomparable to that we display for ourselves from *our* point of view. This is what it is to respect persons, to take them seriously. It is incredibly easy not to do this and to believe whole-heartedly that one has. Thus rationalization cuts against not only the reasoning levels of stage development, but the role-taking levels supposedly necessary to the sophistication of reasoning. What higher stages provide the rationalizer (and there is a bit of her (him) in each of us) is an invulnerable refuge for self-deception as well as the deception and misleading of others. Invulnerability comes from the fact that at the highest stages there are fewer arguments because perhaps there are fewer arguers to formulate and wield them, which might easily unseat the rationalizations in question. Especially in the heat of moral dilemma—self-interest vs. what is right—the tendency to intellectualize backsliding, is heightened. Should it be reinforced?

For the attainment of a higher stage to be better in the full ethical sense, it must be attained in coordination with the maturing of other abilities and the development of their regular use. There are those who have said that Freudian theory, if true, undercuts morality. Kant was especially worried about the problem of our not being able to be certain that our moral motives were pure. Another way to see psychoanalysis (or the gaining of insight into one's motivations by whatever means) is as the necessary precondition for moral choice and action. It allows us (to paraphrase Davy Crockett) to be surer we are right, before we go ahead.

Does anything of what I have said indicate that we should ignore Kohlberg's findings or theoretical interpretation of them? Quite the contrary. At worst, what his work provides us with is great insight into both moral psychology and the pervasiveness of moral ideology of a sort. Much of this ideology is in the theory itself, i.e., the way Kohlberg chooses to amass and interpret relevant data. What we need to do is figure out which is which, how to isolate one from the other. The reasoning dimension, when appended by other psychological findings, will then give us a picture of the psychological limitations and so feasible ranges of moral beliefs and practices. The ideological dimension will provide us with a clear picture of what we must guard against or inculcate through moral education and via a revision of scientific methodology. The account I gave of positive morality as a "better" enterprise, dedicated to high ideals, virtues, and certain moral exemplars as most admirable, is a product of many of the same ideological and psychological influences which yield Kohlberg's philosophy and psychology. Can the positive side of morality, with its tendency to fanaticism, rigidity, puritanical purity, self-flagellation and crusading egomania be trusted so much more than the retributive punishment side? As tempting as it might seem, we should be cautious before buying even *love* as the answer.

Kohlberg, with other deontologists of course, believes love to be a wonderful phenomenon, but hardly an adequate procedure for moral decision-making. Love may be good for motivating kindness, but where it is absent, the yield may be less than justice. Where there is conflict, a love or altruism ethic cannot decide, for it resides equally on both sides of the conflict. Although I cannot pursue this issue here at length, it should be mentioned that love as a decision-procedure, is only seen as deficient in conflicts of interest when viewed on the model of just solutions. Justice may yield one solution where love yields several, or is equally supportive of several. Those in conflict might seek one solution, but is that what they *should* be seeking? They may through justice be seeking satisfaction as we say, but come away with a just compromise that pleases no one. This is a solution, but what does it solve?

A love ethic can send us looking for ways to skirt conflicts, to rise to another level of thinking about and cooperating with regard to the conflict in question, which will reduce its importance. Justice, on the other hand, legitimizes the conflict as it stands and may leave in the wake of its adjudication, lingering resentment and guilt. Without specifying details, what I am saying here might sound a bit soppy. Let me cite an actual case in relevant intellectual history. The Stage 6 or fair solution to Kohlberg's lifeboat dilemma is taken to be the drawing of lots for who must go overboard so that others might stand some feasible chance of surviving. In a recent role-play of this dilemma at a moral development conference, the lifeboat occupants (including myself) undertook somewhat heartfelt discussion with each other, deciding finally that it would be better for us all to go down on the slimmest chance that we would be saved, than to insure the death of two of us, for justice's sake (the sake of the others). Kohlberg was the one dissenting member of our crew who kept calling to our attention how our nobility was killing him (literally), and how this wasn't fair. In the abstract I would find our decision difficult to justify. I certainly would not have opted for it beforehand. But it seemed then and lingers with me now as the most truly beautiful thing we could have done. Of course it might have been better if two of us had jumped off and sacrificed our lives; for Kohlberg's sake, at least. This is what I mean when I say that "love" decisions admit of several and pursue higher-level solutions. (End of sermon.)

As far as I am concerned, however, the love ethic people and those who would accuse Kohlberg of ideological fault (myself, for example) remain more rhetoriticians than theorists or scientists until they can come up with some clear principles of love (as we have principles of justice) and can at least sketch out ways in which to measure the influence of false ideology. At present I am working on such endeavors, and I suggest to those who share my philosophical predelictions to begin becoming more hard-headed than is typical of our type, in this regard also. In the next section I will begin to sketch, for example, a way to psychologically define such concepts as alienation and dehumanization which have been used by Marxists to characterize false ideology. I also attempt to sketch how we might formulate moral principles so as to retain the best insights of deontology and teleology, while eliminating their implausibilities.

III. Natural Psychology—Sick Society

In the initial section of this article I referred to the trade-off problem posed by moral theory. My claim is that morality, as we normally conceive of it, cannot be *determined* by facts about our psychology, universal or not, because it is dedicated to opposing them. Moreover, this dedication, though psychologically based, is not psychologically (cognitively) *determined* in a universal or standard way. There can be no Stage 6, no *ultimate* stage. Morality is rather a matter of creative imagination linked to complexes of self-interest, socialization, superstition, overoptimism or cynicism, striving or insecurity, hope and joy, or self-hate and masochism. People imaginatively form a view of the people they would like to be or the society they would like to have and in various ways pursue these ideals. They are called dreamers and fanatics to the degree that their goals surpass the realms of probable or even possible attainment by normal or even exceptional people. Saints are often disappointed in themselves as a function of having seriously set goals which are apparently beyond the range of human capability, and perhaps fortunately so. In this sense, a moral view may prescribe forms of behavior which not only run contrary to psychological tendencies, but are designed to off-set or outstrip our range of psychological functioning. To see my point more clearly, please accompany me on a little psychopolitical fantasy.

There are some who claim that two of the most morally objectionable phenomena of social life, under a variety of conditions, are alienation and dehumanization. By alienation and dehumanization I will mean especially the treatment of people by others which subverts what would have been their normal or natural development in a way they would and should object to were they able to realize "fully" what was happening. (As children they cannot. As adults they know not.) Alienation and dehumanization could occur by the design of human action, by its foreseeable but unforeseen consequences, or even as a result of natural phenomena. We will center here on the especially morally objectionable forms in which people are manipulated by others, as through education and the media, or subverted through unintended but foreseeable consequences of actions. These two processes of alienation and dehumanization pervert our psychologies and values in such a way as to make us enemies to (competitors with) our fellow beings, as well as to ourselves (obstacles to the attainment of our own true interests). They cause us to measure humans in terms of material goods and often as less valuable than them.

Many attacks on the alienating and dehumanizing elements especially in competitive market and technologized society seem to rest on disputable factual assumptions regarding the essentially social and autonomous (self-liberating) nature of humankind. The problem posed here for psychology is that of defining human nature, the range of natural or normal development and function, in value-free way. Yet we wish this value-free definition to answer our questions about the essential goodness, badness, neutrality, individualism or spontaneous sociability of humankind. Alienation and dehumanization may then be defined as what opposes these facts, what perverts our "true nature." Although most psychologists find this problem laughably hopeless as a project of research, psychological theorists apparently feel free to assume individualistic tendencies found in early childhood as determining basic human motivation throughout life. (Psychological theory and research is very often a tale of ideological bias as well as one of science.)

For our purposes, natural development and function need only be defined insofar as they are relevant to moral objectionability, and therefore in close relation to (on a continuum with) unnatural development and function. I believe that the range of natural development may be defined along three dimensions. The first concerns basic laws of psychology, especially the law of effect or reinforcement which in most ways aligns with a combination of Freud's pleasure and reality principles. Put most generally, this law tells us that people initially and to some extent throughout life, tend to pursue pleasurable experiences of more or less complex sorts, while avoiding unpleasurable ones. Initially pleasure may be accurately defined in terms of basic needs or drives and the operation of our senses in relation to pleasure centers (the limbic system) in the brain. With the development of cognitive and conative capacities the conception of pleasure must be, though rarely has been in psychological theory, modified to include more thought-mediated complexes of satisfaction and equilibration. With the addition of "higher" cognitive and conative (emotional) systems, the pleasure principle becomes incorporated with prudential reasoning (enlightened self-interest) so as to form a motivational principle in which what we often term happiness, is sought. Happiness, psychologically defined involves the predominance of complex satisfactions and equilibrations over complex frustrations, depressions, and disequilibrations. The complexity involved is illustrated by the fact that a simple pain or frustrating need may actually form part of a complex satisfaction when balanced in the proper way with pleasures. This is experienced in tickling, sexual activity, most forms of having fun including athletic or artistic pursuits, and especially in learning—the development of capacities and skills.

Note that the notion of equilibration is not merely a means of structurally or functionally characterizing complex satisfactions. If this were all it did, I would see the happiness principle as overly reductionistic. Equilibrations concern also the stability of motivational functions and principles which are proper to higher cognitive and conative capacities. One example of such a "drive" which might be better termed a pull is that motivation most of us seem to have to render our relation to the world comprehensible. Although what we traditionally term happiness sets some limits on how far we feel we should go with such meaningfulness pursuits, our tendency to pursue metaphysical comprehensibility of more or less grandiose sorts despite great psychological and physical distress seems to indicate the partial autonomy of this motivational system. I see no reason to believe that systems, however complex they become, will always function in all ways, at all levels, by the same initial directives which predominated in their more primitive stages of evolution.

The second dimension definitive of natural development and function concerns degree of stress and integration of the psychophysical system. Particularly, I would hold that natural development and function would fall in the range of those psychophysical systems which would fulfill or at least not predominantly oppose the functioning of the psychological laws of the first dimension. That is, the fulfilling of psychological predispositions to pursue a predominance of complex pleasure over complex pain in experience would not normally (naturally) involve the development of cognitive, conative, or behavioral sets which through their very operation would strongly oppose tendencies toward happiness. Abnormal or unnatural development would involve the formation of such oppositional psychological patterns to a great degree. That is, they would involve a necessary high level of stress (displeasure) in the carrying out of pleasure-seeking activities, and so would be self-defeating or neurotic. (An addiction is of this form.) Extreme abnormal development and function would yield so great a degree of stress as to cause dysfunctions in the ability to pursue pleasure in opposition to the stress thereby created (including the pursuit of pleasure through relieving that stress). This would be accompanied by a breakdown in external coping behavior necessary to competent functioning, further development (given appropriate stimuli), and the satisfying of desires pleasurably through such functioning. It is abnormal then to be unable to maintain internal functional integrity without shutting down one's functional and developmental systems, especially where so doing impedes ability to cope with or interact developmentally with environmental stimuli.

This second dimension is supported by the third which involves facts about our species-success and the selection of competence capacities via the evolutionary process. For those of you who are fond of Darwin, please bear with the account I am about to give. It certainly smacks of being teleological (purposeful) rather than random (in the sense of random selection) and makes claims about evolution and naturalness which are not at all entailed by Darwin's theory. I see Darwin's theory as in many ways inadequate once a certain phylogenetic level is reached, basically because certain of our capacities allow us to be purposeful in our manipulation of factors crucial to species-success. My definition of natural is normative to the extent that it makes note of and evaluates the ways in which we manipulate these factors. When we develop adaptive capacities and then use them in a way which is not foolishly species-destructive but purposefully so, in the sense that some of the species purposefully endanger us all for the chance of certain individual gains in wealth or fame, this is unnatural or sick. It is not unusual. Psychosis is not unusual. (Murder, of course, is relatively unusual.) What I maintain is that what is unnatural comes out of a perversion of capacities selected for by evolution. Freely functioning, these capacities would not be species-destructive. I recognize how debatable and speculatively bold such a view is, but let me at least propose an initial sketch of it in the hopes that it may seem plausible and interesting to some.

Our developmental process as well as the organization and functioning of our capacities have proven enormously successful in the survival and proliferation of our species. As a result, we would expect that the natural functioning and development of these active capacities in general would not involve degrees of stress which would threaten their functional integrity either internally or externally in those environments in which they have proven successful. Rather, we would expect their *optimal* functioning and further development to take place, necessitated partially by the likely results in social complexity yielded by optimal functioning.

Due to the manner of our development as species and individuals thereof, it is not unnatural for us to develop or function in ways that yield some degree of stress. In a changing environment this is necessary to coping behavior for each individual and so, to species survival (which we have already proven successful). Natural motivation, then, will not only involve tension reduction but a complex of tension *arousal* and reduction, where a certain degree of stress or tension can be conceived of and will be experienced as part of complex pleasure. Adaptive learning experiences fall within this category. This way of conceiving motivation ties it to our psychophysical heritage (how we got to be complex and successful organisms) and to our future progression through adaptive learning and the development of relevant capacities for such learning. Equilibration as a higher order pleasure or happiness principle, then, balances off the cycle of greater complex pleasure pursuit and complex pain avoidance with a certain degree of competence which forms the necessary background condition in balance, for the capacity to equilibrate. Competence and its necessary precondition, learning through often stressful accommodation, may be seen then as natural also. Unacceptable stress, stress which impedes accommodation, development, competent functioning and equilibration-potential, represents unnatural stress, and is demonstrative of unnatural development and function. (Because I cannot take up all issues, I will leave aside the question of whether new "non-happiness motivations" arise at the cognitive level which render sensible notions such as "doing X for its own sake," or performing altruistic acts which do not involve any self-interested motivations.)

It may, of course, be that in modern complex societies we create environments to which we are unable to adapt using our currently developed skills and that these environments are created unknowingly and unforeseeably, given our capacities. In this sense it could be said that our species-death is not unnatural, nor the breakdown of our functions and the degree of stress preceding species death. (It is not unnatural for elephants to die out due to their present lack of ability to properly deal with this new situation of rapidly declining resources.) In all cases where environments are manipulated for the short run benefit of some at the expense of others, so as to cause this sort of functional breakdown and stress, the breakdown and stress are natural in the evolutionary sense. Yet these results are objectionable and increasingly so especially insofar as the manipulation and its results are irreversible and were begun in a way that posed such foreseeable, potential dangers. The problem is one of at least morally criminal negligence on the part of those manipulating these environments. We will have to look at the basis of this objectionability claim in a moment.

Note that the characterization of the relation of species success and the development and functioning of useful capacities I have just presented does not do a great deal of work in my characterization of natural development. It is meant merely to provide a plausibility argument for why self-defeating psychological systems are likely to be abnormal, i.e., the result of some perversion rather than expression of our capacities. A fuller presentation of this point would require complicated evolutionary arguments to take account of the relation of materially affluent social systems in the process of natural selection. Piaget's theory moves somewhat away from biological to social coping in this way. The role of moral systems in such social contexts seems in particular need of explanation from the perspective of evolutionary argument. Civilizing influences such as moral norms in society appear directed toward the stifling of a whole range of human capacities which at the least have not been selected against by evolution, e.g., aggression. Are we to say, then, that such social conventions merely represent evolution's (nature's) way of carrying out its processes where instinctual mechanisms have been largely replaced by cognitive capacities? In this sense, should we merely see such social choices as evolution finally achieving the teleology (purposefulness) some had wanted to attribute to the process all along?

We might complicate my notion of unnatural as perversion to include not only adaptive faculties which are being interfered with, but non-adaptive faculties which are not being interfered with as they become and are recognized as becoming more and more non-adaptive to species-success. It is possible, of course, to claim that all of our socio-moral degeneracy is merely a function of previously adaptive capacities which though our morality works to control them, cannot be stopped from coming through at times. Evolutionary selection may prove slower than the industrial revolution and the development of mechanized warfare. In this sense, our moral systems, though imperfect, may be seen as holding the fort until the neural aggression centers and adrenal glands diminish in size and function. (Should we organize our world so that the warriors kill each other off and leave few children?) It seems plausible to me that both of the claims in question are true in that the stifling and sublimating of formerly adaptive capacities is adaptive and that the stifling of adaptive capacities, is not. The former is natural, the latter is not.

Of societies, some may be judged as more or less "natural" or as some say, "sick," not solely in terms of their ability to survive or appear formally stable from the outside, but in terms of how debilitating they are with regard to the psychological and physical well-being of their members. The "sick" society and the "perverted" personality's stability will involve almost constant strain. Members will be plagued with psychological stress and fixation and/or will have to be put through rigorous training designed to suppress a significant range of their capacities, including adaptive ones. This training, because it is so extreme in its opposition to psychological tendencies, will normally prove to be inadequate and will have to be backed by social pressure (positive and negative), as well as legal sanctions. A society may then be seen as sick in two ways from the perspective of its members. It is sick insofar as its members are sick (stressed and dysfunctional) and insofar as it operates through its institutional structure so as to yield such a result. A society which moves its ideals too far ahead of its evolution, so to speak, is sick. Note that a society that is stressful to its members need not be seen as unnatural from the perspective of social forms unless it leads to a degree of psychological debilitation which so seriously threatens its own stability as to threaten species survival. The difference between societies and governments here should be borne in mind. Social breakdown would involve the inability of a large number of the species to peacefully coexist. It would involve a breakdown in customs and even cooperative non-interference in those activities essential to member survival or welfare. Governments come and go in a somewhat less crucial sense.

We may note that for any complex of human traits to flourish, some potential traits must be suppressed or not allowed to develop. In a sense, then, some predominance of traits X over Y may not involve socialization suppression, but the somewhat chance snowball effect of some traits beginning to develop first. I do not know if traits cluster; if personality *types* are *natural* in this sense. Such variance is not troublesome to the point I have made nor hope to make regarding natural psychology or objectionable perversion of such psychology, so long as it does not include dysfunctional clusters.

What many of us would consider civilized or morally admirable societies might fall within the category of "sick" society as I have characterized it. This I regard as a happy consequence of my categorization, since I believe "sick" to capture much of what civilization and moralization embodies socially. It is indeed moral conflict (intra- and interpersonally), taboos, and the so-called moral emotions such as guilt-shame, humiliation, self-condemnation (combined with their Freudian helpers, intellectualization, rationalization, reaction-formation, suppression or denial) which are to blame for much intellectual and emotional strangulation in our societies. They also seem to contribute to a basic lack of gusto, spontaneity, creativity, openness, and flexibility which we might otherwise enjoy as humans. I would argue that norms of this sort threaten us both as a species and as individuals, where they function. The threat is not so much in terms of our survival at present, but in terms of the stifling effect on that degree of psychological development which is proving more and more necessary to our continued survival in our rapidly altering environment. That is, certain of those norms we see as moral and as civilizing are preventing us as members of society from developing and pooling our cognitive and emotional resources in a way that will solve increasingly complex social problems. Where we desire such survival (and all else dependent on that survival) such social developments (norms) become highly undesirable. Our desiring to survive, moreover, is no accidental, arbitrary, or *merely* imaginative ideal.

It is justifiable, I believe, to move directly from the characterization of normal personal development, and the sick society, to a theory of natural morality. In the history of philosophy such a move is thought to involve a logical lacuna, specifically, between the is of descriptive statements and the ought of prescriptive value statements. My move from the "is" of psychological development to the "ought" of natural morality is complicated and cannot be presented in detail here. I trust it is obvious however, that my definition of natural development and the sick society is amply normative already, so as to allow for a smoother is to ought transition. Moreover, given the range of opposition to the positions I will hold regarding alienation, dehumanization and moral education, the complications of my argument become somewhat unnecessary. This is because opposition theories accept a principle of autonomy or respect for persons upon which my argument depends. The move I propose between natural development and natural morality attempts to provide a firm basis for that principle of autonomy and respect for persons which at present I believe to be lacking in moral theory.

Let me sketch, however, at least the outline of what might be termed a natural morality, and draw its relation to alienation and dehumanization as morally objectionable features of social interaction. Value systems are based upon preferences. In terms of development, a natural morality would term good what satisfies the pleasure principle; what satisfies visceral needs at early levels, and what satisfies the happiness principle at later fuller levels of development. Prescriptive words such as should or ought play the role of prudential advice-giving in a very egoistic (egocentric in Piaget's terminology) self-interested way in youth, and a more complex partly altruistic way in adulthood. "You ought to do this in the sense that it will satisfy your needs." At the earliest levels of development, value words and prescriptive ones converge around physiologically based preferences.

Note that, "You ought to pursue pleasure" is not at all a trivial statement, even given that we are psychophysically predisposed to do so. For what it may be seen to claim is that we should follow our physiological predispositions, which is not at all obvious from what we typically see as the moral point of view. Moreover, where we are not following some physiological predispositions due to the influence of competing interests or beliefs, or due to the interference of other people in our activities, the prescription that we ought to pursue pleasure is highly informative. According to philosophers—especially G. E. Moore—we may be able to ask of such pleasure principles whether, although they inform us as what we tend to desire, we cannot ask whether we *should* desire them. In fact, it is held, the *moral* question is precisely this, i.e., "Should we desire what we tend to desire? And supposedly the moral answer is often "No!"

It seems to me that such an answer makes sense in especially the following cases: (a) when we are unclear or incorrect in our practical calculations as to what will satisfy our desires, e.g., in short vs. long-run instances; (b) when our desire systems are out of whack with our deeper interests, e.g., when we want what will hurt us; (c) when our desires do not express relevant capacities in a proper way as regards moral decision-making, e.g., when we do not role-take or weigh fully, competing reasons when making a decision; and (d) when we wish for others to join with us in our way of thinking and interacting. Note that I am including in satisfying our desires and interests the conflicts we would have with others over what we want and the working out of that conflict in a way that would satisfy our selfish and other-regarding wants.

What we must ask of the philosopher when (s)he maintains that moral shoulds and ideals go beyond interests and are yet objectively true (as compared to the mere dreams, biases, and commitments of some), is what such ideals reflect? If they do not reflect interests, why should we give the smallest damn about them? Why should we take them as somehow more legitimate than ideals which reflect interests? The reply of the dominant philosophical tradition in moral thought would no doubt involve the position that such ideals reflect the purified and fully developed choices of Reason alone; Reason purified of emotional interference. Rationalists often seem to give purified Reason the inside track on truth and, after all, where is the competition? Yet we may ask, "And why is what Reason chooses good?" This is an especially useful question when we must suspect that interest is supposedly not guiding Reason in moral judgment cases. Reason must choose moral ends for their own sake, not out of desire for them. What is guiding Reason here? Should we be pleased with its performance as guide? Some say it is false ideology, class privilege and intellectual defense mechanisms which guide Reason. Perhaps we have cause to worry.

Alongside the pleasure principle of natural morality, though hardly differentiated from it, is a primitive and correlative version of the principle of respect for persons, or autonomy. At the earliest level respect for persons is represented by fear of and love for—awe in the face of—the physical power and size of especially our parents and (if Freud is correct) our father. As we develop, the pleasure principle of natural morality gradually transforms into the happiness principle. This is accomplished through the defining of good in terms of preferences or desire systems which reflect complex interactions of earlier and later developing conative and cognitive capacities, combined with life experiences, socialization influences as well as current and foreseen social contexts. The principle of respect tends to develop in the same way. To the extent that Kohlberg's data reflect natural development, respect or valuing of persons is to be defined with increasing complexity in terms of the utility of one's powers and those of other persons in pursuing one's goals, followed by empathetic concern for the feelings, self-esteem, and complex interests of one's friends, fellow citizens, and eventually, humanity as a whole.

Suppose we could create some admittedly unusual environment which would stimulate natural development without *imposing an indoctrinative* stamp of its particular content. Then we might be able to devise a fully developed (adult) principle of autonomy and happiness which would represent the full flowering of natural morality. Such principles would reflect the ways in which various capacities would function in rendering value decisions. It would reflect a view of how valuable persons were in relation to things valued by people. We might be able to argue that given the influence of reason and the lack of total flexibility in desire systems, necessary conditions for all value and/or moral systems could be specified. For example, unless people are respected in general and to a certain degree, it will be impossible to have value systems and for most people to attain preserve and further what they value. Much of what they will value includes themselves and others. This would represent one way in which the facts of our common psychologies provide a basis for objectivity in moral views. On the other hand, there is no reason to believe that these necessary conditions of value systems or moral systems are all that extensive. For example, they should not be expected to be extensive enough when specified, to rule out any of the major theories or even to show any clearly superior to any other. Yet they may exclude some theories such as those which say, "Kill everyone," or "Do not advance the welfare of others."

How may we narrow the variability of plausible alternative moral view or broaden the range of objectivity? One way to accomplish this might involve showing that given common preference, certain moral prescriptions give better practical advice regarding how to act upon them successfully. This is to trade on the functional limits provided by the facts of our psychology. A further strategy might be to present some picture of moral personality, i.e., to specify a standard psychology, by which to render a range of moral judgments less valid than others. Many believe that principles of respect for persons advanced in this way represent the bedrock of objectivist moral theory. Let us test the stability of this bedrock.

The rationalist tradition, represented most recently by the Kantianism of Rawls in his classic book *A Theory of Justice*, holds that some subset of our personality traits is of prime and exclusive relevance to morality. This is so both as regards moral decision-making and as regards the proper treatment of persons. For Kantians, reason and free will—those capacities necessary to play the moral game of deliberating and choosing right and wrong actions—are considered those features which should determine our moral choices. The influence of emotions and interests (often termed by these theorists passions and biases) on moral judgments, are seen as illegitimizing. If one looks to the rationale for the precise form their selectivity in defining moral personhood takes, one finds nothing very substantial. It seems to rest in a somewhat descredited belief, presented most blatantly in Aristotle's function argument, that reason, because it is what distinguishes the human species, should be the prime influence on our activities. Nostalgia for this difficult to support position has been reinforced by the rationalistic biases, lifestyles, and class consciousness of those intellectuals who by and large shape the form which moral philosophy takes. These days we call it, "being out of touch with one's feelings."

Yet we need not only object to the form of selectivity such views of moral personhood take, but to the very notion of selectivity. The latter objection may take two forms. From the naive common sense point of view we can question the utility of being selective in defining moral personality (of defining it as a subset of personality traits) when we already are able to agree on the limits of psychophysical personality. This argument should compel the objectivist who after all is seeking grounds for agreement as regards moral belief. A more daring form of this objection sees the selection of subsets of psychological personality as a betrayal of individualistic bias in defining moral personality. Those who advance such objections would sooner opt for defining moral personhood in terms of psychophysically interpersonal units such as families, tribes, communes or, for certain purposes, even whole societies. Such theorists are often termed socially organismic in their theories, and often are comprised of Utilitarians, social perfectionists, and socialists. Although the case of these theorists appears less plausible than that of the Kantians, I believe it can be made at least as plausible. Since this is not saying much, perhaps, I will forego the attempt.

Variability with regard to theories of moral personality occurs also at the level of treatment; regarding the issue of respect for persons and human rights. Many egalitarian political theorists seem to believe that we deserve equal welfare or at least a guaranteed annual income, simply because we are people and worthy of the dignity at least minimal welfare affords. More libertarian-tending capitalist theorists believe that only certain meritorious or socially useful acts should be "rewarded" with income. Pacifists see just about no action as relevant to the lower limit of how people may be treated, whereas the retributivist is often willing to take the life of someone who has performed immoral or illegal acts of certain sorts, e.g., kidnapping, murder, conspiracy in a robbery which involved murder. We do not respect the total freedom of each person, but are willing to limit it for a variety of reasons. Kantians, of all people are willing to totally ignore the legitimacy of some people's claims to what they hold dear, on the basis that they involve the violation of rights, principles of justice or certain perhaps unjust laws, in being pursued. If theories of moral personality are to function as means for shoring up respect for persons as the bedrock of objectivist ethics, we might expect more objectivity or especially better grounds for it, than one generally finds in the literature (Kant, 1956; Rawls, 1971, p.p. 251-57). Although I cannot take up the issue here, I believe that much of the respect for persons argument is based not on the necessity of free will to the very enterprise of morality, but on the somewhat disguised proposal of personal autonomy, an active self-determining lifestyle, as the highest ideal of life. In this sense I believe that deontologists are complicated perfectionists. Of course deontologists deny this explicitly (Nozick, 1974, pp. 28-33). It seems clear to me that a principle of respect for persons, of taking persons seriously, is crucial to morality, but that it need not and should not be posed as independent of a principle of happiness.

Natural morality expressive of later and fuller development should be expected, I would hold, to represent the principles of autonomy (or respect) and happiness, in combined form. Perhaps such a combined principle could be characterized by the following sorts of statements: *One should prefer what one does prefer when one's preference system has not been interfered with by influences which oppose one's psychophysically and developmentally defined interests. One should think and act out of the fully functioning unperverted aspects of one's developed personality and one should not pervert but should rather further the developing and functioning personalities of others.* Ignoring limitations of practical wisdom and the like, the rationale for these developed principles corresponds in form to those used in supporting the earlier stage pleasure principle. One should further one's own development because this will render more probable the attainment of complex happiness. One should not pervert others because this will likely mitigate against the attainment of complex happiness. Recall that complex happiness involves interest in the welfare of others. This welfare in turn clearly rests upon social morale and the ability of society to solve social and environmental problems. With regard to respect for others it is assumed that the interaction of general prudential considerations or self-interest with fairness or altruism (as the result of role-taking and empathetic development and skill) will provide grounds of interest for predicting the unlikelihood of evolving extremely egoistic theories within the range of natural morality. The same might be said for the likelihood of evolving saint and martyr moralities. Note, however, that natural morality admits of a range of legitimate moral views. It is in this sense relative in its objectivism.

One disturbing and complex complication of the combined principle has to do with adaptive versus maladaptive traits. Should we stimulate or fail to interfere with maladaptive traits? Should we help people's cruelty to flourish, and their aggression? The answer is, of course, no. The problem, then, is one of defining which traits are maladaptive and when. There are those theorists who believe that all aggression against other humans is the result of perversion by others. Some theorists maintain that traits are so broad in their function that they may be both crucially adaptive and maladaptive. The power of aggression may also be the power (sublimated) of ambition, intellectual striving and the like. Although these controversies are difficult, they must eventually be faced.

It should be noted that natural morality is *prima facie* in its stance. It consists in the range of cases to which an exclusivist ethic (a system being advanced as objectively true for all people) must address its arguments. The exclusivist case must demonstrate the superiority of one view to the entire range of views which might be generated by freely functioning and developed people with different though not perverted desire systems and ways of thinking. Consider how difficult this case will be to make, i.e., the case that somehow what free and developed people choose for themselves may not be as valid in form as what would be chosen by certain others for all. By "in form" I mean to note that there may always be arguments which could be advanced to show the superiority of a view on the basis that it utilizes more accurate factual information on what particularly will make people happy, what are efficient means to the attainment of these particulars, what social policies are most feasible to these ends, and the like.

Many objectivists would like to believe that truly free and developed people will converge on the true moral theory because they will see it out there in the world of reason or society (their moral vision being cleared and tuned up), or because we are all that similar under the skin. This latter position would see the facts of our psychology as *determining* true beliefs at ultimately low (drive-based) and ultimately high (reason-based) levels. Yet what evidence is there for believing that such would be the case at a level of organization so inclusive of variables as that of optimal or near-optimal cognitive-conative development? It is just at such levels that so much of what is different about us becomes especially relevant to us. It is at such levels that optimal and extensive flexibility in using our capacities is achieved, i.e., variety in ways of thinking about problems and issues. This is what I formerly referred to as the trade-off posed by morality, the "ought" rather than "is" of morality. Using our later and earlier developing systems in combination we are enabled to formulate ways of living, goals to pursue and a variety of social forms which sacrifice some goods to others. We may be willing and rational in tolerating somewhat stressful environments for the sake of health advantages they yield, e.g., mechanized hospitals and the technology they depend on. Natural morality functions as a backdrop against which to weigh the "sanity" of such choices. It functions as a warning system when the sacrifices we make to imaginative ideals begin to threaten the very source and end of those ideals, i.e., our happiness, autonomy, development and functioning, on which they depend. Natural morality, in taking these principles of life and morality as intrinsically interconnected mitigates against the formulation of moral systems which are "insane" in themselves; i.e., moral systems which allow or prescribe choices in service to self-determination (individual rights) in a way which undercuts the attainment of individual happiness of which autonomy is only a part. It is this point which I feel Marxists wish to make in their arguments against the alienating effects of political rights in Capitalist systems.

The objectionability of alienation and dehumanization may be defined now in terms of natural morality. This is accomplished via the notion of perversion of personality which will have to be spelled out at length. Many influences may interfere with "natural development." Some of these may be judged good despite their initial undesirable effects on the growing child. Here we may include certain forms of justified paternalism, i.e., "You can't play in the street," and types of competence training. Other obstacles to natural development will involve the limitations or contingent facts of physical and social environments. In this regard, natural morality may speak to our obligations regarding actions designed to alter our societies in ways which will be more propitious to natural and full human development and function. Environments which are optimal for spurring what I have termed natural development may seem unlikely, as natural occurrences, as opposed to designed ones. Of course, designing is natural, given human cognitive capacities. The easiest case for natural morality against aliena- tion and dehumanization is represented by the actions of those who pervert others in ways which violate their autonomy and happiness. By allowing natural morality a range of legitimate moral views, we do not circumscribe the capitalist as culprit to the degree a Marxist might perhaps desire in this context. Moreover, we take most of the steam out of the notion of social profiteers as evil demons. Indeed, it is likely that those who choose and/or act out of profiteer dehumaniz- ing and alienating perspectives are the victims of personality and developmental perversion themselves. How can the Marxist deny this?

IV. Freer Than Free Education

In my discussion of Kohlberg's theory, I had suggested that by separating ideo- logical influences from psychologically-based moral reasoning, we could gain a clear picture of (1) what to guard against, or (2) inculcate, via moral education. In proceeding to our discussion of moral education, I would like to pursue these two possibilities, vindicating this essay's title, *Moral Education and Its Cure*, and directly addressing the problem posed at this essay's inception:

> If we do not know what morality is, we cannot teach it. In crucial ways, we do not know what morality is. Yet we must teach it because it is of prime importance and must be learned. Moreover, teaching must not be brainwashing; it must be moral.

The influence of unconscious (unseen political and psychological) factors on our moral thinking and consciousness I see as the reason we do not know what morality is. The effect of these influences in stultifying, fixating, alienating and dehumanizing us is the reason I see for why morality, when we find it, is of prime importance and must be learned. My approach, then, is directed toward finding and using morality. This can be done both within and without educa- tional institutions as they now stand.

Kohlberg and other Deweyites claim that the stimulation of development is the only ethically acceptable form of moral education. If, as Kohlberg holds, people can only develop in one way when they do develop, i.e., *up* the moral stages, it cannot be wrong to stimulate them to do so. I have already questioned the truth of this seemingly uncontroversial claim. Kohlberg himself recognizes the ethical dilemma of raising people to later stages of moral insights when they must live in a social context governed by earlier stage dog-eat-dog rules. Morality can be a disadvantage in a cruel world, as we shall soon see.

When we speak of freedom in regard to our moral political and educational systems, we concentrate on *non-interference* with regard to consciousness, and *gaining power control or competence* with regard to skills. "After all, we do not want to control the child's mind! That's indoctrination!'' Well, we don't want to *control* the child's behaviors either. Rather, we should want the child to gain power, control over, and competence in using both mind and body. We continue to fail to take account of the full indoctrinative influence of the socialization process on free education. The education process begins and is maintained in the home, and we at school normally would rear our students much as their parents do, despite huge differences at certain points. People who enter teaching professions are, even when unconventional, unconventional in a basically conventional way. Even those with the least authoritarian slant recognize "the need for discipline" and are becoming increasingly disaffected with many free-wheeling alternative approaches to education. What this failure of anarchic education may indicate, however, is that people work best when organized and cooperating, not when each is doing her (his) own thing. But the point is that there are more or less authoritarian forms of organization and cooperation.

At the same time, although it is ideal to allow organization to evolve from the needs and interests of, e.g., classroom members, such evolution may indeed not be as voluntary as it would seem. That is, its structure would most likely mirror the authoritarian structure of the family or traditional classroom (leaders-followers) which though inappropriate to peer-relations, is the most powerful if not the only model of interpersonal relations at students' command.

An alternative that is being tried, e.g., by Kohlberg, is the just community approach in both correctional and educational institutions. Although run with some traditional safeguards against too much freedom, these set-ups attempt to remold both the consciousness of leaders and followers (teachers-guards and students-inmates) with regard to justice and fair play. They do this by allowing both groups to discuss and formulate the terms of their own cooperation with each other, toward goals they agree upon. This is done, to some extent, in one vote per person fashion. Here we not only have the autonomy (self-determination) of each person respected as it stands at present. We have also a developmental cycle of self-transformation set up. For as people choose the pattern of their relationships, their social institutions in a sense, so they formulate policies for changing the way they see themselves in relation to others. By legislating their own rules and in such a way as to decrease, e.g., authoritarianism in their social structure, they are likely to become less authoritarian in their thinking and predispositions to behave. Self-determination at best, is self-transformation. Lack of self-determination represents alienation and suppression in that it impedes this process of development.

The freedom which various forms of respect for persons and natural rights arguments seek to uphold, represents the ability to direct and carry out our lives as we see fit. "By our own wills" is the key to autonomy or self-determination. Looked at developmentally, freedom is a paradoxical quality of both persons and societies. It seems to require its opposite, e.g., discipline, direction, law, order, and regularity. On one side, freedom involves lack of obstacles or non-interference. This is the side of public morality to which rights speak primarily in Liberal or Libertarian political systems. On the other side, freedom seems to require power, know-how and any other necessary means for taking advantage of one's right of way. Here we find the basis for equal opportunity guaranteed on annual income, public education and other "welfare" measures which seek to back equal rights with equal power to use them.

There are two special obstacles to freedom with which, it seems to me, education can best deal. They are both unconscious interferences, in an extended sense of "unconscious." The first is being interfered with in one's normal development in such a way that one's interests and one's consciousness are not one's own, i.e., what would have been one's own consciousness had development merely been provided opportunities to progress? We may add to this the acceptability and desirability of some paternalistic interference in so-called natural development which any person would choose to see "perpetrated" on her (him) in retrospect. I characterized autonomy as being able to act through one's own will versus that of others. Laws that protect freedom, concentrate on instances in which we are impeded between our willing to act and our acting. Education must be concerned with those objectionable impediments which occur between ourselves and our will, between our birth and our maturation. When parents, educational institutions, and the media train us to like what we do not like initially, at each developmental phase, they are on dangerous moral ground. When advertising reprograms our wants or turns what we see as weaknesses into addictions, the charge should be breaking and entering with clear intent to harm.

Not all training which positively reinforces what initially seems unpleasant is objectionable, obviously. We are always making such trades between conflicting desires so as to give our life direction. This is to some degree a necessary dilemma where goals are involved, and preferences exist. Because we desire to prolong pleasure we must endure the pain of resisting oversaturation. A parent can justifiably act in the child's behalf, to *some* extent, so as to help that child build competence in such self-control. But we as parents most often go *much* farther than this, both in childrearing and education. We, to a great extent, mold children in our own image both as social and family members.

The problem of self-control speaks to the second form of relevant freedom for education. Again, we train competence in skills, but we do not traditionally deal in education with helping the child become more reflective regarding her (his) own psychology, motivations, drives and the like. When Rousseau speaks of personal freedom as breaking the chains of slavery to our passions, his strong dichotomy between reason and emotion strikes us as dated. Yet there is a sense in which true self-determination involves self-control as thought or intention-directed behavior. This should not legitimize intellectual compulsivity and extreme rationalism. Rather, it should speak to reasonableness and balance. The aim of education in this area should be to help students become aware of the unseen influences on their deliberations, choices, and behaviors whether these be primarily cognitive or emotional. In this way students will be better able to decide whether and to what degree to allow these influences to affect them, as well as to what degree and in what way they may act to alter these effects. Awareness, balance, and capacity to change are of prime importance—not reason controlling emotion.

By becoming aware of why we do things, something most adults are still quite unclear about, we can choose the person we want to be and take steps socially and personally, to become that person. The parallel with regard to socialization and ideology is perfect. In both cases we must provide each other with an awareness of those unseen factors which are causing us to be the way we are, as well as think and act as we do. Through cooperative and also individual effort in altering the way we interrelate and think, we can change who we are; choose the type of person we will be. This is the deepest form of self-determination. We determine not only what we do, but who the person is who does it.

What does this imply in terms of educational policy? As mentioned, it involves both "guarding against," and "inculcation" in a variety of ways. Our educational system must be designed to block and/or counteract social influences which pervert the range of normal development. In Russia and China this is done by taking the child out of the nuclear family and prerevolutionary ideological environment, and indoctrinating what the government feels the child would choose to learn because of its truth. Such a policy is unacceptable in a host of ways for us. A crucial problem here is one of protecting the rights of both parent and child, establishing priority of rights and sanctioning parental obligations, all while hoping to maintain a basis of love rather than obligation in the home. In one sense, *the* problem may be the nuclear family itself. But this is not a problem education can deal with directly and at the moment. (It may be a longer range goal, however.)

How can the government hold parents responsible for their children and yet institute educational policies which will rob them of much of the control to joy, love, and intimacy which parents and children may wish so strongly to share? How can the government "force" people to support through taxes an educational program which would not be fully designed to meet parental expectations, or which would likely have the effect of "turning children against their parents," as the parents would see it? Children who would undergo freer than free education should be expected to think very differently than their parents, and to recognize objectionable authoritarian tendencies in them. Yet if both political (ideological) and psychological reflectiveness are nurtured in a half-way competent manner through such a program, we would expect more understanding of and desire to compromise with and "help" parents in these areas, than is usual in adolescence at present. Any feasible educational policy of the sort I am suggesting should include parental if not social reeducation through the media (e.g., public broadcasting) and perhaps extended PTA-like organizations. I do not mean to paint parents or the socialization process as monsters. Much of childrearing is very beautiful and beneficial to the child. Where it is less so, it may still be to some degree necessary given the world into which children grow and must function. For current purposes, however, I wish to concentrate on the greatest evils of these procedures. Since concentrating on evils is a typical role for justice to play, let's talk justice talk.

We must protect the rights of children as well as of their parents. We are willing to protect the bodies of children to a tiny degree, with laws against negligence, child abuse, and the like. But the sanctity of biological possession scares us from taking extensive action designed to protect their mental welfare and rights to development. When a child is born, it has certain basic rights, e.g., not to be burned alive, not to have life interrupted in an unnatural way. We would not allow parents to stunt their children's growth by feeding them anti-growth pills (e.g., ACTH-inhibitors). Yet we allow, and in adoption cases support, parental rights to instill guilt, mythological belief (from the tooth fairy to a variety of religions and anti-religions) bigotry, dependency neuroses, depression, accentuated insecurities, fixations, unhealthy nutritional and hygienic habits, and the like. Moreover, we allow such treatment at a time in life when its influence may be almost impossible to fully reverse except via concentrated, expensive, long-term effort (e.g., psychological therapy tension and sleeping pills, marriage counseling, yoga and meditation). Early socialization often casts a pall over one's entire life which is hardly noticed, even when noticed, in that we have no "would-have-developed" version of ourselves with which to compare our inverted version. Just because this sort of evil and injustice is so widespread, is no reason to merely acquiesce in it.

Developing a moral sense, conscience, or at least rationale, is a useful if not necessary tool for coping with or fitting into society. Without some assimilation of the conventional morality of the culture one may very likely be a misfit and act in ways which will alienate one from relevant others. Children would have a legitimate complaint against their parents for not providing them with such a socially necessary tool. Yet at the same time can they not also complain about being fed the false hypocritical ethic that so many young people find objectionable and sick today? The moral dilemma for reflective parents is between helping children to become misfits versus hypocrites in a mishapen world. Children will likely come to see certain ideals as superior but difficult if not impossible to attain and maintain given their training in "moral" habits of thought and action, i.e., hang-ups regarding job success, material affluence and the like. The point is not to blame parents. How could they realize or keep from having some of the less savory influences they are having on the child? The point is to do something that will hopefully help and cause the least suffering and damage to all involved.

What can education itself do here? At the least it can provide (inculcate) methods by which students can become aware of unseen socialization and psychological influences on their development. The attentiveness to these influences can come early. Unfortunately, the competence to evaluate them and decide how they should be dealt with comes gradually. To some extent, then, *some* paternalism in inculcating ward-off strategies is justified. Note also that it is not a paternalism that is or need take a form opposed to parental interest, either theoretically or ideally. It is not as if most parents desire to screw up their children. It is because parents are representative of these same influences we see as objectionable as it is transmitted through them to their own children, that provides impetus for our wishing to STOP the process HERE!

Techniques of self and social analysis or reflection are not naturally developed in *our* society especially, and so cannot be merely stimulated. Children must be *urged* to master and utilize them. However, and this is crucial, they must be provided with alternative forms of analysis, to some degree, so as to guard against a deeper form of social indoctrination. I therefore term the introduction of these techniques *inculcation*, and their proper use as one only of guarding against and reversing the influence of right-violations; attempts to rob children of their birthright to unsubverted development. I trust it is obvious why such inculcation used in these ways and amid these social circumstances, is not indoctrination. Although I cannot go into further detail here, I direct your attention to the consciousness-raising literature of, e.g., the women's liberation movement and to several suggested readings (see references) relevant to the type of curriculum development I am advocating. You are free to devise your own, I hope, within or without institutional guidelines. I have attempted to do so in a course I devised called "Lifestyles." (If you would care for a description of this course, please write to me. Perhaps we might develop curricula along these lines together.)

This first phase, then, of the freer than free education process is one of psycho-social (and indeed, moral) consciousness-raising. Once consciousness is on its way up, there can be little justification for additional interference with or failure to adopt student-centered self-development educational policies in Phase Two. Kohlberg notes the dependence of cognitive development on active interaction with the world. In a way, Phase One of freer than free education, safeguards against the tendencies for passivity and lack of freedom to grow. Phase Two takes advantage of phase One's effectiveness while maintaining the use of ward-off techniques for other suitable purposes. With regard to moral education, the developing psycho-social awareness of Phase One and Two should provide just that huge complement to true, de-enculturated cognitive development which is necessary to turn sophisticated moral reasoning into mature overall moral personality development. Empathy and social relating skills will be necessary to and fostered by the guarding of developmental rights process—an uncannily fortunate consequence for personality and character development. But there is more to come.

What this two-phase process of education provides as regards moral education is a real-life theoretical justification for the validity though not necessarily the adequacy of a moral view. It defines validity in terms of whatever views are chosen by children educated in this way. In a sense, freer than free education provides a practical technique for specifying a standard or ideal psychology from which to generate moral principles—as used by ideal observer and veil of ignorance theory in philosophy (Firth, 1952). The deductive justification of a, e.g., moral theory, consists in showing that a certain set of moral beliefs or principles can be derived from certain premises via certain appropriate steps. Through decision theory we may mirror this logical procedure—as Rawls has done—by showing that a hopefully unique set of moral beliefs or principles can be generated by a unique set of psychological traits (people of a certain sort) via certain appropriate ways of thinking termed practical or moral reasoning. Normally, philosophers attempt to provide moral arguments for the appropriateness of how they have specified their standard psychology, moral reasoning procedure, and generation of moral principles. These arguments speak to the greater adequacy or truth of such beliefs, generated by such processes. Yet we may criticize the moral arguments and constructed decision procedures of these philosophers on the basis that they have been generated by a *faulty* process. That is, they have been advanced by philosophers who have been hardly less vulnerable to the perverting effects of socialization. As we cannot trust our moral intuitions, these philosophers should not trust theirs. Their expertise in reasoning has not included psycho-social reflection on the causes for why they advance and hold the moral views they do.

Freer than free educational policy attempts to generate true moral philosophers, cleansed of important biases, in attempting to stimulate and support the process of what may be seen as the range of normal or less objectionably altered development. We of the "freer school" can spur maximal cognitive development with less worry than our free education Kohlbergian predecessors, since the rationalization problem is directly attacked by the psycho-social awareness process, and is therefore less likely to arise. Thus, the preferences, ideals, and justifications, which freer than free graduates would tend to produce, and why, might stand as criteria of validity and as valid views in themselves.

The major area in which the adequacy of these views becomes problematic is in the area of practicality and efficiency. Some ideals or policies chosen by these graduates would no doubt be impractical or found to be unlivable. This is because such graduates lack knowledge and predictive expertise regarding which precise ways to live will lead to what precise consequences. In addition to this practical source, inadequacy in a freer than free moral view can be claimed on the basis of some shoddiness in the free curriculum or its effectiveness. Such ineffectiveness would allow some objectionable perversion of the psychologies of certain students to persist unmitigated. Of course practically this hope of the objectivist will always be founded. No procedure could be near fool-proof. Yet, these very same problem areas are present in all theories and educational programs, in addition to those freer than free theory and policy eliminate.

Should neither of these two attacks on adequacy (factual or consciousness purity) prove fatal in particular cases, then seemingly the only additional ground for claiming greater or less adequacy or truth of the moral views our graduates advance would be on the basis of their cognitive and intellectual maturity. Should we come to agree that several groups of students who hold different moral views are optimally developed, however, then we must accept the fact of another *ultimate* source of relativity in ethics. Of course this notion of high or highest level of development should not be emphasized in a truly developmental approach. Relativity is not an important issue in this context. It is important at all levels of development, however, insofar as we are intolerant of differences in our views. (Where ultimate relativity exists we must be tolerant of the *validity* of different views.)

Who knows how far we can go in our development? And why should the highest or most adequate theory be of special relevance to those on lower levels in governing their relations, except as an incentive for their continually striving to move on? As relativity becomes less important, so does objectivism on the practical level. People have different life histories and experiences when allowed any degree of freedom. These are likely to affect their molding of moral principles and values. Can we term all these differences biasing from the moral point of view? What is the alternative? Should we force people to have like experiences so that we can all avoid the "problem" of having to tolerate differences? Of course even freer than free graduates might choose jointly to do this. If *they* were not those choosing such a course we might well ask why they would choose so, suspecting some conformist indoctrination. We must be prepared, however, to accept free choices that may seem to us from where we now stand, as not quite ideal.

"But what if freer than free graduates started choosing fascist and conquest-oriented moralities rather than Schweitzerian ones?" Why should we worry about this given that so many of *us* have not chosen such views? Is it that in the end we are afraid that we are basically monsters under our superego and that our morality must necessarily be an authoritarian muzzle? Are we afraid that without authoritarian socialization with all its craziness, we will turn out to be even crazier at the core and decide to relate to each other in a way that will make us all more miserable? A psychosocially insightful society will be the last to be lulled into acquiesence toward sick moralities, i.e., moralities which would take such a toll in suffering on them. Are we so afraid of the truth at all levels that we must fool ourselves into submission?

I assume, because it is highly plausible to do so, that what would be chosen by freer than free graduates would be somewhat similar to parts of many traditional moral theories. No doubt there would be some respect for persons component since this is at base, a matter of our psychology. Harming people brings pain in one's own case. Development brings increased empathy with the pain of others. Empathy and cruelty are likely to both be natural to some extent, as is pursuing and attempting to prolong pleasure. Cruel social cooperation seems clearly less likely to be effective, given the social context, in bringing us prolonged pleasure on the whole unless we assume sado-masochism to be natural developmentally, and widespread. *We* would be bothered by our own pain and that of others.

I assume that a certain degree of consistency and responsibility in people's thought and action would be esteemed in most any freely chosen morality. People might choose views which attach greater importance to community and cooperation than to competition and individual achievement. At least this would be expected if typical criticisms of technological market economy systems are at all accurate. I would expect also that freer than free morality would be more body and sensual pleasure oriented than our conventional morality. In this sense the extreme virgin-saint, do-gooder conception of many so-called higher moralities (slave moralities in Nietzsche's eyes) might also appear to us as more pervertedly induced (slave-oriented) than admirable. This will no doubt be difficult for many of us to take. But didn't we say that Truth and Justice would make us free?

Unlike many moral philosophers I would also expect some convergence among more freely than freely educated persons as regards value hierarchies. That is, I suspect there to be some objective basis, though some range of flexibility also, in the ranking of values we would choose if not manipulated by others in our desire systems. Personal qualities such as the ability to be warm, open and nurturant with others would be considered more valuable as goals of life by the non-polluted than the mere accumulation of luxury items. Moreover, I believe that nurturant qualities would be seen as preferable to power-trip qualities, e.g., the ability to manipulate or dominate others. This, of course, is an empirical question.

Suppose that we were to find a large group of people who could be termed natural sado-masochists, i.e., people who need not be perverted by others in their development to prefer what we see as painful life-experiences. Suppose these sado-masochists, freer than freely educated, were to choose a Hell's Angel's morality which crucially involves their interfering with our alternative tolerant systems? In my view such people would and should be allowed to choose such lifestyles on much the same grounds that we would and should be allowed to choose ours. There is the complication of viewing aggression as a maladaptive archaic trait and what should be done about those who perhaps would not see it as such and would not refrain from being aggressive. Do the intolerant forfeit rights to be tolerated? I would hold that whereas they lose rights, our duties toward them may continue.

How this very idea rubs our objectivist tendencies raw. "There must be something objectively wrong with Hell's Angels' ethics and/or with Hell's Angels' mentalities. They aren't just different, they're sick! Scrambled eggs with ketchup can't taste good. Beethoven just is better than Charlie Parker." I may ask where the "must," "sick," and "just" comes from. A delightful reply might be, "From that part of my developed faculties which is unperverted. Now what can you say against it? And now that I have you, I also believe that objectivism is true, and I believe that within my unperverted self."

What such a reply might expose, were it true, is that many of the crucial problems of morality and psychological development do not arise in form but in the practical and factual details of situations, degrees of development, and the actual and differential use of developed capacities. I do not assume that the fully rounded and developed personality (could one version of it be specified) would choose such-and-such moral view. Nor do I assume that we in the presence of freely developed sado-masochists and they given the existence of us would choose merely to follow naturally based but conflicting preferences for one or the other form of pleasure. This is not to be rational, and rationality is one of the complexes of the developed mind. Each group would perhaps choose to tailor their behavior and to perhaps even alter their preferences by one means or another so as to yield some forms of feasible coexistence. This is one of the implications of the prima-facie nature of natural morality. It does not determine but rather sets certain limiting conditions on the validity and appropriateness of our choices. The use of our faculties may still vary. We may still debate and disagree. Yet in the end, the view I have proposed may indicate to us that fundamentally we *should* disagree; that your advice may be good for you but bad for me—that you are being unkind in offering it to someone like me versus you. Of course this need not be the case if what we are both after is a way of seeing where we stand and how we might change whatever things about us can be changed (with few ill effects to all) so as to lead to our mutual advantage. Our mutual advantage, we might expect, would also consist for each of us of what advantages the other. Natural morality provides us with a home base in changing ourselves. It can warn us of hidden fanaticism behind seeming saintliness in our personal ideals.

Let us be clear that as I have portrayed things, there are at least two important ways in which psychology places limits on objectivism and relativism. The first has to do with the degree of stretch allowed by psychological laws and tendencies in interaction, e.g., the workings of the pleasure principle in basic need versus noble ideal conflicts. The second has to do with level of development. The natural Stage 1 child should not, all things equal, accept a Stage 6 ethics because it really will not be even understood, much less useful and beneficial to her (him). A sado-masochist should not, all things equal, accept a pacifist-genteel ethics for the same reason. ("All things equal" is added to note that I am ignoring the utility of social compromise.) There is a difference, however, between people with like psychologies at different levels of development as compared to people with different psychologies at the same level. An implication of this difference might be, e.g., that paternalistic interference by a more developed person of one psychological type on a less developed member of that type could be seen as more justifiable than paternalism across types. Moreover, developing persons should and will, as they develop naturally, take into account how they will change in both their cognitive and conative ways. At present, we are all somewhat ignorant of the development we are likely to go through, whether we be adults or children. This is a fault of our education as well as a sign of the current limits of research in the area. As we become more knowledgeable, however, there will be better grounds for adopting a principle of responsibility to oneself on the basis of projected phases of a later life and more developed view of moral and other issues. Traditionally, reference to moral exemplars, wise old men (people) has served a primitive version of this function. For example, we may act to develop habits which are unpleasant to develop and of no use to us at present so that for the most of our later life we will be able to enjoy their benefits in helping us live by higher stage principles.

We should recognize moreover that one's natural "psychological type" is not physiologically determined. There may clearly be a predominant influence of physiological differences on psychological types, e.g., sado-machochists, depressives, even to the extent that cognitive styles or structures may typically reflect one certain physiological influence. For example, dogmatism, bigotry, humanitarianism, rationalism and existential authenticity may each reflect physiological predispositions which influence cognition and intellectual behavior in certain standard situations. Natural types, however, are more likely determined by a complex interaction of physiological, cognitive, conative, socialization and experiential influences in life histories. For this reason, changing a person's mind on a deeply important issue such as whether to be a right-wing isolationist or an aggressive left-wing radical can change thereby, through its influence on other aspects of the psychological system, a person's natural type. Such flexibility puts limits on, among other things, even the degree of inter-type paternalism which may be justifiable.

As much as we should be accepting of value differences which are freely chosen in the deepest sense, to this extent should we be suspicious at present of moral views which are insensitive to human suffering and dedicated to protecting wealth and property over human development. My stress on relativism should be seen at the level to which it is directed. Our psychologies and our most basic human needs, do provide guidelines of feasibility and "health" in the construction of moral views, i.e., views, which would be chosen from the perspective of social freedom and self-understanding. We must ask where the role-taking skills went in views which on principle permit the extinction or benign neglect of "those people."

Kohlberg's objections to the relativism of the values clarification approach are aimed at the tacit legitimization this approach gives to the equating of all preferences as mere preferences. Some preferences come out of our natures. Others stem from our perverters. The source makes a difference as well as the relation of the preference to human welfare versus, for example, men's fashions. Kohlberg's objections to behavior modification are deeper and cut appropriately at this technique's lack of respect for what I have termed rights to development. Behavior modification is directly opposed to the self-determining aspect of the moral enterprise. As a technique it wholly embodies the disease of moral education—its use as a tool for social control and oppression.

In the end, then, the objectivity of morality is not being characterized here as groundless. It is rather seen as based on our needs, our unfolding development, and our choices in a somewhat flexible way. The morality likely to derive from programs I have just suggested pays great respect to reality, to our health, and to the legitimacy of what brings us progressive happiness. It also recognizes the important relationship between our happiness, our ideals and our free and knowing choices.

Different moral systems represent, to a great extent, different social causes, and should be addressed to others as appeals. We must await the views of those less polluted than we, to know with great surety which appeals we should or should not listen to and which of us should or should not listen. Of course there are good grounds for probability statements in the meantime. To the degree that these are uncertain, we should see at the least that we err on the side of the children; on the side of their potential to flourish.

References

Firth, Roderick. "Ethical Absolutism and the Ideal Observer." *Philosophy and Phenomenological Research*, Vol. 12 (1952).

Kant, Immanuel. *Groundwork of the Metaphysics of Morals.* New York: Harper & Rowe, 1956.

Kohlberg, Lawrence. "From Is To Ought." In T. Mischel, ed. *Cognitive Development.* New York: Academic Press, 1971.

——————. "Stage and Sequence." In D. Goslin, ed. *Handbook of Socialization Theory and Research.* New York: Rand McNally, 1969.

——————. "The Claim to Moral Adequacy of a Highest Stage of Moral Development." *Journal of Philosophy* (1973).

Nozick, Robert. *Anarchy, State and Utopia.* New York: Basic Books, 1974.

Raths, L.; Harmin, M.; and Simon, S. *Values and Teaching.* Ohio: C. E. Merrill, 1966.

Rawls, John. *A Theory of Justice.* Cambridge, Mass.: Harvard University Press, 1971.

Suggested Reading

Kanter, R. *Commitment and Community.* Harvard University Press.

Rowbotham, Sheila. *Woman's Consciousness, Man's World.* Penguin Books.

Rush, Kent. *Getting Clear.* Random House.

Schumacher, E. F. *Small Is Beautiful.* Harper and Row.

Sennett, R. *Hidden Injuries of Class.* Random House.

The Just Community Approach to Corrections. (A Manual) Moral Development Center, Larsen Hall, Harvard University, Cambridge, Mass.

WHO IS TO SAY WHAT SHOULD BE TAUGHT IN VALUES EDUCATION

Robert Litke
Department of Philosophy
Wilfrid Laurier University

Who is to say what is the most appropriate content and method for values education? The answer proposed in Part I is: that, initially, everyone should have his say—teacher, student, parent, School Board, the ministry, society at large; that the teacher in the classroom, however, must finally decide what is to be done in light of all such suggestions; but that, in the final analysis the student and society must remain free to reject the teacher's final decision. Because of this the values educator remains in a state of unavoidable tension.

In Part II it is suggested that the only adequate way for the teacher safely to decide upon the content and method of values education is from the perspective of one's own theory or philosophy of values education. A model and strategy for formulating such a theory is offered. The model is then illustrated with a partial analysis of *Circular P1J1,* a curriculum policy statement, recently published by the Ministry of Education of Ontario.

Part I

Who is to say what should be taught in values education? The question is often asked because of a concern that children may have false values imposed on them. Some ask the question because they have it in mind to impose true values on the children, thereby protecting them from false values which others would impose on them. These people lack no confidence in the educational value of their own values. Such confidence sometimes springs from the belief that one has final, absolutely right, answers to all the important questions. Others ask the question precisely because they lack this kind of confidence and assume that they are therefore inadequate as values educators. Their concern is that they may impose false values, perhaps inadvertently. The sense of inadequacy apparently springs from the thought that one's own values are *merely one's own* and surely one's *personal* moral perspective is not fit to be taught. (One wishes to ask, of course, if it is also not fit to live by!) This is obviously a variation on the common subjectivist theme: "Who's to say what is right and wrong?" a theme usually accompanied by that characteristic expression of lack of moral nerve: "Not me."

Obviously these two groups of people are expressing divergent concerns with the same question. They would be satisfied only by quite different answers. Moreover, there is something right and something wrong with each set of concerns: Do values have to be imposed at all? If so, which ones? If not, how do we educate? Do *personal* views have to be discounted just because they are personal? How do we get from the personal to the interpersonal? etc. We cannot do justice to all the important concerns which lie behind the question we have posed. We can, however, make a start at answering it.

The Context

Everyone involved in values education has experienced the tension which always and necessarily exists between the rights and concerns of the individual and the rights and concerns of society. This tension is a fundamental characteristic of the moral life as we know it, and so, it is something we must learn to live with. Hopefully, we learn to do so in an open and creative manner. Openness and creativity are important because the moral dimensions of things are changing. What counted as the appropriate balance point between the individual and society yesterday may no longer appear appropriate today or tomorrow. New facts, new sensitivities, deeper understandings emerge and demand that we reassess and, perhaps, change our commitments. The balance point may have to be relocated.

As values educators we should invite our students to join us in learning to live with this tension between the individual and society. We should also make them aware of the possibility and the need for creative response to it. Actively working out some appropriate balance between the individual and society is an ongoing requirement of the moral life. And getting this point across is an ongoing requirement of moral education.

In a recent public policy statement the Ministry of Education of Ontario shows itself to be clearly aware of this tension between the individual and society. Under the curriculum topic "Values," the recommendation is made that Primary and Junior Division students be given the opportunity to

- become aware of the values that Canadians regard as essential to the well-being and continuing development of their society—namely, respect for the individual, concern for others, social responsibility, compassion, honesty, and the acceptance of work, thought, and leisure as valid pursuits for human beings;

- begin to develop a personal set of values by identifying value alternatives and their consequences, selecting personal values from the alternatives, internalizing the values selected, and acting in accordance with the values selected.[1]

We can see, then, that the ministry would have its students develop so as to be morally concerned both with themselves as individuals and with the society in which they live.

Now there is a hard question which should be asked at this point. Which takes precedence in the case of unresolvable conflict? Should it be the values selected by the individual or the values that members of society regard as essential to society? It is to be noted in this regard that the Ministry makes no

[1] The Ministry of Education of Ontario, *Circular P1J1* (Ontario, 1975), p. 20.

attempt in this document to say how such a conflict should be settled. Under another curriculum topic, "The Individual and Society," the recommendation is that the child be given opportunities to "develop self-respect, respect for the rights of others, and respect for the rule of law."[2] But whether respect for self or respect for others in society should be given the highest priority is left completely in the dark.

And this is how it should be. For to try to say in advance of specific cases whether the value commitments of individuals or those of society should take precedence is to try to avoid that tension which we regard as fundamental to the moral life. It is not something for scholars and educators to take out of our hands and resolve for us. This tension is something we must learn to deal with in our lives. It is something we must help our students to appreciate and live with.

If this is agreed to, the question then arises: How can this best be done? What is the best content and what is the best method for values education, given a commitment to helping students deal with this tension between the individual and society? These are important questions: the answers are far from obvious. Questions about which virtues to inculcate, which duties to teach, which ideals to promote must all be faced. Concerns about indoctrination, closing minds, and the like would also have to be dealt with. These are matters that I cannot now pursue. Underlying them is a prior and deeper issue which is the concern of this paper, namely, who shall decide the answers to these questions.

The Question

Who is to say what is the most appropriate content and method for values education? Should it be the individual educator, the individual student, or should it be the society which has decided that the student needs to be educated, the society on whose behalf the educator educates?

It would be ironic if this question were thought to be entirely answerable in advance. Surely this question points up yet another case of unavoidable tension between the rights and concerns of the individual and the rights and concerns of society. As such, it must also be dealt with in the concrete form and in the complex context in which it arises. To assume otherwise, however, may be a more serious matter than one of irony. To assume otherwise may well undermine in advance all prospects of ever getting students to appreciate this tension as a fundamental characteristic of the moral life. If morality were consistently taught under the assumption that society should unilaterally decide upon the content and method of moral teaching, then it may well turn out that one lesson that is sure to be learned is that, in the last analysis, society takes precedence over the individual. The opposite seems equally likely. If morality were consistently taught under the assumption that the individual (teacher *or* student) should unilaterally decide upon the content and method of moral teaching, then the lesson which may be best learned is that the individual always takes prece-

[2] Ibid., p. 22.

dence over society. The remaining alternative also has some promise of being true: teaching morality from the point of view that decisions about content and method of moral education should reflect both the concerns of society and the concerns of the individual (teacher *and* student) may help establish the conviction that both types of concerns should be reflected in one's own moral decisions, that some appropriate balance between the individual and society must be sought in living out the moral life.

Well then, how *is* one to decide what is the most appropriate content and method for values education, given such a point of view? Who is to say what should be taught in values education? The answer I would propose is a simple one to state: first, everyone concerned should have his say—teacher, student, society at large; second, the teacher in the classroom is the one who must finally decide what is to be done in light of all such suggestions; third, the tension between the individual as teacher, the individual as student, and society at large can, nevertheless, be preserved. Let me explain why and how this is to be done.

The Answer

Teaching is an intentional activity. The teacher, therefore, is an agent, and a moral agent among other things. As such, what the teacher does should be compatible with or be the realization of his moral ideals, moral obligations and the like. Stepping into the classroom obviously does not entail stepping out of the moral point of view.

Thus what the individual teacher must first do is figure out what are his moral concerns and moral rights insofar as these having a bearing on his teaching activities in general and on his teaching of values in particular. As we shall see shortly, these concerns are not only important in their own right, but they are centrally and ultimately important in relation to the other relevant concerns.

Secondly, students are human beings and must be respected as such. Entering the classroom does not entail leaving their humanity behind them. What must be determined then is what concerns and rights they should therefore be considered as having, both from the moral perspective of the teacher and in consideration of what the students themselves tell us they are concerned about and what they think they have a right to. Failure to take into account the students' perception of these matters would be to discount them in an unwarranted way as a source of relevant information about the actual immediate effects of certain educational measures taken on their behalf and about the desirability of certain longer run objectives which allegedly justify such measures. It is hard to imagine that anyone would wish to deny that such information should be deemed relevant unless it is mistakenly thought that "taking into account" is the same as "acquiescing to demands of." Failure to take into account one's own perceptions of these matters would be to irresponsibly suppose that one is not a moral agent in the situation, that one is merely following orders, as war criminals so often claim.

Thirdly, assessment must be made of the rights and concerns of society at large—parents, School Board members, ministry officials, politicians, the tax-payers. It is society at large, and the organizations which represent its many interests, that have created and actively maintain much of the context in which teaching and learning take place. At the very least, prudence would require that society should have its say. But it is also morally right that the many voices of society should have a bearing on decisions about the content and method of values education. Thus information about the rights and concerns of society should be obtained by the teacher from two sources: his own moral opinion of society's legitimate concerns and rights regarding values education and the opinions of the many others who speak on society's behalf. As before, failure to take into account one's own perceptions of these matters would be irresponsible and failure to go beyond one's own perceptions of them would be to discount in an unwarranted way various persons as legitimate sources of relevant information. But there is here an additional reason why the views to be found in society at large must be heard and taken into account. Failure to do so would be to attempt to avoid the unavoidable tension between the individual and society. And it is not simply that this is undesirable in itself. It has been argued that this may ruin in advance all attempts to get our students to live creatively with this tension.

So we find there to be three separable sets of rights and concerns: those of the teacher, those of the student, and those of society in general. We also find that there are at least two sources of information concerning these rights and concerns for two of these sets. Moreover, it has been argued that all of this information should somehow figure in considerations leading up to decisions about the content and method of values education. The next task for the values teacher is to find some appropriate resolution or balance point for the contending parties and opinions. About this several things can be said: (1) this is no easy matter; (2) the teacher cannot avoid this difficult task; (3) the teacher's moral perspective will be both central and ultimate.

It is not easy because of the wealth of relevant factors and because there is no clear formula that one can rely on for all occasions. What would count as an appropriate balance point in one situation may not count on another occasion for a variety of reasons—sophistication of the students, the level of tolerance in society, the moral climate of the times, etc. Thus the values teacher must be content to be like the professional in so many other fields. Complex and shifting circumstances demand sensitivity and judgment, not the mechanical application of some pat decision procedure. Nerve and hope are required, not blind trust in how things have been done before.

So the task of finding the balance point is not easy. Nor can the teacher avoid it by trusting it to someone else's hands. Obviously it is the teacher in the classroom who must finally translate learning objectives into relevant learning experiences for the student. This means, of course, that the teacher is the one who must finally decide and who is ultimately responsible for the content and method of values education. And it is precisely because of this that the teacher's moral point of view unavoidably plays a central and ultimate role in all such decisions. What would the teacher's "ultimate responsibility" be, if it did not have a moral character to it? And where would its moral character come from if not from the teacher's moral point of view? And so it comes out that after everyone has had his say, the teacher has the last word—a morally informed word we would hope.

Now it may be argued at this point that I have failed to preserve the allegedly unavoidable tension between the individual and society. Have I not just suggested that the individual as teacher takes precedence over society! Well, in one sense, the teacher *does* have the last word. But in another sense, the teacher clearly does not. Those who receive the services of the teacher have the right and option of refusing to accept these services. The students can do this by refusing to learn or take seriously what the teacher intends them to learn; society at large can do this by having the teacher removed from the teaching position he requires to serve as a teacher. Let us look at this a little more closely.

We have come around to the interesting matter of how to preserve the autonomy of both the teacher and those who receive the teacher's services. And I take this to be but one specific type of case of the more general matter of how to protect the freedom or autonomy of both members of any professional-client relationship. Looking at the two extremes we get the following conceptual fix on the relationship.

To allow the client to prescribe for the professional what is to be done would eventually destroy the profession and the practices, skills, knowledge, and aspirations which constitute it. To allow the professional to force persons to be recipients of his services would be to destroy a fundamental freedom protected by both law and morality—a freedom which gives substance to our concern for such things as informed consent and which makes contractual relations possible. We can protect the autonomy of each only if the professional is allowed to finally decide what services he is prepared to offer and only if the recipient is allowed to finally decide what services he is prepared to accept.[3] So the teacher must be allowed to make the final decision concerning what he is prepared to do with respect to the content and method of values education; the student, the Board, and society at large must be allowed to make the final decision as to

---

[3]These are admittedly two extremes; they are chosen because they bring out in a clear fashion what I believe is at the heart of the professional-client relationship. There is much room for interaction in most actual cases of this type of relationship. The recipient can often suggest or request that certain services be offered, not to mention other forms of influence or pressure. The professional also has considerable influence, even power, over potential recipients of services in many cases. What I would argue, however, is that the influence that each may properly be allowed to have over the other must have certain controls on it. The outline of the argument that I would give for this view is that presented in the paragraph to which this is a footnote. I would like to thank my colleagues in the Department of Philosophy, Wilfrid Laurier University, for making this matter clearer than I had.

whether values education of that sort will be accepted. In this way basic free-doms are protected and in this way the fundamental tension between the indi-vidual as teacher, the individual as student, and society remains intact as a challenge to our creativity.

This brings to an end the line of considerations which began this paper with the question of who is to say what should be taught in values education. The answer we have proposed is this: (1) initially, everyone concerned should have his say; (2) the teacher has the last word concerning what he is prepared to do in light of all such suggestions; (3) society at large has the final say as to whether to accept the teacher's last word.

It will have been noticed that no suggestion has been made about what the teacher's last word should look like, except to say that it should be at least compatible with his moral convictions. Since the latter will vary from one teacher to another there is little more to be said in a general way about the teacher's last word. What can be done in advance of knowing the content of anyone's moral perspective is to suggest a way of handling the diversity of information which I have argued is relevant for formulating this last word about the content and method of values education. Let us turn to that now in Part II.

Part II

A Model

William Frankena, an ethicist and philosopher of education at the University of Michigan, has proposed a model for analyzing philosophies of education in sev-eral places.[4] Because I have found Frankena's model useful in my own studies I have introduced it to students during the last five years. A very high proportion of them have assured me that they also have found it a valuable tool. What I shall offer is a version of this model which is a simplification in some ways and an elaboration in others.

As I see it, the model can serve three distinct kinds of function: (1) it can be used to analyze a continuous discussion in educational documents such as *Circular P1J1* by the Ministry of Education of Ontario, *Pedagogy of the Op-pressed* by Paulo Freire, even shorter policy statements of individual school boards; (2) it can be used to keep track of disconnected remarks about educa-tion and to put them into some coherent order; (3) it can be used to guide one in the construction of a theory or philosophy of education which is both coher-ent and comprehensive. I would argue in general that only if one has some such theory about what one is doing as an educator can one be at all sure that he is doing more good than harm. I would further argue that this is especially true of values education.

[4]William Frankena, "A Model for Analyzing a Philosophy of Education," *The High School Journal* 50, 1 (October, 1966):8-13; other versions appear in William Frankena, *Philosophy of Education* (Macmillan, 1965), pp. 1-10, and William Frankena, *Three Histori-cal Philosophies of Education* (Scott Foresman, 1965), pp. 6-12.

Suppose then that an educator wished to construct a philosophy of values education. It has already been argued that decisions about the content and method of values education should reflect the views of the teacher, the students, and society at large and that such decisions should ultimately be compatible with the individual teacher's moral perspective. It should be noticed that some of these views will appear in continuous documents (*P1J1*), some will come forth in isolated directives (from a principal or a Board), some will arise as casual remarks (of students or colleagues), and some will emerge as brief insights into the implications of one's own moral convictions. In the first place, then, the model can help us notice, keep track of, and begin to order these various bits of initial information. Next the model can serve as the framework for working these into a complete and adequate philosophy of values education. At this stage, the educator fills out the various components of the model with that information which is a balanced and reasonable reflection of both his own view of what are the rights and concerns of everyone involved and the parallel views of the students and society at large. The model can serve us then in all three of its functions if our purpose is to construct a theory of values education. It can help us live in that creative tension insisted upon in Part I.

The model makes essential use of two kinds of statement: *factual* assumptions and *evaluative* claims. While the difference between facts and values continues to be a matter of debate the distinction nevertheless continues to be useful. The *factual* would of course include empirical claims of various sorts but as used in the model it is a much broader category. In addition to theoretical claims about narrowly empirical matters it would also include various non-empirical claims such as those which make up the bulk of common sense and those we expect to find in philosophy and theology, not to mention most of the humanistic disciplines. For the model, the essential difference between the factual and the evaluative is this: the former are claims about *how things are,* while the latter are claims about *how things should be.* Evaluative claims then would include ideals, duties, and in general, recommendations about how things should be or be done. Educational goals and objectives are obviously recommendations, then. Thus the first thing that the model would have one do is to divide up the various bits of relevant information into two classes: the factual assumptions and the evaluative claims.

The second thing the model would have one do is to integrate these two types of claim into a coherent argument or rationale for doing what one proposes to do as an educator. To accomplish this one must first arrange the various educational objectives in a certain order.

For the sake of illustration, let us suppose that there are four distinct objectives that one is working with. They are to be placed in a sequence of means to end relationships as follows: the fourth objective is a means to the third, which in turn is a means to the second, which in turn is a means to the first. Diagrammatically they could be represented in the following way:

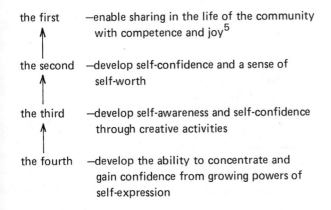

the first   —enable sharing in the life of the community
              with competence and joy[5]

the second   —develop self-confidence and a sense of
              self-worth

the third   —develop self-awareness and self-confidence
              through creative activities

the fourth   —develop the ability to concentrate and
              gain confidence from growing powers of
              self-expression

The diagram is a plan of operation which openly shows its rationale: the reason for doing what is recommended in the fourth objective is that it leads to the third one, and the reason for pursuing the third objective is that it leads to the second one, etc. Typically, lower level objectives are more specific than higher level ones and lower level objectives are shorter run than higher level ones. The key to ordering them, however, is the means to end relationship. It should also be noted that for the argument to be adequate the highest level objective must be capable of rationalizing all the lower level educational objectives. This is where one places very general aims of education such as "happiness," "individual survival," "competent and joyful sharing in community life," "self-actualization," "eternal beatitude," "enlightenment," or whatever one thinks is the overall point of education. So, once the factual and evaluative claims are sorted out, one then must order the evaluative claims (educational objectives) in a means to end relationship.

That done, the next thing one must do is relate various factual assumptions to the ordered objectives to strengthen the argument. The essential idea here is this: presumably there is some reason for thinking that some particular educational objective would (likely) be a means to some other objective. This reason, then, is to be stated, thereby establishing some support for the view that there is a relationship between the two objectives. Diagramatically this could be represented as follows:

.

[5]As a matter of interest it can be noted here that these and most subsequent examples used to illustrate the model are taken from *P1J1*. Full references shall be given later.

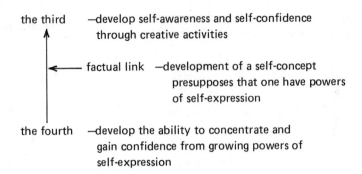

the third   —develop self-awareness and self-confidence
                through creative activities

            ◄——— factual link —development of a self-concept
                              presupposes that one have powers
                              of self-expression

the fourth   —develop the ability to concentrate and
                gain confidence from growing powers of
                self-expression

Putting this all together we get the following:

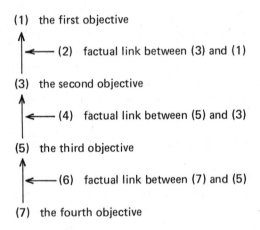

(1) the first objective

    ◄——— (2) factual link between (3) and (1)

(3) the second objective

    ◄——— (4) factual link between (5) and (3)

(5) the third objective

    ◄——— (6) factual link between (7) and (5)

(7) the fourth objective

We now have the outline of a highly integrated and fairly comprehensive rationale: the reason for doing what is recommended in (7) is that it is believed that it
leads to what is recommended in (5) and the reason for believing that is stated in
(6); further, the reason for pursuing what is recommended in (5) is that it is
believed that this will lead to what is recommended in (3), the reason for
believing this is stated in (4), and so on up to (1), the main point and ultimate
justification of all one's educational endeavours.

It must be allowed that there is room for further argument in at least two
places and so one may wish to supplement his theory of values education so as
to be prepared for this additional argument. First, there may be some dispute
over any of the factual linkage claims. Presumably a response would be a matter
of bringing in further factual claims (broadly conceived) to support one's view
that a certain factual link does obtain between two objectives. For example, a
psychological claim in (2) to the effect that the objective in (3) does lead to the
objective in (1) may be supported by a psychological theory (2a), which in turn
may be supported by claims of its superiority over alternative theories in the
field (2b), all of which may be supported by a certain philosophy of science

(2c). Thus (2a) would support the claim of (2) that (3) leads to (1), and (2b) would support the claim of (2a), etc.

The second place where dispute may arise is over the content of (1), i.e., over what really is the overall point of education. Suppose that the claim in (1) were that the long run goal of education is "competent and joyful sharing in the life of the community." Such a claim may then be supported by some social or political theory or ideology about what competent and joyful sharing can be like and what community life should be like (1a); this in turn may be backed up with some rationale for adopting this theory or ideology (1b), the kind of thing one finds in social philosophy or theology. In this case, (1a) would support the claim of (1) that competent and joyful sharing in the life of the community is the aim of education, and (1b) would support the claim of (1a). All these supplementary matters may be diagrammed as follows:

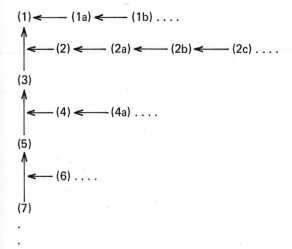

The suspension dots indicate the possibility of making as many additions as one's commitments require.

We now have explicated the essential relationships captured by the model. However, because education is a rather complex business, there are two further complications we might wish to make provision for. The first one arises from the recognition of the obvious point that at any level there may be various objectives which *jointly* serve as the means to some higher objective. For example, sharing in the life of the community with competence and joy (1) would require more than self-confidence and a sense of self-worth. Let us suppose that the joint means to (1) were thought to include the following: (i) self-confidence and a sense of self-worth, (ii) knowledge and attitudes presupposed by active participation in Canadian society, (iii) moral and aesthetic sensitivity. Thus (3) would have three items in it, all of which are means to (1). It may also be thought that each of these items in (3) may require that certain joint means be satisfied before they are realized. Thus (5) would have a variety of items in it as well. Finally, it is easily imagined that the factual linkage between various components in (3) and (5) may be somewhat differentiated as well. These complexities may be captured by listing the various items and by making parenthetical remarks about what is connected with what:[6]

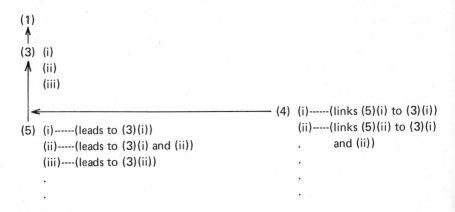

The parenthetical remarks about what leads to what and what links with what enable one to keep track of finer grained connections *if that seems important to one.* As we shall see later when we analyse *P1J1* some of these connections may have an important bearing on the matter of where and when values education takes place. Obviously they may sometimes be important for planning classroom activities as well. On the other hand, the main value of the model is that it gives one a synoptic view of things. It would be a mistake, therefore, to allow oneself to get buried in details of this finer grained sort.

It sometimes happens that the specific means we choose to realize our purposes effectively ruin all chances we had to realize those very purposes. This criticism has often been made about the use of physical violence to achieve certain ends: The use of violence often breeds more of the very thing it was supposed to eliminate. Certainly educational practices are sometimes criticized in this way. The claim is that the chosen practices themselves are sufficient to preclude any chance of reaching our educational objectives. Such higher level objectives as "creativity," "autonomy" or "independence" seem particularly susceptible to this kind of ironic failure. Just why human behavior should be subject to this sort of ironical twist is worth pondering, but that it is must be accepted.

---

[6]This use of parenthetical remarks was devised by a student, Terry Skeats.

Recognition of this brings us to the second complication. It is not uncommon for there to be special recommendations about the implementation of educational objectives, recommendations which specifically seek to prevent the objectives from being undercut by our very efforts to realize them. What I suggest is that these recommendations be noted in the model by attaching them to the relevant objective:

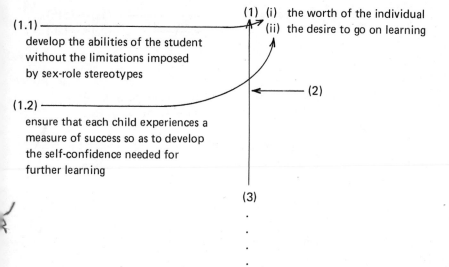

(1) (i)   the worth of the individual
     (ii) the desire to go on learning

(1.1)
develop the abilities of the student
without the limitations imposed
by sex-role stereotypes

(2)

(1.2)
ensure that each child experiences a
measure of success so as to develop
the self-confidence needed for
further learning

(3)

Noting them in this way in the model not only gives them the prominence first accorded them by their author(s) but it also eliminates trying to fit them into the means to end relationships already established, something which often leads to rather contrived and unsatisfying results. Again it would be important to not let the addition of this type of detail interfere with the overall perspective afforded by the model.

This brings to an end the explication of the model. In summary, this is what has been suggested:

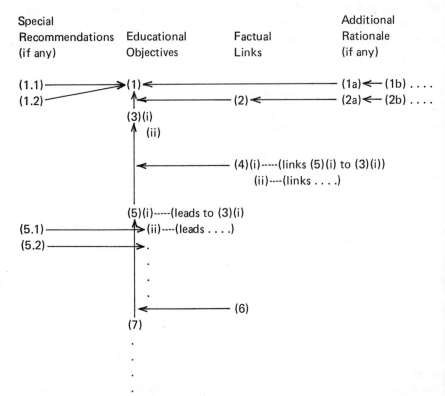

Special
Recommendations   Educational   Factual   Additional
(if any)   Objectives   Links   Rationale
                                                          (if any)

(1.1) ─────────────▶(1)◀────────────────────── (1a)◀─(1b) . . . .
(1.2) ───────────────▲◀──────────── (2)◀─────── (2a)◀─(2b) . . . .
                    (3)(i)
                      ▲ (ii)
                      │◀──────────── (4)(i)-----(links (5)(i) to (3)(i))
                      │   (ii)----(links . . . .)
                    (5)(i)-----(leads to (3)(i)
(5.1) ─────────────▲▶(ii)----(leads . . . .)
(5.2) ──────────────▶ .
                      ·
                      ·
                      ·
                      │◀──────────── (6)
                    (7)
                      ·
                      ·
                      ·

To illustrate how the model actually works I shall now use it to analyze *Circular P1J1.*

An Example: A Partial Analysis of P1J1

Circular P1J1 is the provincial curriculum policy for the primary and junior divisions of the public and separate schools of Ontario. It was published in 1975 by the Ministry of Education. What follows is an analysis of this document which is partial for two reasons. First of all, I shall pay attention only to those parts of the document which have an obvious and direct bearing on values education; secondly, I shall do so only for the sake of illustrating the model, not for the purpose of rendering a thorough examination of the educational policy of the Ministry of Education.

In all, I find the educational objectives forwarded in *P1J1* to fall into four levels of analysis, ranging from general aims such as promoting the worth of the individual to somewhat more specific objectives such as developing an appreciation of the outlooks of various ethnic and cultural groups and developing respect for the rule of law. While we may intuitively sense that such general and specific objectives are somehow related to each other we may not be clear as to precisely what the relations are. And failing to know this may seriously impair the implementation of such objectives. Now it is precisely this sort of thing that the model can help us with, for it enables us to determine in an explicit fashion the extent to which various objectives can be arranged in a structure of means to end relationships. And this information should be especially relevant to the educator since the educational process is a purposive or intentional one.

I find the Ministry of Education committed to five general aims of education in *P1J1*, (all page references are to this document):

(1)
  (i)   promote the worth of the individual (p. 4)
  (ii) develop each child as completely as possible in the direction of talents and needs (p. 4)
  (iii) provide the child with a fuller life while in the Primary and Junior Divisions (p. 4)
  (iv) enable the child to continue his or her education with satisfaction (p. 4)
  (v)   enable the child to share in the life of the community with competence, integrity and joy. (p. 4)

While complex relations obviously obtain among items (i) - (v), none of them serve primarily as means to any of the others. In this sense, all five objectives are on a par with each other.

In addition, several special recommendations are made regarding the implementation of the above objectives. Attaching to (1)(i) is the general requirement that sex-role stereotypes not be imposed on students: (p. 4) students are to be treated and valued primarily as individuals, not differentially as male or female sorts of individuals. Attaching to (1)(ii) is the requirement that the teaching program be adjusted to the student's level and rate of learning (p. 5). Maximum development of each child clearly requires this sort of fine-tuning, whatever the practical difficulties of doing so in the actual learning situation. Finally, there is a rider that attaches to (1)(iv): ensure each child enough success to that the self-confidence needed for further learning occurs (p. 5). Diagrammatically these would be displayed as follows:

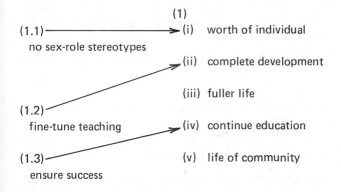

At the next level of analysis I find four objectives, all of which are a means to one or more of the objectives listed in (1). These four objectives appear as a list on page four of *P1J1* and I quote them in full (adding the relevant numerals):

(3)   It follows that the curriculum will provide opportunities for each child (to the limit of his or her potential):
(i)   to acquire the basic skills fundamental to his or her continuing education;
(ii)   to develop and maintain confidence and a sense of self-worth;
(iii)   to gain the knowledge and acquire the attitudes that he or she needs for active participation in Canadian society;
(iv)   to develop the moral and aesthetic sensitivity necessary for a complete and responsible life.

What needs to be noted are the specific means to end connections between items in (1) and these four objectives in (3). This can be done in the following way:

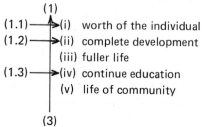

(1)
(1.1)——▶(i)   worth of the individual
(1.2)——▶(ii) complete development
        (iii) fuller life
(1.3)——▶(iv) continue education
        (v)   life of community

(3)
(i)   basic skills (leads to (1) (iv))
(ii)   confidence and self-worth (leads to all items in (1))
(iii) knowledge of society (leads to (1) (v))
(iv)   moral and aesthetic sensitivity (leads to (1) (ii) (v))

Up to this point I have attempted to include everything in *P1J1* that is relevant to these two levels of analysis. Hereafter this is not the case. For example, I somewhat arbitrarily restrict the list to seven items in the next level of analysis and to sixteen items in the level that follows. The Ministry, on the other hand, lists thirty-one curriculum topics, including the seven I make use of at level (5), and it forwards almost two hundred objectives at level (7), where I mention only sixteen. In the fact of so much relevant information one cannot be both thorough and illustrative.

The seven chosen items which serve as means to the four objectives listed in (3) are as follows:

(5)
(i)   increase sensitivity of perception through the use of all the senses and develop the ability to express it; (p. 17)
(ii)   develop self-awareness and self-confidence; (p. 17
(iii)   promote understanding of physical and emotional nature; (p. 20
(iv)   begin to develop a personal value system in the context of society while recognizing the integrity of the individual; (p. 20)
(v)   develop the ability to make informed and rational decisions; (p. 21)

(vi)   acquire knowledge of Canada and pride in Canada; (p. 23)
(vii) understand social relationships. (p. 22)

Again, the specific means to end relationships may be noted parenthetically in the diagram:

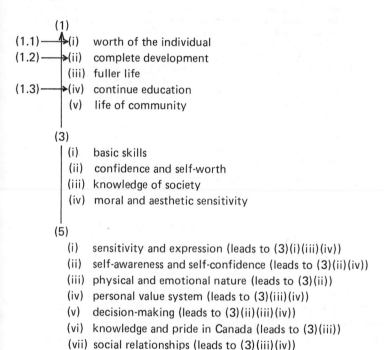

(1)
(1.1)——►(i)   worth of the individual
(1.2)——►(ii)   complete development
        (iii) fuller life
(1.3)——►(iv)   continue education
        (v)   life of community

(3)
        (i)   basic skills
        (ii)   confidence and self-worth
        (iii) knowledge of society
        (iv)   moral and aesthetic sensitivity

(5)
        (i)   sensitivity and expression (leads to (3)(i)(iii)(iv))
        (ii)   self-awareness and self-confidence (leads to (3)(ii)(iv))
        (iii) physical and emotional nature (leads to (3)(ii))
        (iv)   personal value system (leads to (3)(iii)(iv))
        (v)   decision-making (leads to (3)(ii)(iii)(iv))
        (vi)   knowledge and pride in Canada (leads to (3)(iii))
        (vii) social relationships (leads to (3)(iii)(iv))

At the next level of analysis I have included only those items which are clearly related to values education, i.e., items which serve as means to objective (5)(iv)—the development of a personal value system. Similar lists of items would have to be worked out for the other six items listed in (5) to do justice to the Ministry's proposal. This narrowing of focus not only serves the purposes of illustration but is in keeping with the main concern of this paper, namely, values education.

The items I find to be means to objective (5)(iv) are as follows:

(7)
(i)   appreciate that one's ideas and feelings have value and are worth expressing; (p. 17)
(ii)   become aware of and accept reactions to sensations; (p. 17)
(iii) develop freedom of thought (p. 17)
(iv)   discover assumptions, points of view, and emotional reactions and an awareness of roles; (p. 17)
(v)   develop the ability to concentrate and powers of self-expression; (p. 17)
(vi)   develop an appreciation of the relation between physical development and ability, emotions and behaviour; (p. 20)
(vii) acquire an understanding of mood and behaviour modifiers; (p. 20)

(viii) promote an understanding of sexuality; (p. 20)
(ix)   become aware of the values that Canadians regard as essential to the well-being and continuing development of their society—namely, respect for the individual, concern for others, social responsibility, compassion, honesty, and the acceptance of work, thought, and leisure as valid pursuits for human beings; (p. 20)
(x)   begin to develop a personal set of values by identifying value alternatives and their consequences, selecting personal values from the alternatives, internalizing the values selected, and acting in accordance with the values selected; (p. 20)
(xi)   identify and analyse public value issues; (p. 20)
(xii) understand one's nature and needs as a basis for understanding others; (p. 22)
(xiii) understand that one's actions have physical and cultural consequences; (p. 22)
(xiv) develop self-respect, respect for others, and respect for the rule of law; (p. 22)
(xv)   develop personal identity through a sense of continuity with the origins of one's community and culture ; (p. 23)
(xvi) begin to understand and appreciate various ethnic and cultural points of view. (p. 23)

It should be noted, however, that the above items not only serve as means to (5)(iv) but quite obviously to other items in (5) as well. As before, this information may be added parenthetically. In summary, then, here is overall analysis we have come up with:

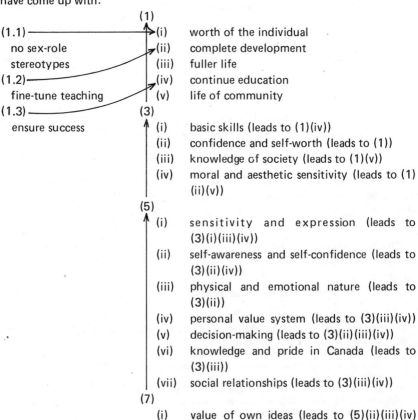

(1)

(1.1) ————————————→ (i)   worth of the individual
  no sex-role   →(ii)   complete development
  stereotypes   (iii) fuller life
(1.2) ————————————→ (iv)   continue education
  fine-tune teaching   ↗ (v)   life of community
(1.3) ———————————   (3)
  ensure success   ↑ (i)   basic skills (leads to (1)(iv))
                            (ii)   confidence and self-worth (leads to (1))
                            (iii) knowledge of society (leads to (1)(v))
                            (iv)   moral and aesthetic sensitivity (leads to (1) (ii)(v))

                        (5)
                          ↑ (i)   sensitivity and expression (leads to (3)(i)(iii)(iv))
                            (ii)   self-awareness and self-confidence (leads to (3)(ii)(iv))
                            (iii) physical and emotional nature (leads to (3)(ii))
                            (iv)   personal value system (leads to (3)(iii)(iv))
                            (v)   decision-making (leads to (3)(ii)(iii)(iv))
                            (vi)   knowledge and pride in Canada (leads to (3)(iii))
                            (vii) social relationships (leads to (3)(iii)(iv))
                        (7)
                            (i)   value of own ideas (leads to (5)(ii)(iii)(iv)(vii))

    (ii)   own reactions to sensations (leads to (5)(i)(ii)(iii)(iv))

    (iii)   freedom of thought (leads to (5)(i)(ii)(iv)(v))

    (iv)   awareness of assumptions and roles (leads to (5)(ii)(iii)(iv)(v)(vii))

(7)

    (v)   concentration/self-expression (leads to (5)(ii)(iv)(v))

    (vi)   physical development and ability/emotions (leads to (5)(ii)(iii)(iv)(vii))

    (vii) mood and behaviour modifiers (leads to (5)(ii)(iii)(iv)(v))

    (viii) understanding sexuality (leads to (5)(ii)(iii)(iv)(vii))

    (ix)   Canadian values (leads to (5)(iv)(vi)(vii))

    (x)   personal set of values (leads to (5)(ii)(iv)(v))

    (xi)   public value issues (leads to (5)(iv)(vi)(vii))

    (xii) understand own nature (leads to (5)(ii)(iv)(vii))

    (xiii) understand consequences (leads to (5)(ii)(iv)(vii))

    (xiv) respect for self/others/law (leads to (5)(ii)(iv)(vii))

    (xv) personal identity (leads to (5)(ii)(iv)(vii))

    (xvi) other ethnic points of view (leads to (5)(iv)(vi)(vii))

Now, as has been noted several times, the above analysis is quite incomplete as an account of the proposals contained in *Circular P1J1*. Much of the document has been deliberately ignored for the sake of simplicity. However, even at that it still has become a rather complex matter. Indeed, what we do as educators is complex!

One kind of incompleteness, however, is traceable to the document and not to decisions on my part, namely, the complete lack of factual links. *P1J1* is essentially a set of educational objectives which the ministry would have teachers in Ontario adopt. It does not provide anything in the way of factual support for thinking that the overall proposal is feasible, i.e., that one level of objectives will indeed lead to the next level, and so on. Analyzing *P1J1* makes this quite evident.

Another interesting feature which the analysis brings out is the high degree of interrelatedness among various parts of the curriculum. The ministry mentions only three specific objectives as means to (5)(iv) values education, namely, (7)(ix)(x) and (xi). Nevertheless, all the objectives I have given in (7) would seem

to be important means to (5)(iv). I have taken them from the following topics in
P1J1: Perception and Expression, Drama, Health, Values, Decision-Making, The
Individual and Society, Canadian Studies. Moreover, I have no doubt that there
are other parts of the curriculum which would also be relevant. We now have an
immediate answer to the question of where values education may be taking
place, for good or ill, and something of an answer as to who should be doing it.
In short, values education does indeed happen all over the educational place, and
so we should all be prepared to do it well, wherever we figure in the curriculum.

A Strategy

Now that we have a better grasp of what the Ministry of Education is
saying about values education in *P1J1*, what should the values educator do with
it? On this point the ministry is quite clear. The educational objectives set forth
in *P1J1* are to be adopted, the responsibility of teachers, principals, and super-
visory officials being to plan and implement programs consistent with these
objectives.[7] Though I have misgivings about this as a general policy, I have
nothing to say against it now. What I have argued in Part I, however, is that this
would be a serious mistake for the values educator. First, to uncritically acquiesce to the ministry guidelines would be morally irresponsible. Teachers do
not simply take orders, they also must take responsibility for the learning experiences of their students. Second, to simply adopt and implement ministry objectives may ruin in advance all chances of getting our students to appreciate a main
feature of the moral life, namely, the need to understand and live creatively with
the tension which always and necessarily exists between the rights and concerns
of the individual and the rights and concerns of society. If the ministry, *as the
respresentative of society,* properly overrides the teacher *as individual* then the
lesson which the students may learn from their values education is that society
properly overrides them as individuals as well, in the conduct of their moral life.
Thus, while I have no specific argument with what the ministry recommends we
do in values education in *P1J1*, I must take issue with the background assumption that its recommendations must be accepted.[8] To do so removes the tension
I take to be so important to the moral life as we know it, as well as the
possibility of conveying this to the next generation.

It was argued in Part I that a philosophy of values education which had as
one of its objectives inviting students to live creatively with this tension would
be characterized by two things: (1) it would always attempt to reflect the views
of the teacher, student, parents, School Board and society at large about the
rights and concerns of everyone involved in values education—not only the views
of the Ministry of Education; (2) ultimately, the theory would contain information which was a balanced and reasonable reflection of all the above mentioned

[7] Cf., *Circular P1J1,* pp. 2-5.

[8] Items (ix), (x) and (xiv) in (7) specifically reflect the tension between the individual
and society.

information, with the teacher's moral point of view being the final arbiter of what is included in the theory—not the final views of the Ministry of Education. Not only does such a theory show some promise of not undermining one of its main objectives, but it also would have the benefit of keeping the values educator in a state of creative tension, not to mention the considerable benefit of not having one's conscience violated by what one was required to do on the job.

It should be noted that I am not *blaming* the Ministry of Education for insisting that its published objectives be adopted by Ontario teachers. It is not clear to me who should be held responsible for this mistake, if it is that. In fairness, several things should be pointed out: (a) Ontario law requires that the Ministry exercise this type of authority; (b) the public probably would demand that it show this type of leadership; (c) the teachers themselves typically insist on receiving such guidelines.[9] It can be said, then, that the Ministry of Education is simply a reflection of various segments of the society it seems to serve when it prescribes educational objectives for teachers. It might also be suggested that allowing the teacher to have the last word on what values educational objectives will be pursued presupposes more in the way of professional training and experience than teachers typically have. This is to say that teachers cannot be professional in the manner I have proposed in Part I. So, in the absence of this capacity the Ministry must have the last word on what should be taught in values education.

But if what I have suggested in Part I is correct, none of this will do. Values education apparently requires that teachers take final responsibility for the values educational objectives they implement. It follows, then, that they should obtain the requisite professional training and experience to properly shoulder this responsibility before they teach. Finally, the law, the public, and the teachers' self-concept must be changed so that teachers are encouraged to take this responsibility, apparently so necessary for any genuine education in values.

Now I would not suggest scrapping the theory of values education to be found in *P1J1*. The ministry's proposal *is* a valuable one. The role of values education in the broader educational context appears to be rather well thought out—see the interconnections between (5)(iv) and (3) and then to (1) in the analysis of *P1J1* given above. Also, many useful recommendations about how to educate one in values are offered—see the relations between (7)(i)-(xvi) and (5)(iv) of the analysis. The proposal is almost certainly to be much better than anything an individual is likely to produce in an afternoon.

I would suggest, therefore, that one *start* with the analysis of the ministry's proposal. One should then add to it information about educational objectives from other documents (school board policies, ethical writings, other theories of values education), information from isolated directives from prin-

9For these points I am indebted to Vern Cunningham, Midwestern Ontario Regional Office, Ministry of Education.

cipals and board personnel, information contained in casual remarks of students and colleagues, and finally, those suggestions which emerge from one's own moral convictions. The next thing to do is to make sure that this wealth of information fits together in a coherent way according to the means to end relationships required by the model. One should then add to it factual assumptions one is prepared to make about what may be expected to serve as a means to what. This is to assure one that the entire proposal has some feasibility, that it is a reasonable undertaking and not merely a collection of ideas that look attractive on paper. This factual information may come from one's own educational experience, common sense, theories of human behavior and human learning, etc. Finally, and most importantly, one must make sure that *everything* contained in the theory of values education now constructed according to the model is an expression of one's own deepest moral convictions or at least that it does not violate them.

In this way one could end up with a philosophy of values education which was coherent, comprehensive, and informed, a theory which also did not violate one's own conscience. Moreover, developing such a theory would obviously be one creative response one could make to one instance of the unavoidable tension between the individual and society.

It is often said, and I am one of those who say it, that one cannot educate others in values until one is reasonably clear about one's own value commitments. Though it is not an effortless way, the model and strategy offered in this paper are one way of obtaining this much needed clarity.

PART TWO

THE LEARNING ENVIRONMENT

PEDAGOGICAL IMPLICATIONS FOR STIMULATING MORAL DEVELOPMENT IN THE CLASSROOM

Diana Pritchard Paolitto
Research Associate
Center for Moral Education
Harvard University

Richard H. Hersh
Visiting Professor
Ontario Institute for Studies in Education

Introduction

Teachers are constantly confronted in the classroom with values conflicts and moral issues. Values are private concerns, we think, to be left to the family, church, and other institutions outside the school. But in a world of "future shock," accentuated by television and travel, our exposure to a myriad of values is multiplied. Such issues as war, political deceit, racial conflict, and unemployment bombard teachers and students and demand attention. Yet teachers fear these issues, not because they are unaware of what is happening, but because values issues represent a complexity not easily reducible to "right or wrong" on a test.

There is another set of values inherent to the classroom itself and often more hidden from teachers and students than the values conflicts presented by the society at large. These are the values reflected in *how* students and teachers interact in the classroom and school—the process of schooling itself, identified by Jackson (1968) as "the hidden curriculum." Teachers tell students what to do, where to sit, when to talk. They judge what is right and wrong behavior in school. Teachers express their values when they stress individual competition for grades rather than cooperation. They reflect their values in their dress, language, and non-verbal communication patterns.

What values are being taught? Conformity to authority? Valuing the thoughts of others more than one's own? Deceit? A teacher's emphasis on the establishment of order and the maintenance of rules may be justifiable in the creation of an atmosphere conducive to learning, but such practice may inadvertently lead to the formation of values not intended by the teacher. In a democratic society which ideologically disclaims unquestioned obedience to authority and conformity to the group, educational institutions often teach values which are antithetical to our stated democratic beliefs.

Perhaps the most pervasive attempt to recognize the legitimacy of the study of values in schools is the values clarification approach (Raths, Harmin & Simon, 1966). Proponents of values clarification acknowledge that values are not absolute. In addition, they are concerned with the descriptive "is," rather than the prescriptive "ought." "What *do* you do?" demands a different type of explanation than "What *ought* you to do?" The absence of prescriptive (should/ought) questions in values clarification is related to a failure to distinguish between moral and non-moral issues. What this educational approach lacks is the substance to help students confront questions of ethics, issues "of basic principles, criteria, or standards by which we are to determine what we morally ought to do, what is morally right or wrong, and what our moral rights are" (Frankena, 1963, p. 47). This limitation tends to reduce the complexity of values issues, to avoid moral controversies which values conflicts usually engender, and unwittingly to teach a system of values relativity that prevents rather than promotes resolution of conflicting values. For these reasons teachers require a broader conception of values education.

Lawrence Kohlberg's work in moral development offers an approach which confronts these limitations. His work in developmental psychology, based on the work of John Dewey and Jean Piaget, requires reconsideration of the role of teacher. Teaching within a cognitive developmental framework demands a philosophical, psychological, and educational perspective that is significantly different from that provided by traditional teacher training or in-service education. Such a reformulation of the teacher's role does not mean that what teachers presently know or do is ineffective or unnecessary. Rather, an understanding of moral development may provide an explanation of the complexity of the interaction between teacher and student which may help to inform teacher behavior.

A major goal of the teacher who embraces cognitive developmental psychology is not simply to help students accumulate knowledge but to help them develop more complex ways of reasoning. In essence, the teacher wants to facilitate intellectual, or cognitive, development. Moral judgment is defined as that aspect of intellectual functioning which focuses on a person's ability to reason about moral questions. The purpose of moral education from a cognitive developmental framework therefore becomes the stimulation of the student's capacity for moral judgment.

Development as the Aim of Education

Kohlberg and Mayer (1972) assert that two major ideologies dominate moral education. The first of these, the "romantic" ideology, stems from a maturationist theory of development, in which the child's growth is a naturally unfolding process. According to this view, the aim of education is to nurture the individual, to help the child to realize the full potential that already exists inside him or her. The educator's task is to eliminate any restrictive environmental barriers which might obstruct the flowering of the individual. Kohlberg and Mayer maintain that educational objectives within this ideology are characterized by a "bag of virtues" approach—that is, by a set of broadly-conceived traits which together characterize a "healthy" personality.

The second and most common ideology to American schooling is the "cultural transmission" approach to learning. The task of the educator within this framework is to teach students the knowledge and virtues of past experience, including the social and moral rules of the culture. Educational goals within this ideology demand adjustment or "socialization" to the prevailing norms. The cultural transmission model is also considered by Kohlberg and Mayer to rely on a "bag of virtues" rationale, one which does not examine any philosophical principles to justify moral education. Thus, important questions are neglected by educators within the cultural transmission framework: What is the basis on which certain "prevailing norms" are selected? What should a person believe when one cultural belief comes into conflict with another?

Kohlberg and Mayer argue that neither of the above ideologies results in effective moral education. Both stress the relativity of values. Both leave unresolved the question of how to walk the tightrope between indoctrination and capricious laissez-faire values education. Values clarification, for example, has been hailed for its welcomed reversal of moral indoctrination. But after teachers have helped students "clarify" their values, two questions remain: How does "clarifying" one's values relate to the development of a consistent moral philosophy? And how does one face the problem of values relativity if each value is "different" rather than "better" than another?

The third ideology, which Kohlberg and Mayer label "progressivism," attempts to confront these philosophical questions as part of its conception of moral education. The "progressive" school of thought suggests that education ought to promote the child's natural interaction with a changing society and environment. Development is not a naturally unfolding process as assumed by the romantics; rather it is a progression toward greater logical complexity through an invariant sequence of stages. The goal of education is the attainment of higher stages of development in adulthood, not merely a healthy childhood. Thus an educational environment should stimulate moral development by providing genuine moral problems or conflicts to be resolved. Educative experience should require the child to think in increasingly complex ways. Knowledge is seen not as a "thing" to be acquired but as an active change in the child's pattern of reasoning brought about by resolving moral conflict.

The "progressive" conception of cognition assumes that mental processes are structures—internally organized wholes or systems which relate one idea to another. These systems or structures function according to logical "rules" for processing information or connecting events. The cognitive structures consist of active processes which depend on experience to produce change, or development, in the way the individual makes sense of the world. Cognitive development therefore results from the dialogue between the child's structures and the complexity presented by the environment. This interactionist definition of moral development demands an environment which will facilitate dialogue between the self and others. The process of moral development involves both stimulation of reasoning to higher levels and expansion of reasoning to new areas of thought. The more people encounter situations of moral conflict that are not adequately resolved by their present reasoning structure, the more likely they are to develop more complex ways of thinking about and resolving such conflicts.

The Teacher as Developmental Educator

The teacher who intends to stimulate moral development must first do some careful thinking along several main dimensions. As in any area of teaching the moral educator needs to acquire a certain body of knowledge, in this case the theory of moral development and the pedagogy of moral education intervention. As a developmentalist the moral educator must become more than a specialist in a specific body of knowledge. The teacher's knowledge of moral development is the starting point and the means by which the student's education becomes possible. The teacher's theoretical understanding is the basis on which interaction is stimulated between what is inside the student's head and what exists in the world. The teacher's task is to empower developmental theory with substantive meaning for a specific population who are at a certain period in their development; that is, to think about the developmental characteristics of a particular group of children or adolescents with whom one is working in order to be able to design appropriate educational experiences that will enhance their development (Mosher, 1975).

On the one hand, thinking about moral development is an expansive activity, since the development of moral reasoning parallels such other areas of human development as intellectual and ego development. In addition, the biological model of cognitive developmental theory is in itself expansive, based on the organism's struggle toward adaptation through increasing differentiation (i.e., complexity) in its interactions with the environment. Still a further feature of expansive thinking for the teacher as developmentalist involves the philosophical aspects of moral development theory. In a very real sense, the teacher is asked to become a moral philosopher. The moral educator is asked to test one's own limits as a rational adult as a prerequisite for asking students to reason philosophically.

Learning about moral development with regard to a particular period of childhood or adolescence is, on the other hand, a narrowing and refining activity for the moral educator. The more that a teacher's developmental knowledge about a particular group of children or adolescents is specific and defined, the more likely will educational experiences designed to stimulate development be effective. The junior-high-school teacher working with children at the transition to conventional moral reasoning ability, for example, will be thinking about educational experiences effective in stimulating their development to conventional moral reasoning. Moral conflicts surrounding friendships, family, or other small groups of people tend to elicit stage-three reasoning. The teacher working with high school seniors, who are likely to be at the conventional level of moral reasoning, needs to consider situational conflicts that are very different. Issues focusing on the law, authority, and religious beliefs for example, relate to the developmental transition to post-conventional thinking, appropriate for this group of adolescents.

The stimulation of moral development requires not only a reconceptualization of teacher as developmentalist and philosopher, but also a focus on skills which help the teacher create the conditions for specific modes of classroom interaction. Such interaction requires that students go beyond the mere sharing of information; they must reveal thoughts which concern their basic beliefs. The theory of moral development demands self-reflection stimulated by dialogue. The teacher within this framework must be concerned with four types of interaction: (1) student dialogue with self, (2) student dialogue with other students, (3) student dialogue with teacher, and (4) teacher dialogue with self. Ultimately the interaction-dialogue process is intended to stimulate student reflection upon one's own thinking process. It is the student's dialogue with self that creates internal cognitive conflict. The need to resolve such conflict eventually results in stage change. Teachers may stimulate student reflection by encouraging and facilitating dialogue between students and between teacher and student. These interactions expose students to stages of thinking above their own and thus stimulate them to move beyond their present stage of thinking. Finally, such a process should also result in the teacher's dialogue with self, since the teacher may also grow in such a process.

Further, a climate of fairness must be created as a pre-condition to such dialogue. The concept of fairness, or justice, involves a regard for the rights of each individual in the classroom. A "fair" decision-making process therefore takes into account the rights and interests of each member (Kohlberg, Wasserman, & Richardson, 1975). The most effective environment for this task is postulated to be as close an approximation of democracy as possible, since in a democratic setting each person is equal to every other.

Lewin (1948) suggests that only through actual experience with democratic methods can one learn the peculiar conduct of a democracy. These experiences include responsibility toward the group, ability to recognize differences of opinion without the condemnation of others, and "readiness" to accept and give criticism in a sensitive manner. The climate for democratic learning should be free from autocratic methods and should include active participation, freedom of choice, freedom to express one's ideas, and heightened group identification or sense of belonging. Hunt and Metcalf (1968) argue that climate-building is an important part of a teacher's method, and that the climate of democratic groups be used to stimulate and maintain reflective thinking in the classroom.

Prerequisite Conditions for Stimulating Moral Development in the Classroom

The need for a person's existing thought structures to adapt, or assimilate and

accommodate, when confronted with new perspectives on a given conflict eventually leads to a more adequate structure of reasoning. Such interaction requires
environmental conditions which permit and support individuals to share their
struggles to comprehend complex social reality.

The teacher initiates those conditions necessary to all subsequent interaction that develops at the teacher-student, student-student, and student-with-self
levels. This prerequisite does not imply that the teacher is the center and controlling force of the moral education classroom. Rather, the teacher enters the
moral education classroom with deliberate and systematic pedagogical skills
which are based on the developmental and philosophic rationale previously described. In using these skills the teacher becomes the catalyst whereby interaction leading to development may take place.

Two conditions are fundamental to an environment which will stimulate
development: *trust and respect,* and *social role-taking.* A classroom with these
two requirements does not simply "happen" as a result of teacher and students
being together over time. The teacher is instrumental in creating such an atmosphere by modeling specific behaviors from the very first teacher-student interaction that takes place. Students are often not accustomed to participating in
discussions which center on listening to one another's opinions. It may take time
and patience, for example, to help students understand the importance of sitting
in a circle, and to encourage them to do so. In addition, students sometimes
"yell out" their responses and impulsively interrupt each other without realizing
it. Time must be taken as part of the core of the moral education classroom to
teach listening and communication skills.

By virtue of the teacher's own developmental difference as an adult, he or
she has a different social, personal, and emotional perspective, and probably a
more complex moral reasoning level than that of the students. The teacher
brings interpersonal and pedagogical skills into the classroom which hopefully reflect this more complex developmental pattern. Recognition of this difference is
fundamental to all other areas of creating a climate within which student development can take place, since the teacher needs to be able to comprehend the
perspectives of the students and thereby stimulate their thinking to more complex levels. The reverse of this process is not likely to be true, however. That is,
the students may not have the ability to take the cognitive perspective of the
adult. In this very crucial sense, the teacher is therefore "first among equals"
(Sullivan, 1975), not simply one among equals.

Trust and Respect. Given that the goal of a moral education classroom is
to enhance students' development, an atmosphere of mutual trust and respect is
essential. There is an interaction between the level of structural development and
a student's ability to conceive of a particular concept like "trust." A seventh-
grade youngster who reasons primarily at stage two in moral judgment, for
example, has a limited ability to take the perspective of others within a hedonis-
tic framework of bargaining, characteristic of stage two. That person might

conceive of trust as "doing what you can get away with" or not being open with anyone "until you can prove they'll be honest with you too." A person with a stage-three conception of trust, on the other hand, has the ability to take into account what others believe to be "good" behavior; that individual can then reason out his or her own behavior and that of others according to the standard of another person or group. At stage three trust is perceived as helping to maintain relationships.

It takes time for mutual trust and respect to evolve in the moral education classroom, especially among students who are at the preconventional level of moral reasoning. That is to say that *development* takes time. Certain activities like role plays and interviews require the group to cooperate in order to organize themselves effectively in deciding what to do and what is fair to expect of each other in accomplishing a task. For students to learn to evaluate their own discussions and role plays means that critical self-reflection and evaluation of others are encouraged in relation to developmental goals.

The teacher's respect for individual autonomy is a related and important aspect of a trusting learning environment which fosters development. Initially the teacher needs to channel any focus on personal disagreements into setting a contract involving what is fair to expect of one another in the group. Before students know each other, the teacher can also refocus personality clashes into an examination of disagreement about *issues.* Later, as trust develops, personal conflicts in the group can be presented as "real" moral dilemmas to be worked out by the group.

Part of the respect for autonomy involves the capacity for empathy. Understanding what the students in the class are experiencing from their point of view is a critical aspect of a developmental classroom. Cognitive developmental theory defines the structural aspect of empathy as *social role-taking,* or the ability to put oneself in the place of another and see the world through the other person's eyes (Selman, 1969).

Social Role-Taking. Taking the perspective of others is a necessary precondition for moral development. Selman (1976) notes that the link between intellectual development and moral development may be found in the ability of a person to take an increasingly differentiated view of the interaction between oneself and others. Hence, teachers must create classroom conditions which call upon the student to practice taking the perspective of others. This process involves helping students to perceive others as similar to themselves but different in respect to their specific thoughts, feelings, and ways of viewing the world. Also important is the development of the ability to see oneself from the viewpoint of others. The four levels of social role-taking ability identified by Selman are presented in Table 1.

TABLE 1

SOCIAL ROLE-TAKING STAGES

Stage 0 — Egocentric Viewpoint
(Age Range 3-6)[a]

Child has a sense of differentiation of self and others but fails to distinguish between the social perspective (thoughts, feelings) of other and self. Child can label other's overt feelings but does not see the cause and effect relation of reasons to social actions.

Stage 1 — Social-Informational Role-Taking
(Age Range 6-8)

Child is aware that other has a social perspective based on other's own reasoning, which may or may not be similar to child's. However, child tends to focus on one perspective rather than coordinating viewpoints.

Stage 2 — Self-Reflective Role-Taking
(Age Range 8-10)

Child is conscious that each individual is aware of the other's perspective and that this awareness influences self and other's view of each other. Putting self in other's place is a way of judging his intentions, purposes, and actions. Child can form a coordinated chain of perspectives, but cannot yet abstract from this process to the level of simultaneous mutuality.

Stage 3 - Mutual Role-Taking
(Age Range 10-12)

Child realizes that both self and other can view each other mutually and simultaneously as subjects. Child can step outside the two-person dyad and view the interaction from a third -person perspective.

Stage 4 — Social and Conventional System Role-Taking[b]
(Age Range 12-15+)

Person realizes mutual perspective taking does not always lead to complete understanding. Social conventions are seen as necessary because they are understood by all members of the group (the generalized other) regardless of their position, role, or experience. (Selman, 1976, p. 309)

---

[a]Age ranges for all stages represent only an average approximation based on Selman's studies to date.

[b]Higher stages of role-taking have been defined by Byrne (1973).

A theoretical understanding of the function of social role-taking is important as a basis of teacher and student behavior in the classroom. Moral conflict results from being able to take the perspective of others. The "cognitive dissonance" described by Kohlberg occurs as a result of one's own point of view being confronted by a different perspective. This conflict requires resolution. Individuals realize that their own answers to the problem are inadequate. If people could not assume the role of another, they would see no conflict. The individual's network of social relationships and social interaction forms the basis of each person's primary role-taking opportunities (Kohlberg, 1969). The family, the peer group, and school are the major social institutions in which children have the opportunity to consider the viewpoint of others in making decisions and in understanding the implications of their decisions on others. The more the structure of the group is democratic, the more the individual learns to experience taking the perspective of others.

The teacher in a moral education class is the primary role-taker in the group. The ability of the teacher to take the perspective of each student is a vital "skill." It is all too frequent that during a teacher-student dialogue, the teacher is unaware of how the student perceives a given situation. This failure often leads to a belief on the part of both student and teacher that each is not hearing the other. In one sense this problem is a case of not communicating. Within a cognitive developmental framework this lack can be further identified as an instance of not understanding or not accepting a particular complexity of perspective taking. The onus of failure in this regard, however, must be placed on the teacher, since the teacher will most often be in a better position to take the perspective of the students rather than the reverse. At the same time the teacher will need to create conditions in which student-to-student dialogue helps to develop an increasingly more differentiated and integrated social role-taking perspective. Questions like, "What do you think so-and-so is thinking about this situation?" or "How would so-and-so think *you* would resolve this question?" are as important to the development of social role-taking as the question, "What do *you* think about the problem?"

In summary, then, the development of trust and respect, and social role-taking ability are basic to establishing a fair atmosphere in which moral development can be fostered. As philosopher, the teacher realizes that children and adolescents have the capacity to reason philosophically and to become aware of themselves and others as reasoners. As developmentalist, the teacher wants to stimulate students' thinking to the next higher stage of moral reasoning. And finally, as an interventionist in the educational process, the teacher needs to establish core conditions to facilitate effective interaction which leads to development.

The process of leading a discussion of a moral dilemma is an example which captures the essence of the synthesis of these aspects of teacher preparation for moral education. Tracing the pedagogical steps involved in conducting a moral discussion helps to elucidate the interrelationship between moral development theory and educational practice.

Moral Discussion: A Vehicle for Stimulating Moral Development

The purpose of presenting students with moral dilemmas to discuss is to create thought-provoking dialogue that probes the moral basis of people's thinking from many different perspectives. A moral dilemma is an open-ended conflict situation, hypothetical or real, that requires a resolution of competing rights or claims among people, and for which there is no clear, morally-correct solution. Beyer (1976) summarizes the characteristics of an effective moral discussion:

> Regardless of the specific techniques used in conducting a moral discussion, however, the process of confronting a dilemma, taking a tentative position and examining and reflecting on the reasoning behind various positions remain essential activities. Crucial, too, are the student-to-student interaction, the constant focus on moral issues and reasoning, and the emphasis on a supportive trusting, informal classroom atmosphere. The extent to which the teacher can direct the entire process without assuming an expository or authoritarian role largely determines the success of a moral discussion.

The teacher needs to develop enough competence to facilitate a discussion based on students' moral reasoning patterns. In other words, the teacher must constantly keep in mind the *structural* level of discourse, including the fact that students often move between different stages in their thinking and that they often seek to avoid issues or entangle themselves in a web of complexity that may result in frustration or withdrawal.

The discussion of moral dilemmas in the classroom is a new experience for most children and adolescents, as documented by the intervention research on moral discussion curricula (Grimes, 1974; Paolitto, 1975; Sullivan, 1975). Moral dilemmas are often not perceived as such by students because parents and teachers make decisions for them before situations have the potential to become those of conflicting obligation or moral choice. In addition, children at the first level of moral development (stages one and two) respond to external rules in making moral decisions and therefore do not see a separation of self from external sources of judgment. Moral conflict often does not exist as stage one because, after all, "it's wrong to steal, period." Confusion is also evident when students create moral dilemmas out of non-moral situations. As one thirteen-year-old described, "Of course whether to paint your bike blue or green can be a very important moral dilemma! I'd paint my bike from green to blue any day to hide it if I stole it!"

In the initial phases of leading moral discussions, the teacher must be very active in teaching a process of inquiring into moral issues. Helping students to recognize that they are indeed thoughtful reasoners and to articulate elements of conflict in a situation are important first steps for students to experience. Posing questions that provoke cognitive dissonance, as a result of students' exposure to more complex ways of seeing the world than their own (i.e., a higher stage of reasoning), is a second step. The teacher has the responsibility of ensuring that students are exposed to the stage of reasoning above their own (Blatt, 1970; Blatt and Kohlberg, 1975). This the teacher may do by either utilizing his or her own higher stage arguments or by eliciting those same arguments from students.

When leading moral discussions for the first time, teachers often experience a disappointment that accompanies a simple "Yes" or "No" answer to a "Should" question, or a mere "Because" reply to a "Why?" question. A paucity of response is particularly true from students who are not highly articulate or verbal. The sequencing of qualitatively different types of questions and comments is therefore important for the teacher to consider:

(1) *Asking "Why?" questions.* Asking why somebody should resolve a certain moral conflict in a particular way helps students identify situations as dilemmas which require resolution from a conflict of choice. Such questions also, of course, elicit one's level of moral reasoning more easily than most other types of questions. Questions like, "Why do you think your solution to the dilemma is a good one?" or "What is the main reason you decided to resolve the problem as you did?" are two examples.

(2) *Complicating the circumstances.* Adding new situations to the original dilemma increases thoughtful, differentiated responses to a problem. This strategy also helps students to avoid "escape hatches." "Escape hatches" involve changing the nature of the facts of the dilemma, thereby effectively solving the dilemma by eliminating it as a conflict situation. For example, in a dilemma concerning the decision to throw certain people overboard from an overcrowded lifeboat drifting at sea, students commonly avoid confronting the dilemma by asking to tie the extra people to the side of the boat with ropes. To help students face the moral question in this case, the teacher might say, "Suppose there were no ropes in the lifeboat." The teacher might also complicate the dilemma in this instance: "Suppose holding the ropes would sink the lifeboat—if you had to choose between a mother and her eighteen-year-old son, who should be cast overboard?"

(3) *Presenting "personal" examples.* Such examples give students the realization that moral dilemmas are a part of their daily social interaction, as well as the source of many problems and solutions in the society at large. "Personal" in this sense implies situations within the experience of students and the teacher. A dilemma in the news or on a television program is as much a personal one in this context as a "personal problem." If a dilemma is personal, then there is likely to be high interest and emotional investment on the part of students. Such situations give a person pause to think about daily problems in new ways. Conflicts over different people's rights in the cafeteria, corridors, and classroom are especially fruitful sources of personal dilemmas. Real dilemmas can be written and presented by students themselves, such as this example co-authored by two eighth-grade girls:

> One table of girls constantly leaves their trays on the table. Because of this the cafeteria workers say that everyone who eats that period can't have ice cream until those trays and a few other scattered trays start getting cleared on a regular basis.
> Unfortunately, the girls at that table don't buy ice cream anyway, so they don't care.

> Should everyone get deprived of ice cream because of a few people? Why or why not?
>
> What should they do now that they know the ice cream punishment isn't working? For instance, should they punish each individual who doesn't clean his or her tray, individually? Why would the solution you choose be a good one? (Paolitto, 1975, p. 362)

(4) *Alternating real and hypothetical dilemmas.* This format helps to expand the range of the students' notion of what constitutes a moral problem. This variation also takes into account the range of student interests in the class.

Hypothetical dilemmas are imaginary conflict situations which highlight and often polarize particular rights or obligations to dramatize the *moral* components of a problem. "The Desert" (Blatt, Colby, & Speicher, 1974) is one such dilemma:

> Two people had to cross a desert. When they started, both had equal amounts of food and water. When they were in the middle of the desert, one person's water bag broke and all his water ran out. They both knew that if they shared the water they would probably die of thirst. If one had the water, that person would survive.
>
> What should they do? Give your reasons. ("Why" question)
>
> Suppose the two people are husband and wife. Should that change the issue and the decision? (Complicating the circumstances)

Hypothetical dilemmas in early sessions of the class also help students to develop trust through sharing the common experience of discussing crucial situations. At the same time, students do not feel prematurely "pushed" toward self-disclosure before the group is ready to respond at a level of personal acceptance.

For adolescents in particular, a combination of hypothetical and real, personal dilemmas makes sense developmentally and "works" in the classroom (DiStefano, 1976). For those at the beginning stages of formal operational thinking, or Piaget's conception of abstract reasoning ability, the intriguing aspect of hypothetical dilemmas may be the abstract dimensions which they entail. Part of this development of abstract intellectual thinking involves the ability to be self-reflective. Real, personal dilemmas, therefore, can complement hypothetical dilemmas, since they stimulate reasoning about the self in relation to others. Given the self-consciousness that accompanies the discovery of self, it seems important to provide a variety of opportunities for adolescents to move between the hypothetical and the real.

These four considerations constitute the "core" of the introduction to moral dilemma discussions. They involve an exposure to the breadth of the notion of moral dilemmas. How long the teacher concentrates his or her efforts on teaching students to consider the range of moral considerations in conflict situations depends on the nature of the particular group of students.

The second phase of a moral discussion format involves a *focus in depth.* The teacher's questioning techniques parallel this change in effort.

(1) *Presenting few questions.* Fewer questions means a sustained focus

through to a resolution of conflict. Questions should probe many sides of the same issue. A "Why?" question is not sufficient at this point. Students need to hear extended arguments from each other so they can understand the reasoning and challenge each other's logic. Beyer (1976) offers five types of probing questions:

I.   Clarifying probe—anything from Why; to What do you mean by . . . , or Then are you saying . . . ?
II. Issue-specific probe—asks student to examine their own thoughts about one of the major issues identified by Kohlberg—obligation, contract, authority.
III. Inter-issue probe—asks what to do when two issues conflict, e.g., loyalty to President versus loyalty to Constitution; loyalty to friend versus obligation to the law.
IV. Role switch probe—asks student to put self into the position of someone in the dilemma in order to see the other side.
V.   Universal consequence probe—asking person to consider what would happen if such reasoning were applied to everyone.

Probing usually involves role-taking questions that are effective in pursuing motives, intentions, and personalities of characters in dilemmas. Spontaneous role plays when students are "stuck" trying to resolve a certain issue can be tremendously helpful. Students are ready to role play when trust and acceptance have developed in the group. Concentration in depth also alleviates the problem of escape hatches. We assume that this in-depth period of questioning is the part of the moral discussion process where sustained cognitive dissonance leads to structural change.

(2) *Referring to the history of the group.* The teacher can link the present discussion to earlier discussions to help students see commonalities and differences. It is especially important to refer to earlier solutions of particular students. This helps students become aware of changes in reasoning in themselves and their classmates.

(3) *Clarifying and summarizing.* The teacher's role changes to that of clarifier and summarizer, rather than that of major initiator of topic questions. Students by this phase of discussion have learned how to approach questions of moral conflict; *they* can ask "Why?" questions. The teacher therefore becomes a more active listener in order to link crucial elements of discussion.

Conclusion

Teachers, like their students, are moral philosophers. Teachers too must ask questions of what is right and what is good before entering the classroom as well as during actual classroom interaction. The classroom itself confronts teachers and students with a myriad of potential moral dilemmas surrounding issues like cheating, stealing, truth-telling and keeping promises. The teacher must also be a developmentalist, with a knowledge of the psychology of moral development and the pedagogy of moral discussions. At best aspects of these two roles have always been a part of some teachers. The developmental perspective as a rationale for education demands that teachers become competent not only in knowledge and skills in their content area, but also in the ability to create the conditions for social interaction conducive to developmental change. To realize the teacher's function as developmental educator, one must be able to take the social perspective of each of the stages reflected in the reasoning of one's students, and to create an environment in which students are brought into contact with those differing perspectives.

The teacher who engages in a cognitive developmental approach to moral education is not only a moral discussion leader. The essence of moral education is that the teacher create the opportunity for students to organize their own experience in more complex ways. The moral educator is actually teaching the students a cognitive developmental approach for pursuing their own education after the formal educational process has ended. To learn the tenets of rationalism, or learning by reasoning, as well as to see the world in the eyes of another—these are the fundamental experiences of moral education.

References

Beck, C.; Sullivan, E.; & Taylor, N. "Stimulating Transition to Post-Conventional Morality: The Pickering High School Study." *Interchange* 3 (1972):28-37.

Beyer, B. K. "Conducting Moral Discussions in the Classroom." *Social Education* (April, 1976).

Blatt, M. "Studies on the Effects of Classroom Discussions upon Children's Moral Development." Unpublished doctoral dissertation, University of Chicago, 1970.

Blatt, M.; Colby, A.; & Speicher, B. "Hypothetical Dilemmas for Use in Moral Discussions." Cambridge, Mass.: Moral Education and Research Foundation, 1974.

Blatt, M., & Kohlberg, L. "Effects of Classroom Discussions upon Children's Moral Development." In L. Kohlberg and E. Turiel (eds.), *Recent Research in Moral Development.* New York: Holt, Rinehart and Winston, 1975.

Byrne, D. "The Development of Role-Taking in Adolescence." Unpublished doctoral dissertation, Harvard University, 1973.

Colby, A. "Values Clarification—Book Review." *Harvard Educational Review* 42, 1 (1975):134-143.

DiStefano, A. "Teaching Moral Reasoning About Sexual and Interpersonal Dilemmas." Unpublished doctoral dissertation, Boston University, 1976.

Frankena, W. K. *Ethics.* Englewood Cliffs, N.J.: Prentice-Hall, 1963.

Grimes, P. "Teaching Moral Reasoning to Eleven Year Olds and Their Mothers: A Means of Promoting Moral Development." Unpublished doctoral dissertation, Boston University, 1974.

Hickey, J. "The Effects of Guided Moral Discussion Upon Youthful Offenders' Level of Moral Judgement." Unpublished doctoral dissertation, Boston University, 1972.

Holstein, C. "Parental Determinants of the Development of Moral Judgement." Unpublished doctoral dissertation, University of California at Berkeley, 1969.

Hunt, M., & Metcalf, L. *Teaching High School Social Studies.* New York: Harper & Row, 1968.

Jackson, P. *Life in Classrooms.* New York: Holt, Rinehart & Winston, 1968.

Kohlberg, L. "Stage and Sequence: The Cognitive Developmental Approach to Socialization." In D. Goslin (ed.), *Handbook of Socialization Theory and Research.* New York: Rand McNally, 1969.

————————. "Stages of Moral Development as a Basis for Moral Education." In C. Beck and E. Sullivan (eds.), *Moral Education.* Toronto: University of Toronto Press, 1970(a).

————————. "Education for Justice: A Modern Statement of the Platonic View." In T. Sizer (ed.), *Moral Education.* Cambridge: Harvard University Press, 1970(b).

————————. "Continuities in Childhood and Adult Moral Development Revisited." Address to Life Span Psychology Conference. University of West Virginia, 1972.

Kohlberg, L.; Colby, A.; Fenton, E.; Speicher-Dubin, B.; & Lieberman, M. "Secondary School Moral Discussion Programs Led by Social Studies Teachers." In L. Kohlberg, *Collected Papers on Moral Development and Moral Education.* Vol. 2. Cambridge, Mass.: Moral Education Research Foundation, 1975.

Kohlberg, L., & Mayer, R. "Development as the Aim of Education." *Harvard Educational Review* 42 (1972):449-496.

Kohlberg, L., & Turiel, E. "Moral Development and Moral Education." In G. Lesser (ed.), *Psychology and Educational Practice.* Chicago: Scott, Foresman, 1971.

Kohlberg, L., & Turiel, E. *Recent Research in Moral Development.* New York: Holt, Rinehart & Winston, 1975.

Kohlberg, L.; Wasserman, E.; & Richardson, N. "The Just Community School: The Theory and the Cambridge Cluster School Experiment." In L. Kohlberg, *Collected Papers on Moral Development and Moral Education.* Vol. 2. Cambridge, Mass.: Moral Education Research Foundation, 1975.

Lewin, K. *Resolving Social Conflicts.* New York: Harper Bros., 1948.

Mosher, R. "Knowledge From Practice: Clinical Research and Development in Education." *The Counseling Psychologist* 4, 4 (1974):73-82.

————. "Funny Things Happen on the Way to Curriculum Development." In H. Peters and R. Aubrey (eds.), *Guidance: Strategies and Techniques.* Denver: Love Publishing, 1975.

Mosher, R., & Sprinthall, N. "Psychological Education: A Means to Promote Personal Development During Adolescence." *The Counseling Psychologist* 2, 4 (1971):3-82.

Mosher, R., & Sullivan, P. "Moral Education: A New Initiative for Guidance." *Focus on Guidance* (Jan. 1974).

Paolitto, D. P. "Role-Taking Opportunities for Early Adolescents: A Program in Moral Education." Unpublished doctoral dissertation, Boston University, 1975.

Raths, L. E.; Harmin, M.; & Simon, S. B. *Values and Teaching: Working with Values in the Classroom.* Columbus: Charles E. Merrill, 1966.

Rest, J. "Developmental Psychology as a Guide to Value Education: A Review of 'Kohlbergian' Programs." *Review of Educational Research* 44 (1974):241-259.

Rest, J.; Turiel, E.; & Kohlberg, L. "Level of Moral Development as a Determinant of Preference and Comprehension of Moral Judgments Made by Others." *Journal of Personality* 37 (1969):225-252.

Selman, R. "Role-Taking Ability and the Development of Moral Judgment." Unpublished doctoral dissertation, Boston University, 1969.

————. "The Relationship of Role-Taking to the Development of Moral Judgement in Children." *Child Development* 42 (1971[a]):79-91.

————————. "Taking Another's Perspective: Role-Taking Development in Early Childhood." *Child Development* 42 (1971[b]):1721-1734.

————————. "Social-Cognitive Understanding: A Guide to Educational and Clinical Practice." In T. Lickona (ed.), *Moral Development and Behavior: Theory, Research, and Social Issues.* New York: Holt, Rinehart & Winston, 1976.

Sullivan, P. J. "A Curriculum for Stimulating Moral Reasoning and Ego Development in Adolescents." Unpublished doctoral dissertation, Boston University, 1975.

Turiel, E. "An Experimental Test of the Sequentiality of Developmental Stages in the Child's Moral Judgement." *Journal of Personality and Social Psychology* 3 (1966):611-618.

————————. "Developmental Processes in the Child's Moral Thinking." In P. Mussen; J. Langer; & M. Covington (eds.), *New Directions in Developmental Psychology.* New York: Holt, Rinehart & Winston, 1969.

————————. "Stage Transition in Moral Development." In R. M. Travers (ed.), *Second Handbook of Research in Teaching.* Chicago: Rand McNally, 1973.

————————. "Conflict and Transition in Adolescent Moral Development." *Child Development* 45 (1974):14-29.

SOME THOUGHTS ON THE NATURE OF CHILDREN'S SOCIAL DEVELOPMENT*

William Damon
Department of Psychology
Clark University

In this paper I shall discuss some striking yet often overlooked characteristics of a young child's social development. In the past few years there has been a strong tendency for educators and psychologists to shift their interest from the intellectual to the social side of children's lives. Programs in moral education, values education, and social-emotional growth are fast becoming common in elementary schools across North America, partly as a result of the upsurge in psychological research on these topics. Still, our understanding of how children actually acquire social or moral maturity is remarkably shaky. To begin with, we have only the haziest idea of what society itself means to a young child.

My focus in this paper is on the child's acquisition of social knowledge. As will become clear, however, I am using the word "knowledge" very broadly. I wish it to include knowledge not only as it is expressed by the child verbally or cognitively, but also as it is expressed in the child's active dealings with members of his social world. In other words, the kind of knowledge of which I write can be seen in a child's nonverbal social conduct as well as in his judgment and reasoning. It can be expressed in a real life social situation as well as in response to a hypothetical story or dilemma. As we shall see, there are legitimate distinctions to be made concerning such different expressions of social knowledge; but to begin with we shall think of knowledge in the most general possible sense: in the manner of William James (1890), both as reflective knowledge *about* something as well as active knowledge *of* something.

As adults, we rarely appreciate the complexity and subtlety of our own understanding of society. We quite naturally tend to think of our social world simply as a collection of familiar individuals and institutions. Typically, these may include our friends, family, working associates, our governments, companies, churches, as well as countless media figures and nameless "persons on the street." We think, then, of understanding society as getting to know the important characteristics of these individuals and institutions. A socially sophisticated adult should know the traits that distinguish his wife from his sister and his secretary from his boss, just as he should know the codes and rules that govern

*This article has been excerpted and adapted from the Introduction to William Damon's forthcoming book, *The Social World of the Young Child*. Preparation of this chapter was supported by a grant from the Carnegie Corporation of New York. The author is indebted to conversations with James Youniss for many of the ideas expressed in the first part of this article.

the several institutions in which he is engaged. Similarly, from this point of view, a child's task in understanding his social world seems to be acquiring such knowledge. This may mean learning how adults differ from children, how Joey is different from (and yet similar to) one's other friends, what the school honor code and the law of the land are, and a host of other social facts.

Such learning indeed would appear to be a considerable accomplishment. But we shall soon see that it cannot account for the essence of a child's development of social knowledge, primarily because social knowledge is far more complex, dynamic, and subjective than we normally consider it to be. In fact, learning the characteristics of persons and institutions contributes only marginally to the process of understanding the social world. More central and more difficult is understanding the nature of the *relations* between persons (or between persons and their institutions); and understanding the *transactions* that serve to maintain or to transform these relations. It is only through gaining knowledge of such social relations as authority, attachment and friendship, and of such social transactions as fairness, kindness, and hostility, that a child comes to experience and make sense out of society.

It is perhaps surprising to note that learning the particular traits of individuals and institutions does not help a child much in understanding the social relations that bind these entities to one another. We would not, of course, want to claim that a relation between persons could exist independently of the persons themselves; nor that the individual characteristics of the persons involved would not influence the nature of the relation. And yet, as we shall see, there do exist certain powerful and archtypical social relations that organize a child's social world, and that do not depend upon person or institution-specific attributes for their fundamental character.

Consider, for example, authority—a relation central to the social world of childhood. Authority, from a child's point of view, is invested in a number of persons, usually including mother, father, policeman, teacher, peer-leader, team captain, and even supernatural figures, e.g., God. It is also invested in a number of social institutions which engage the child, particularly school, family, church, city law, and so on. Now to some extent, it is important to know the specific expectations of each of the various authority figures. Mother may demand that you wipe your feet before coming into the house, whereas father may be more concerned about verbal politeness. Similarly, school may forbid blue jeans, whereas the city may not allow bicycling in the park. But children do not endeavor to learn all the demands and rules of the world verbatim as they emanate from individuals or institutions, and, if they did, it would do them little good. For the crux of the authority relation is not a catalogue of all the rules and demands of all potential authority figures, but rather the very rationale of obedience itself.

To understand and to cope with the multiplicity of demands from various kinds of authority in his world, a child must discover why one obeys at all, and under what circumstances one ought to obey. It is also important to determine

whom one ought obey: that is, what attributes of a person call for the investment of authority in that particular person. Such attributes cannot be given
merely by a learning of the objective characteristics of persons. The same person,
with the same objective traits, may legitimately wield authority in one circumstance but not in another, or over one group of persons but not over another.
The child himself may be placed in a position of authority at times (perhaps over
a baby sibling, or as a captain of a team), and still be subservient at other times.
How does one decide when to obey and when to command in all of life's shifting
circumstances? Perhaps most significantly, a child must determine a basis for
disobedience as well as obedience. As conflicting expectations from conflicting
sources of authority are recognized, a child must decide how one best accepts
some and rejects others. No catalogue of rules will help the child deal with these
kinds of considerations.

   As are all important social concepts, authority is best understood as a
subjective, dynamic relation between social entities. It is subjective because one
man's leader is another's follower. It is dynamic because, even between the same
two parties, authority need not be permanently and irreversibly invested in one
or the other: a child may some day find himself giving directions to his parents,
just as a citizen may some day find himself rewriting the laws of his government.
Now it is certainly true that such transformations in the authority relation
depend to some extent upon certain characteristics of the persons (and the
institutions) participating in the relation. For example, well-educated individuals
are more likely to rewrite laws than are poorly-educated ones, and citizens are
more likely to rewrite laws in a democratic society than in a despotism. But
these transformations are not comprehensible without an understanding of the
nature and purpose of the authority relation itself, quite apart from the individuals engaging in it. In order to know when authority should be maintained and
when (and how) it should be changed, when an authority relation serves a useful
purpose and when it should be terminated altogether, when one authority
should be respected in lieu of another, as well as countless other decisions vital
to social existence, it is primarily necessary to be able rationally to deal with
subjective and dynamic qualities inherent in this relation. But herein lies the
complexity and elusiveness of this kind of social knowledge. As Piaget has shown
in his many studies of children's mathematical, physical and moral conceptions,
it is the subjective and dynamic properties of the world that are the least easily
grasped early in development.

   Unfortunately, very few psychological studies of children's social development have attempted to capture the complexity and subtlety of a child's developing social knowledge. Like most adults, psychologists have tended to under-
estimate the process of understanding society, and consequently have overlooked its most important features. American child psychology until ten years
ago was dominated by the social learning approach (Sears, Maccoby, Levin,
1957; Bandura, 1963), which considered social development to be mainly a
process of the child's "internalizing" information and social norms that he has

observed or experienced in his environment. From this point of view, a child has no special difficulty in acquiring any aspect of social knowledge, as long as it has been adequately presented to him by his environment. If one conceptual achievement is regularly seen to develop in children at an earlier age than another conceptual achievement, a social learning theorist would claim that this is because children are not normally exposed to the second concept as early as they are the first concept. For example, Bandura (1969) offered a social learning analysis of the old Piagetian finding that children normally evaluate moral acts on the basis of the consequences of the act (e.g., how much harm was done) at an earlier age than they evaluate acts on the basis of the intention behind the act (e.g., whether the act was meant to be helpful or selfish). Bandura claimed that this age differential was not a result of one concept (intentionality) being more complex and subjective than the other (objective consequences); but rather that it was a result of the kinds of information that parents offer children at different ages of childhood. His assertion was that parents do not normally bother to instruct or discipline children in terms of intentionality until the child has reached middle childhood, because, for such reasons as safety and child management, a parent considers it more important that a young child obey for any reason than for him to consider the motives and intentions behind his acts. Later when the child's world becomes more varied and complex, parents and others introduce these new notions, which then become part of the child's repertoire. Bandura was making a real case for the chicken coming before the egg.

In the past ten years, developmental psychologists have shown a greater respect for the uniqueness—as well as the limitations—of the child's own way of knowing the world. The assertion that a child can directly absorb information from his social environment (or that he would if he could) has been by and large discarded. Psychologists have come to doubt, for example, that the consequences-intentionality progression observed in the development of children's moral judgments would be reversed if only parents would reverse the order in which they introduce these notions to their children (Cowan, Langer, et al., 1969). In place of the social learning model of the child as passive receiver of social instruction has appeared a model of a child actively constructing his social knowledge out of an interaction between his own unique experience in the world and his own conceptual abilities and limitations.

The usefulness of this positive trend in developmental psychology has been subverted, however, by the kinds of social thinking that developmental psychologists have persisted in investigating. The predominant interest in recent years has been in "social cognition," with particular emphasis upon what has been called "person perception" (Livesley and Bromely, 1973), or "understanding other persons" (Mischel, 1974). The assumption behind this approach is that the child learns about his social world by discovering the important characteristics of other persons, just as the child learns about his physical world by discovering the important properties of objects in the world around him. The child learns that Mommy gets mad when you slam the door in much the same ways as he learns that ice melts when you heat it. Much of this work on social cognition does show, to its credit, an appreciation of the relatively greater conceptual difficulty behind certain kinds of person understanding than behind others. For example, Flavell (1974) has described the complex process of inference necessary for a child to understand covert properties of persons like motives and feelings, as opposed to the easier and more direct "reading" of observable features and behavior needed to discover overt personal traits and dispositions of others. Still, it is rare to glean from this line of work an indication that developing social knowledge entails anything more than increasing one's understanding of other persons and their characteristics. Such a view is inadequate for explaining the child's greatest difficulties and accomplishments in learning to understand and work with his social world.

There have been, however, a few recent exceptions to this person-centered approach to the study of children's social knowledge, most notably Youniss' work on children's understanding of interpersonal interactions (Youniss, 1975), Selman's work on the development of social role taking (Selman, 1974; Selman and Byrne, 1974), and Turiel's work on children's conception of social custom and convention (Turiel, 1974). In the present essay, we shall discuss each of these works, as well as the classic works of Piaget (1932) and Kohlberg (1963), both pioneering attempts to describe some radical differences between primitive and mature reasoning about one central type of social transaction, *morality.* The present effort follows the lead of these predecessors in focusing chiefly on the child's developing understanding of the relations that constitute human society and on the interpersonal transactions that serve to maintain or transform these relations. As in the earlier works, we shall again see some surprising and dramatic differences between children's and adults' perspectives on society, and even between the perspectives of children themselves at various ages. Hopefully, we shall make some progress in understanding how children acquire knowledge of some vital social concepts, and how developmental changes in children's knowledge of society influence and alter their mode of interacting with the persons and institutions of their social world.

Four Important Theoretical Distinctions in the Study of Social Development

The major arguments here rest upon a few basic theoretical assumptions about the nature of human social development. Rather than force the reader to uncover these assumptions as they reoccur, they shall be presented at the start, unadorned for full scrutiny. The assumptions will be offered in the form of four key distinctions assumed to be crucial in social development. Though these distinctions are not new to this work, neither are they widely accepted or even understood beyond the circles of a few developmental psychologists. Around some of the distinctions whirl the fiercest controversies in psychology today.

1. The Distinction Between Primitive and Advanced Modes of Knowing the World

All developmental psychologists are interested in, as Wohlwill (1973) writes, "changes in the individual's behavior as he grows older." But in most of the major developmental theories, including those of Freud, Piaget, Werner, Erikson, and Kohlberg, there is an additional assumption that the most important age-related changes tend to improve the functioning of the individual. Put different-ly, implicit in each of these theories is the notion that there exist primitive and advanced modes of being in the world, that primitive modes tend to be replaced with advanced modes as a child grows older, and that the advanced modes tend to work better than do the primitive ones. "Working better" generally means, in a broad sense, enabling the individual to adapt better to his world. But its exact meaning differs in each of the theories, depending upon what aspect of human functioning is emphasized by the theorist. In Freudian theory, it means being capable of healthy, reproductive sexual selection; in Piagetian theory it means being able to reason powerfully, creatively, and logically; whereas for Kohlberg it means being able to solve virtually all conceivable moral problems according to universal and consistent principles of justice.

Beyond the improved functioning of advanced modes over primitive modes, some theorists have suggested that there exist intrinsic properties of advanced modes which can be used to distinguish them from primitive ones. For example, Werner (1948) described advanced states as being more differentiated and hierarchically integrated than primitive states. Werner's metaphor for all organic development, whether biological or psychological, was one of cell divi-sion: at the beginning, all of an organism's functioning is fused into one global cell, and then later becomes differentiated into discrete but integrated parts, e.g., hands, eyes, etc. Piaget (1967), on the other hand, uses relative degree of equilib-rium as the main criterion for how advanced a structure is. With development, psychological modes of interacting with the world become increasingly able to establish an equilibrium between one's mode of apprehending reality and reality itself. In Piaget's view, a person processes and restructures reality in attempting to understand it (assimilation), but in addition, each new aspect of reality de-mands that a person alter his mode of processing a bit if it is to be truly understood (accommodation). The better the equilibrium between the two pro-cesses, the closer one gets to the true and accurate representation of the world necessary for optimal adaptation. The model here, borrowed from physics rather than biology, is one of balance: the more stable the balance, the less easily it is upset, and the more quickly it returns to equilibrium once it is upset. Kohlberg (1971) has drawn from both Werner's and Piaget's models in establishing descrip-tive criteria for his advanced stages of moral development.

It is important to note that the underlying assumption of this kind of theorizing is that the improved functioning of advanced states actually can be attributed to intrinsic properties of the kind described by Werner and Piaget. In other words, it is precisely the increased differentiation of a structure, or its more stable equilibrium, that makes it work better in this world. One example, analyzable by both Werner's and Piaget's criteria of development, is the child's struggle to understand what makes things float. Floating, like many physical and social concepts, represents a complex phenomenon not easily understood by young children. Only gradually, and late in childhood, does a child construct the notions (like weight and density) that enable him to explain why some objects float and others do not. Prior to this, children offer bizarre and inconsistent theories about floating, e.g., that a sailboat floats because it is light, a piece of wood floats because it is heavy, and a stone sinks because it is not strong. Werner (1948) discussed such childish theories in terms of qualities like fusion and lack of differentiation. The primitive thought of the child, he wrote, confuses properties of objects like strength, weight, and density, so that these are often used interchangeably. Once these properties have been differentiated from one another in the mind of the child, each may attain a consistent and unique meaning, a conceptual advance which will yield more logically adequate reasoning.

Piaget (Piaget and Inhelder, 1958), on the other hand, discusses this same conceptual achievement as one product of formal operational thinking, an attainment that bestows upon the child a new and more equilibrated way of organizing his world. The gist of Piaget's argument is that for a child to construct the crucial notion that materials have different densities he must understand the notion of differential size-weight ratios in objects, a notion that employs the sophisticated concept of proportionality. Such reasoning, according to Piaget, cannot occur in the absence of "proportionality schemes" unique to formal operational reasoning. There is no incompatibility between the developmental criteria offered by Piaget and Werner, only a different focus. Both sets of criteria legitimately may be used together to describe differences between advanced and primitive thinking.

However reasonable the distinction between primitive and advanced may seem while discussing children's understanding of a concept like floating, many uses of this distinction have provoked storms of controversy. Particularly provocative has been the tendency of many developmentalists to compare Western children's thinking with the thinking of adults from tribal cultures around the world. Piaget (1929), Werner (1948), and Kohlberg (1969), for example, have all compared children's belief in magic and in the reality of their dreams with similar beliefs of adults in tribal societies like the Bakairi of Brazil or the Atayal of Taiwan. In addition, these and other psychologists have noted that in many non-Western cultures adults do not seem to use advanced thought structures like formal operations or higher-stage moral judgment.

Probably the most renowned attack on such comparisons, and ultimately on the very distinction of "primitive-advanced" itself, came from the anthropologist Levi-Strauss (1969). Levi-Strauss made two main points. First, he pointed out that there was more similarity than meets the eye between "primitive" and "advanced" thinking. For example, all persons, whether child or adult, savage or civilized man, organize their world according to basic forms of catagorization, such as grouping things on the basis of similarity and constructing oppositions on the basis of contrast. Second, he claimed that the differences that do exist are best conceptualized as distinct yet *parallel* means of coping with different kinds of environments, rather than as more or less adequate modes of dealing with the world in general.

It is the second of Levi-Strauss' arguments that must be taken seriously, for the first only reflects the anthropologist's confusion between varients and invarients in development. No developmental psychologist would claim that all things change in the course of development, or that there are no constancies in the progression from primitive to advanced. Piaget called those important features of thought which remain constant throughout development "functions." Organizing and catagorizing the world would be classic examples of Piagetian "functions," and should be found in both primitive and advanced thought structures. What distinguishes primitive from advanced in this case, as Piaget (Inhelder and Piaget, 1964) has shown in his study of children's classification behavior, is that the child's *mode* of organizing and categorizing his world changes radically as the child develops. For example, early in life a child may group a number of objects together because they are often seen together (e.g., as table and chair, a hammer and a nail, etc.), whereas older children normally use more abstract and consistent criteria (e.g., all wooden objects, all blue ones, etc.) and think in terms of hierarchies, nesting objects into sub- and super-ordinate classes. Thus, though the type of activity remains constant, the way in which a child performs it changes with age and development.

But the problem raised by Levi-Strauss' second objection remains. Put generally, it is the argument that what works best in one setting may be maladaptive in another, and so it makes little sense to evaluate disparate modes of dealing with the world according to a common standard. Levi-Strauss described in great detail the considerable daily accomplishments of "primitive" peoples, including some feats (such as crop measurement) which are routinely performed with accuracy and efficiency that would rival any Westerner's techniques. Is the savage mentality actually best for the savage world? He also made a similar case for the young child, claiming first of all that children are capable of more sophisticated thinking than we give them credit for, and secondly, that any qualitative differences that do exist in the child's thinking are likely to enable the child to adapt optimally to his own world (which, of course, is a different world than that of an adult). Extrapolating this line of reasoning to our earlier discussion of the authority relation, we would say that the child has a different conception of authority than an adult because the child is in a subordinate role more often than an adult. It would then be our task to show how the child's conception was adaptive to the child's position in the world, and how the adult's conception was more adaptive to the adult's position.

Levi-Strauss' argument takes on yet another dimension when applied to that central sphere of social development, moral judgment. The issue of what works better aside, on what grounds do we claim that one moral code is more advanced, and by implication better, than another? Many would claim that, ethically, we have no right even to ask this question. The extension of Levi-Strauss' argument into the realm of the moral coincides with the philosophical position of cultural relativism. The assertion of the relativist is that all values are inextricably related to the context in which they must operate: hence the impossibility of ever deriving a set of "universal" moral principles against which all moral codes may be evaluated.[1] Further, without universally valid moral principles, no culture's values may be compared with any other's. Each set of values must be viewed in relation to its own functioning among the specific customs and conventions, as well as the unique needs, of the society that produced the values. An extreme relativist would maintain the same argument for persons at different ages within the same culture. Children have their own social worlds, and the moral rules that they use to regulate their social worlds must be right for them, just as ours are right for us.

An example of a problem in relativism was presented to me by an Indian doctoral student who had attempted to use the Kohlberg stage system in her native country. One of the characteristics of the Kohlberg stage system is that, at its highest level (Stage 6), there is an irreversible relation between life and property. In other words, reasoning at Stage 6 maintains that no property may ever be more valuable or more worth protecting than any human life. The Indian student was troubled by her failure to find Stage 6 subjects in her native population, even among adults whom she considered highly moral and religious. She concluded that Kohlberg's system was hopelessly culturally biased, because one line of Indian tradition, even as upheld by the most sophisticated moral reasoners, views the relation between certain kinds of property and human life differently than does Kohlberg's Stage 6. Certain property of man, such as family land or cows, is deemed sacred and may indeed have more moral worth than the life of a human individual, which is considered transient and renewable through reincarnation. To claim that the Indian view of life's meaning and moral worth was somehow more primitive or inferior to the Western view upon which Kohlberg's system is founded would not do justice to the depth and subtlety of the Indian tradition, the student felt.

Fortunately, my own work deals only with young children of middle-class America, and thus avoids the questionable practice of comparing one society's relative degree of development against another's. Still, I do follow this practice with regard to the children who are the subjects of my studies, and in this sense the distinction between primitive and advanced is very much in use. I find justification of this practice in showing how changes with age in a child's mode

---

[1] Kohlberg, who is able to assimilate most any philosophical position to his six-stage moral judgment system, has responded to the relativist's attacks by placing their position at Stage 4 Transitional (Kohlberg, 1971; Turiel, 1974).

of social functioning can be described as advances in that mode; and how the very qualities which lead us to call a new mode more advanced than the one it replaces are indeed responsible for important improvements in the child's social functioning.

2. The Distinction Between Practical and Moral Orientations to the Social World

Roger Brown (Brown and Herrnstein, 1975) has expressed a concern about recent attempts to "morally educate" prisoners and other social delinquents. In form, Brown's concern is very similar to the "relativistic" argument of Levi-Strauss presented above. Brown has been troubled by one of Kohlberg's moral intervention projects that Brown had witnessed in a Connecticut prison. In the episode that he relates, a group of women prisoners was given the responsibility to sit in judgment on two of their peers who had been accused of illegally bringing liquor into the prison. The group's response to this task was to unquestioningly support the two women, without ever attempting to deal with the issue of the women's guilt or innocence. The group's operative code was to stick together against prison authority, and to help one another through a reciprocal exchange of favors.

Although such behavior on the part of the group was clearly lower-stage in Kohlberg's system, Brown found it nevertheless to be "penetratingly intelligent" given the entire context of the group's social situation. Prisoners, Brown points out, are powerless to do anything about rules of a prison, which are laid down by fiat. Moreover, many prison rules—like those against alchohol—are without parallel in the outside society, and thus often seem arbitrary and devoid of important principles backing them up. Why, then, should a group of prisoners feel an obligation to uphold such rules? Also, Brown suggests that it would have been dangerous, or at least foolish, for any woman or group of women to recommend disciplining peers, given the "general vulnerability" of all inmates within the prison society. Brown concludes that "the higher levels of moral reasoning may be luxuries that only persons in privileged or carefully protected circumstances can afford," and that we ought to be careful about "encouraging young people or adults to reason about moral questions maladaptively for their circumstance" (Brown and Herrnstein, 1975, p. 325). The implication is that low-level moral judgment may be the most intelligent and realistic adaptation to a low-level social world.

The argument that Brown makes actually fuses two concerns into one. The first of these concerns is what we shall call *practical*, the second *moral*. It is a concern of a practical nature that would lead one prisoner to support another because, as Brown writes, she could not "afford" to do otherwise. It is a concern of a moral nature that would lead a prisoner to reject prison rules as arbitrary and authoritarian, and to adhere instead to peer codes out of a sense that the peer codes are fair, important, and self-initiated.

The distinction between practical and moral considerations may be defined in the following manner: practical considerations focus upon the realistic consequences of actions, especially consequences affecting the self or those associated with the self; whereas moral considerations ultimately focus on the issue of how justice is best served. Like in all dichotomies, however, there is often considerable overlap between practical and moral concerns. For example, the age-old debate about the relation of means to ends always fuses practical and moral considerations. To whatever extent one accepts the aphorism that ends justify means, one's arguments are almost invariably made in both practical and moral terms. Will a temporary suspension of moral considerations gain practical results that will end up being fairest for all? Or, will adherence to moral principles actually work best in the long run? Such questions reflect common attempts to deal with the interplay of practical and moral problems normally encountered in the real world.

Still, the means-ends questions posed above show an implicit recognition that practical and moral considerations are distinguishable, even though in most social situations one normally encounters both together. Not all thinking shows such a recognition. In fact, one of the salient characteristics of lower-level social thinking is that it confuses practical concerns with moral ones. Take, for example, the following bit of reasoning, quoted by Turiel (1969) from a five-year-old. Thoreau's act of civil disobedience had to be bad because it landed him in jail. All acts that lead to punishment are automatically bad, and all bad acts will and should be punished because they are bad. Here we see the total fusion of moral with practical, manifested in the determination of right or wrong by reference to consequences, and, reciprocally, the determination of consequences by reference to the rightness or wrongness of the act. Kohlberg (1969) called the first part of this practical-moral equation a "punishment and obedience orientation," and Piaget (1932) called the second part "moral realism."

In a Wernerian sense, then, we see a *developmental* relation between practical and moral orientations to the social world. In primitive thinking, these orientations are fused, whereas with development they become increasingly differentiated and coordinated. Advanced social reasoners have the ability to consciously decide which orientation, practical or moral, they will bring to bear on a social problem. They may even decide that they will place one in service of the other. A citizen may, for example, engage in practical political or business activities for moral ends; or, conversely, may hold with Ben Franklin that moral virtues like honesty are the best "policy" in a very practical sense. Such reasoning is not possible until moral and practical considerations have been distinguished and some integration has been established between them, i.e., until a person establishes some sense of how the two are related in the social world.

3. The Distinction Between Theoretical and Real-Life Social Knowledge

Herman Melville in *Billy Budd* credited an unknown writer with this bit of wisdom:

> Forty years after a battle it is easy for a noncombatant to reason about how it ought to have been fought. It is another thing personally and under fire to direct the fighting while involved in the obscuring smoke of it. Much so with respect to other emergencies involving considerations both practical and moral, and when it is imperative promptly to act. The greater the fog, the more it imperils the steamer, and speed is put on though at the hazard of running someone down. Little ween the snug card players in the cabin of the responsibilities of the sleepless man on the bridge.

In this fine piece of writing, Melville is describing a distinction that psychologists normally call either the "judgment-conduct" or the "thought-action" problem. Simply stated, the issue is that we often cannot infer how a person will act from what the person says he would or should do. This problem is particularly acute in the study of social development, where the most powerful method of investigation has been hypothetical—verbal stories of the type developed by Kohlberg (1963) to study children's moral judgments. How relevant to a child's daily actions are his answers to a Kohlberg-type interview? As Roger Brown (Brown and Herrnstein, 1975) has noted, "the connection between 'story problem morality' and conduct is still . . . mostly unknown."

One of the chief obstacles to our gaining more understanding of this "connection" has been the unfortunate way that psychologists have conceptualized the original distinction. In actuality, there can never be a split between judgment and conduct, nor between thought and action. These are inseparable activities, since every human social interaction by necessity involves both judgment and conduct, both thought and action. It is not possible to imagine, for example, a person engaging in a social action without some corollary mental process which we would call "thought." Likewise, we could not possibly assess a person's social judgment without reference at least to his verbal behavior, which is certainly an aspect of conduct. Some may perhaps wish to distinguish between verbal and non-verbal conduct, but this would not help much, since even in real-life situations most of what we mean by "conduct" is still verbal. In fact, most of the great moral "acts" of history have been comprised solely of, or at least were accompanied by, extensive verbal statements. In any case, this is still not the distinction between thought and action. It should be noted that most philosophers and cognitively-oriented developmental psychologists (e.g., Bruner, Vigotsky, Piaget) consider thought and action to be very much part of the same system, thought being simply one kind of internalized, covert act.

Yet most psychologists who have worked on the "connection between story problem morality and conduct" have approached it as a problem in relating moral thought (or judgment) to moral action (or conduct). This has led both to theoretical confusion and to a paucity of experimental results. The confusion springs from the impossibility of isolating one from the other of two inseparable activities. As Kohlberg (1969) and Brown (1975) have pointed out, any social act can reflect a variety of different judgmental dispositions; and, conversely, any judgment may lead to a variety of different acts. Perhaps the most notable example of this is the difficulty of predicting a subject's dilemma choices within the Kohlberg moral judgment system: a person may, for example, argue either for or against stealing a life-saving drug at any of Kohlberg's six major judgmental positions. The subject's choice or prescribed action (to steal or not to steal) is morally neutral and cannot be assessed unless it is considered together with the reasoning that accompanies it. In other words, it is impossible to consider, or to "operationalize" in any way, moral thought and moral action apart from one another. Still, psychologists persist in dealing with these as two distinguishable "variables" which may be independently measured and correlated.

It is not surprising that experimental studies based on this impossible distinction have without exception failed to yield informative results. Take, for example, the classic experiments of Hartshorne and May (1928-30), upon which all further judgment-action studies (e.g., Grinder, 1964) have been modelled. Hartshorne and May operationalized moral thought by assessing children's knowledge of social rules like the Boy Scout code and the Ten Commandments. They then operationalized moral conduct by observing children's nonverbal behavior in experimental situations which offered children opportunities to cheat, to lie, etc. To their apparent surprise, they found low or non-existent correlations between children's performances across such tasks. The problem, however, was that Hartshorne and May never attempted to find out what an act like "cheating" in one of their experiments meant to the children who "cheated." The tasks on which the children cheated required children to perform such feats as placing pencil marks within rows of circles without opening their eyes, or to list names of countries without looking at the efforts of peers. It is entirely possible that some children may have seen nothing immoral or wrong about disobeying the experimenters' rules on such seemingly arbitrary tasks, and may indeed have seen some value in cooperating with peers. In such cases, child morality may have actually been on the side of the "cheating" action! Without considering the actions of their subjects in the context of the subjects' judgmental interpretations of these actions, Hartshorne and May had no chance of making sense out of the immense amount of data that they collected.

But there is a way of approaching the problem described by Herman Melville, Roger Brown, and a host of others, without attempting to make an impossible distinction between thought/judgment/reasoning on the one hand, and action/conduct on the other. This is to consider both judgment and action together as inseparable components of knowledge, and to recognize that knowledge may be expressed in different contexts. One possible context is the hypothetical-verbal context of an interview composed of story-dilemmas, and we might say that the kind of knowledge tapped by such an interview is a theoretical, reflective knowledge. Another context, of course, is the immediate context of real-life social situations. We may call this a real-life, "practical" knowledge (that is, knowledge in *practice,* rather than in theory); although we must be careful to distinguish this use of practical from our earlier use of it to describe pragmatic, non-moral orientations to social problems.

In the present work, therefore, we shall redefine the original problem as the connection between theoretical, hypothetical knowledge and practical, real-life knowledge, rather than as the connection between thought and action. Once it has been redefined in this manner, the problem may be investigated in a very straightforward manner. One simply designs a methodology that assesses all aspects of subjects' knowledge in both hypothetical and real life social situations. The major implication of this new approach is that both verbal judgment and active conduct must be elicited from subjects in the real-life situations if we are to accurately assess the subject's practical social knowledge. Put differently, we must find out what a person's overt conduct means to him if we are to make sense out of it. In some beginning studies (Damon, 1975b), I have described some experimental work that brings this new approach to bear on the old problem that we have been discussing. Though this work is too young to draw final, powerful conclusions from, it at least has yielded some suggestive and even intriguing findings.

Forgetting for a moment the scarce empirical work that does exist, we might ask ourselves, to start with, how we might predict that a child's theoretical social knowledge should relate to his real-life social knowledge in the course of his development. I think that common sense normally tells us that real-life knowledge does not always "live up to" theoretical knowledge. In other words, a child may have a sophisticated understanding of right and wrong, or may have a good theoretical knowledge of how to best get along with his peers; but under the pressures of an immediate social situation may not fully employ this knowledge. This is clearly the gist of the passage quoted above from Melville. The implication is that factors such as self interest and distracting time pressures interfere with the full utilization of theoretical knowledge in real-life social situations. If this view is correct, we should often see a child's practical knowledge lagging behind his theoretical knowledge all through the course of his development.

The only point that I wish to make at this time is that there is another plausible relation between theoretical and practical social knowledge, a relation which actually consists of an opposite sequence to that described above. It was Piaget (1932) who first suggested practical knowledge is always at the forefront of the theoretical, and thus that we should find a child's moral judgment (for example) often at a higher level in a real-life situation than in verbal response to a hypothetical dilemma. Piaget's assertion is that all knowledge is worked out first on the plane of practical activity, and only later becomes reflective, theoretical, and hypothetical. Social knowledge is no exception to this general principle. I do not wish to try to resolve this issue here, only to note that there are at least two contradictory, yet plausible, predictions that may be made concerning the relation between theoretical and practical social knowledge; and that any comprehensive model describing this relation in children or adults must take into account both types of prediction.

4. The Distinction Between Whole and Partial Social Structures

In the associationist tradition that, under the guise of learning theory, dominated American psychology for so many years, it was assumed that children
acquire knowledge bit by bit, storehousing discrete pieces of information. No
relation was hypothesized between the individual pieces beyond "associations"
formed through regularities experienced by the child in his environment. In
other words, a child learning the concept "Italian" would get no help from his
already having learned the concept "Frenchman," though he might learn
through experience that Italians and spaghetti often go together. Conceptual
achievements in the social realm supposedly occurred in the same piecemeal
fashion. For example, one assertion (Berkowitz, 1964) was that moral values are
learned one by one, in the order in which they are introduced to the child by his
environment. Kohlberg (1969) has called this a "bag of virtues" approach, the
metaphor being one of a child gradually accumulating discrete virtues, each
independent of all the others, and then storing them for future use.

The structuralist tradition, in opposition to the associationists, has maintained that concepts are by no means independent or unrelated, but rather that
they are bound to one another by common structural features. The concept
"Italian" is similar to the concept "Frenchman" in that both concepts rely on
notions like geographical boundary, ethnic heritage, national citizenship; etc.
Further, the structuralist assertion is that understanding one concept implies an
ability to understand any similar concept. If a child learns how to construct and
recognize the class of Italians, he ought to be able to do the same for French-
men, since each of these concepts rely on identical structural underpinnings. The
implication of the structuralist tradition is that there are predictable regularities
in a child's development of knowledge, due primarily to a human tendency to
construe the world according to universal structures or patterns. With development, these patterns become more complex, differentiated, and adaptive.

Certainly the most extreme manifestation of structuralist assumptions in
the study of social development has been Kohlberg's moral judgment model.
Kohlberg, in his strongest statements (Kohlberg, 1971), has maintained that
both children and adults organize their entire social worlds through one or more
of the six basic "justice structures" that comprise his six-stage moral judgment
sequence. The assertion is that justice is the essential factor in human social life,
and consequently that human thinking about social relations and institutions is
structured primarily by notions of justice. Of course, notions of justice may
differ among persons—hence the six distinct forms or "stages" of justice structure. Nevertheless, whatever its specific nature, justice reasoning serves the same
function for all persons, that of a primary organizer of one's social world.

Some who accept Kohlberg's basic model believe it nevertheless to be too
ambitious and too global. The question is whether any justice structure is general
enough to organize the range of human social interactions. For example, sexual
and romantic relations between persons are probably best understood with refer-

ence to notions like intimacy and attraction rather than to notions like justice (though justice, too, may play some part). Turiel (1975) has made this point most forcefully, and I shall draw heavily on his arguments in this discussion.

Turiel has written that accepting the assumptions of structuralism does not entail believing that there is one unitary structure that governs all thinking. In fact, even structural-developmental psychologists like Kohlberg have always drawn distinctions between thinking about the physical world and thinking about the social world. Turiel argues simply that distinctions should further be made between different conceptual realms within the social world. He quotes from Piaget: "I must emphasize that these (structural) systems are merely partial systems with respect to the whole organism or mind. The concept of structure does not imply just any kind of totality and does not mean that everything is attached to everything else" (Piaget, 1967, p. 143).

In his own work, Turiel distinguishes social-conventional concepts from moral ones. His claim is that conventions like manners, customs, etc., do not have a justice component, and thus have a different structural core than do moral rules. This is not to say that the two are totally unrelated or independent, but rather that each is unique in some way and that neither is reducible to the other. Turiel calls each a "partial system within the structure of thought." The task for psychologists and educators interested in social development is to dis-cover how unique and how general are the various structures that make up a child's social knowledge. If some structures, like logic or role taking, are more pervasive and more general than others, we certainly ought to focus on them in our educational efforts. On the other hand, we must respect the uniqueness of all conceptual aspects of social knowledge, and consequently we cannot expect change in one domain of knowledge to bring immediate or direct change in another. But once we are able to decide "how partial" are each of the various facets of a child's social understanding, we shall better know what to expect.

References

Brown, R., and Hernstein, R. *Psychology.* Boston: Little, Brown, 1975.

Bandura, A. *Social Learning and Personality Development.* New York: Holt, Rinehart and Winston, 1963.

————. "Social Learning and the Shaping of Children's Moral Judgments." *Journal of Personality and Social Psychology* 11 (1969):275-283.

Cowan, P. A.; Langer, J.; Havenrich, J. and Nathanson, M. "Social Learning and Piaget's Cognitive Theory of Moral Development." *Journal of Personality and Social Psychology* 11 (1969):261-274.

Damon, W. "Early Conceptions of Positive Justice as Related to the Development of Logical Operations." *Child Development* 46 (1975):301-312.

————. "Studying Early Moral Development: Some Techniques for Interviewing Young Children and for Analyzing the Results." In J. Meyer, B. Burnham and J. Cholvat (eds.). *Values Education.* Waterloo: Wilfrid Laurier University Press, 1975.

Flavell, J. "The Development of Inference About Others." In T. Mischel (ed.). *Understanding Other Persons.* Oxford, England: Blackwell Basil and Mott, 1974.

Inhelder, B. and Piaget, J. *The Early Growth of Logic in the Child.* New York: Harper and Row, 1964.

James, W. *The Principles of Psychology.* Vols. 1 and 2. New York: Henry Holt.

Kohlberg, L. "The Development of Children's Orientations Toward a Moral Order." *Vita Humana* 6 (1963):11-33.

————. "Stage and Sequence: The Cognitive-Developmental Approach to Socialization." In D. Goslin (ed.). *Handbook of Socialization Theory and Research.* New York: Rand McNally, 1969.

————. "From Is to Ought: How to Commit the Naturalistic Fallacy and Get Away With It in the Study of Moral Development." In T. Mischel (ed.). *Cognitive Development and Epistemology.* New York: Academic Press, 1971.

Levi-Strauss, C. *Elementary Structures of Kinship.* Boston: Beacon Press, 1969.

Lively, W. J. and Bromley, D. B. *Person Perception in Childhood and Adolescence.* London: John Wiley and Sons, 1973.

Mischel, T. *Understanding Other Persons.* Oxford, England: Blackwell, Basil, and Mott, 1974.

Piaget, J. *The Moral Judgment of the Child.* Glencoe, Ill.: The Free Press, 1948 (originally published, 1932).

————. *Six Psychological Studies.* New York: Random House, 1967.

————. *The Child's Conception of the World.* London: Routledge and Kegan Paul, 1929.

Piaget, J. and Inhelder, B. *The Growth of Logical Thinking from Childhood to Adolescence.* New York: Basic Books, 1958.

Sears, R.; Maccoby, E. and Levin, H. *Patterns of Child Rearing.* New York: Harper and Row, 1957.

Selman, R. "Perspective Taking and the Analysis of Conceptions of Interpersonal Relations." Unpublished manuscript, Harvard University, 1974.

Selman, R. and Byrne, D. "A Structural Analysis of Role-Taking Levels in Middle Childhood." *Child Development* 45 (1974):803-806.

Turiel, E. "Developmental Processes in the Child's Moral Thinking." In P. Mussen, J. Langer and M. Covington (eds.). *Trends and Issues in Developmental Psychology.* New York: Holt, Rinehart and Winston, 1969.

————————. "Conflict and Transition in Adolescent Moral Development." *Child Development* 45 (1974):14-29.

Werner, H. *Comparative Psychology of Mental Development.* New York: Science Editions, 1948.

Wohlwill, J. *The Study of Behavioral Development.* New York: Academic Press, 1973.

Youniss, J. "Another Perspective on Social Cognition." In A. Pick (ed.). *Minnesota Symposia on Child Psychology.* Vol. 9. Minneapolis: University of Minnesota Press, 1975.

THE REFLECTIVE, ULTIMATE LIFE GOALS' APPROACH TO VALUES EDUCATION*

Clive Beck
Coordinator of Graduate Studies
Ontario Institute for Studies in Education

1. Ultimate Life Goals and the Reflective Approach in Value Education

Discussion with teachers and students and detailed interviews continue to confirm that the great majority of human beings pursue ultimate life goals, or fundamental human (and humanistic) values, such as survival, happiness (enjoyment, pleasure, etc.) health, fellowship (friendship, love, etc.), helping others (to some extent), wisdom, fulfillment (of our capacities), freedom, self-respect, respect for others, a sense of meaning in life, and so on. Even people of a strongly religious persuasion keep referring to such values, implicitly or explicitly, when talking about their way of life.

We continue to be of the opinion that such ultimate life goals must be central to any viable program of value education. However, we acknowledge that there are two aspects to value education: (a) determining what one's values should be (including one's fundamental life values and goals); and (b) coming to live in accordance with these values. The former aspect of value education may be described as the "value inquiry" aspect. Although inquiry into values cannot be separated sharply from trying out values in practice, we have tended in this project to concentrate on the value inquiry aspect of value education because of the limitations imposed by the usual school classroom situation.

In our approach to value inquiry in schools, the key term that has emerged is "reflection." This reflection is carried out either upon ultimate life goals or in the light of such goals. We have arrived at the following breakdown of the reflection process, which we think will be of assistance in curriculum building.

(i) First, reflection on values—specific, intermediate or ultimate—is obviously important in order to ensure that one is not making a straightforward mistake about "the facts of the case." For example, one may value a business associate for his honesty and resourcefulness but find on reflection (including appropriate inquiry) that he is neither honest nor resourceful. The need for this kind of reflection on values is unproblematic and widely acknowledged.

(ii) Second, one must through reflection bring the values one is not sure about into line with the values one is sure about. For example, one may, upon

*Adapted from the 1975 Annual Report of the O.I.S.E. Moral Education Project funded by the Ministry of Education, Ontario.

reflection, be somewhat unsure about the value of competitive sport. By reflection upon a complex of values one is sure about—health, happiness, friendship, and so on, in certain forms— one may arrive at either a rejection of competitive sport as valuable or a conception of competitive sport such that one can legitimately value it. Adjustment of one's values to one another in this manner may appear so obviously sensible as not to merit mention. However, it is amazing to what extent people compartmentalize their valuings, not noticing that certain values which they have no sound basis for can be rejected, modified or justified in the light of other values that they are sure about for good reason.

(iii) Third, one must through reflection bring means-values into line with end-values (insofar as one is sure that the end-values in question really are valuable). One may believe, for example, that promotion in one's profession is a good means to happiness and security but recognize on reflection that one would be happier and more secure at the promotional level one has at present. Here again, it is common for people not to engage in reflection of this kind and to value things which in fact militate against the achievement of their fundamental life goals.

(iv) Fourth, it is necessary through reflection to arrive at and constantly revise and refine a set of fundamental or ultimate life goals—things that one values for their own sake—in the light of which one can assess specific and intermediate values. A list of such values was presented above, but of course the list is always open to question, and people vary in the emphasis they give to the values mentioned in the list: part of the reflection process involves determining the emphasis one is going to give to each value. Further, one has to refine the *type* of survival, health, happiness, etc., one is after (for oneself and others) and under what circumstances.

It should be noted that in teaching students how to reflect on values, one is not merely teaching a *process* that they must then go away and use by themselves. A pure "process" or "skills" approach to value education must be rejected. In order to reflect successfully on values, a student must already have arrived at a relatively sound value outlook, which is usually achieved through reflective dialogue with others. As well as teaching reflection skills, then, the school must, over the years, provide contexts in which the student may, through reflection, build up a sound set of values which he may bring to his reflections on problems outside the school. The school must teach both skills and content.

2. Indoctrination and Value Education

Talk of teaching content may arouse the fear that what is being proposed is indoctrination or the inculcation of moral precepts. However, the process of "teaching" that is envisaged is such that the terms indoctrination and inculcation are not appropriate. It is true that the teacher will feel free to express his or her views on the issues under consideration and present arguments for them. Further, various other points of view and arguments will be injected into the discussion through study materials, books, films, newspaper clippings, visitors, and so on, as well as by the students themselves. But this is imply because, in the absence of clearly articulated views and arguments, students will have few new insights and very little learning will take place. One cannot reflect in a vacuum. At the same time, the atmosphere and organization of the classroom will be such that students will feel genuinely free to disagree, propose alternatives, make modifications, and so on. They will be stimulated by the classroom "teaching" and will make progress toward sounder value positions but they will be doing so with as much freedom as it is possible for humans to attain.

It must be stressed that the progress toward sounder value positions that is envisaged here is *not* necessarily movement toward a consensus. Indeed, there may be even greater diversity of value positions in a class at the end of a successful discussion than at the beginning. The concern is merely that each student should have a more adequate, better informed, sounder set of value ideas at the end than he had at the beginning, not that all students should have the same value ideas. It may be entirely appropriate that students differ on a particular point, either because they are at different stages in their thinking on the issue or because their circumstances differ in such a way that different value outlooks are required. Of course, there are limits to the extent to which people can differ in their value outlooks and still live together satisfactorily in the same society; but the precise nature of these limits is itself a subject of inquiry and each suggested limit must be assessed on its merits.

If students are to progress in the content of their valuing, as we have proposed, a very wide range of value topics must be studied during their school years. Skills approaches and stage approaches in value education have tended to leave the impression that if one concentrates on certain key matters in values— *how* to solve value problems, or *forms* or *principles* of moral thought—the child will progress to higher levels of value functioning. This, however, imvolves presuppositions about the transfer of learning that the facts of common experience would seem to contradict. While it is true that a particular insight may for a particular person open up a whole vista of new wisdom, the same insight may not have the same effect on another person. Transfer of learning, it would seem, is a very individual matter, and there is no alternative in value education to the careful study of a great many different topics and sub-topics. Once again, one cannot teach form or process alone and neglect content.

We have proposed that the teacher should deal with value topics—content—explicitly and should feel free to express his or her views on these topics and present arguments for them. It is commonly assumed that such an approach will introduce a higher risk of indoctrination than currently exists in the classroom. We would like to suggest, on the contrary, that the risk of indoctrination will be lower. On the one hand, if all teachers adopt this approach, students will be impressed with the diversity of viewpoints on various value topics throughout the school and will learn to pick and choose among them. On the other hand, a student is at present subject to a very strong process of implicit indoctrination through the "hidden curriculum" of the school: be neat, be tidy, be clean, be punctual, be obedient, be quiet, the study of classical literature is invaluable, knowledge of history is an end in itself, a high school diploma is priceless, and so on. He is quite vulnerable to this indoctrination because it is largely subliminal, reasons are rarely given and the values are never openly questioned. An explicit program of value education, then, conducted in the manner proposed, would be less indoctrinative than present programs since students would have a genuine opportunity to assess the values of their teachers, by virtue of both the training they would receive and the open and systematic nature of the assessment process.

3. The Role of Tradition, Authority, Family and Religion in Value Education

Why should the school get into the act of value education at all? Our studies have shown that the field of values is so vast that the task of value education cannot possibly be left to one or two societal agencies, such as the home and the church. All societal institutions that can assist, including the school, must do so. Learning not to break one's promises (or *when* not to break one's promises), for example, is not simply a matter of learning that "it is wrong to break one's promises." The institution of promise keeping alone is so extensive in its ramifications and so complex in its justification that the school must help in teaching children about it. The family and church remain very important, but they are not sufficient by themselves. This fact is becoming more and more widely accepted. In contacts with parents in the course of our studies we have rarely if at all encountered the view that the school should not engage in value education. The main concern of parents is that the process be an appropriate one, so that their children arrive at an *adequate* value system, which may, they acknowledge, be different in certain respects from their own. Parents often have less fixed ideas than teachers about what values their children should have, since teachers can easily become preoccupied with the values required for classroom management. The parent, having the child's interests very personally at heart, is mainly concerned that the child should go out into the world with *some* adequate value system with which to confront his problems.

Given this concern, a parent may wonder whether our proposed reflective approach to value education is satisfactory. Is it being suggested that the child should start "from scratch," disregarding all that he has previously been told about values? Is it assumed that adults have nothing to contribute to the value outlook of a child? What is the place of tradition and authority in the proposed approach to value education? These are legitimate queries and some assurances must be provided.

To begin with, it should be noted that the reflection that gives rise to sound values need not be carried on in a highly skeptical, critical spirit. One can be thoughtful about values without adopting a negative stance toward existing values. One may reflect on the value of promise keeping, for example, without being predisposed to reject promise keeping as a principle of living. The result of reflection on commonly accepted values will in many cases—perhaps the great majority of cases—be simply that one will refine the values in certain ways, come to understand their point more fully, learn how to implement them more effectively, and be more solidly committed to them than one was before.

Further, reflection on values may take place with full respect being given to the weight of tradition and authority relevant to the values in question. For example, the values proposed by a particular religion may be taken very seriously. A value that has stood the test of time or that is strongly advocated by a reliable authority is for that reason to be given careful attention. Tradition and authority provide much of the essential raw material for the development of values. Traditions and authorities must be assessed in terms of the likelihood that the values they support are sound. But very often one will not be in a position to develop a value for oneself and will have to accept it from a tradition or an authority that one has good reason to believe can be relied upon with respect to the value issue in question.

Again, while one reflects on values as an individual, one very often does so in a context of dialogue and social participation in which it may be very difficult to distinguish one's own judgment from that of others. A whole group or set of interconnected groups engage in joint inquiry into values and we are inevitably influenced by the values of our community even when we have been unable to make an independent assessment of these values.

Yet again, reflection on values does not exclude the influence of feelings, intuition and conscience in guiding us toward sound values. In many cases we are aware that we do not have the time or the capacity to question the directions suggested by semi-automatic mechanisms of these kinds. We may plan at some future date to assess our intuitions or educate our conscience, but we recognize that we cannot do better than rely on them at this moment on this particular issue. Reflection is still operative here, but it moves to the higher (or lower) level of acknowledging that an assessment "from scratch" is not appropriate under the circumstances.

Finally, reflection on values involves drawing on information and ideas supplied by adults, including parents. Children have a great deal to learn from their parents, and a major task in value education is to help students overcome prejudice against parental advice and example, prejudice which is largely a function of peer indoctrination and over-reaction to parental authoritarianism. Children have a tendency to throw out the parent with the bathwater, so to speak, and while this is understandable at a certain level, it can be highly dysfunctional. A truly reflective child, in value matters, will not for long adopt such an arbitrary and negative stance with respect to parents.

4. The Relation Between Values and Religion

In the previous section some comments were made concerning the role of religious institutions and religious traditions in value education. It was suggested that value education through formal religious teaching must be supplemented in a major way by value education through the school (and other societal institutions, such as the family). Some people may feel that the proposed liaison between religious institutions and educational institutions has been accepted too easily, and that a fuller treatment of the issue is required. Accordingly, some additional remarks will now be made, although they must be limited in scope for reasons of space and because our Project has not been centrally concerned with the relation between moral education and religious education. We have, however, had a considerable opportunity to note the issues that arise when value education programs are proposed for religious schools or for "secular" schools in semi-religious communities.

By way of illustration, let us look at the question in terms of a theistic religious position, namely, Christianity. It might be argued that the "ultimate life goals" mentioned earlier are not ultimate enough: that such life goals require in turn a further justification of a religious nature. It has bqen said that the principles of Christian ethics are to be followed not because they are self-justifying but because they are found in God's revealed Word or, more simply, because God wills that we follow them. This, it is said, is the ultimate justification for being moral. Now there is perhaps some truth in this view for some people, for it would seem that a sense of meaning in life is a fundamental human value, an ultimate life goal, and if one's sense of meaning in life is bound up with a Christian perspective, reference to the will of God may have some place at the ultimate level. But it can only have a limited place at the ultimate level. For the question any reflective, mature Christian must be able to answer is: "*Why* does God want me to follow the principles of Christian ethics?" And the same is true of any other religion.

The inadequacy of a purely authoritarian, unreflective approach to Christian ethics is brought out by the question: Is an action good because God wills it or does God will it because it is good? The latter alternative is rather obviously the correct one. And if God wills good actions because they are good, we can presumably find out the criteria of good actions and hence be in a position to arrive at value conclusions by a non-authoritarian, reflective process. Further, we—and our students—*must* find out the criteria of good actions; for unless a person understands at least in part why a principle of action is sound he will not be able to follow it satisfactorily. To some extent the argument over inculcation *versus* education in values is a non-argument, for values cannot be inculcated. Unless a person is allowed to explore and reflect upon the nature and purpose of a value principle, he will not know when the principle applies, when to make an exception, when to modify the principle, and so on. He will simply not have the principle. Thus, even within a religious context, attempts at the unreflective inculcation of values are self-defeating.

How, then, does the reflective, "ultimate life goals" approach to values and value education relate to a religion such as Christianity? In the first place, Christianity, along with all other major religions, endorses ultimate life goals of the kind listed earlier. God is represented as wanting people, by and large, to survive, be happy, be fulfilled, have friendships, and so on. Accordingly, general theory of reflective valuing can be applied and developed in a religious context.

Second, because of this common ground between religious and "non-religious" approaches to life, people of religious and "non-religious" persuasions can help each other in value matters. (We put the term "non-religious" in quotation marks because it is not clear what it would mean to be non-religious; but that raises issues too large to be discussed here.) Despite metaphysical differences, then, a "non-religious" teacher can help a religious child to a considerable extent in value matters, whether in a counselling situation or in general value inquiry; and equally a religious teacher can help a "non-religious" child.

Third, while not everyone may need religion (in a traditional sense of the term), it is very likely that many do, in order to have optimally sound values. One does not have values in a cultural and metaphysical vacuum; and a person's most satisfactory cultural and metaphysical context may include a traditional religion, depending upon his background, upbringing, temperament and general outlook. The main issue is whether religion is functional in a person's life, and one cannot prejudge this question for a particular individual.

This reasoning would suggest, then—and our experience confirms it—that religious education deriving from a traditional religious institution and value education in the school can play complementary roles in the total value education of students. There is sufficient common ground to permit many insights to be transferred from one body of thought to another and to enable people of religious and non-religious persuasions to help each other.

5. The Need for Growth in the Capacity to Reflect on Values

If in discussing value education one stresses the need for increased reflection on values, one is implicitly claiming that people at present do not reflect sufficiently on values. This, of course, is our position, and it is supported not only by observation of how school students (and teachers) handle particular value issues, but also by normative data (for Ontario) on the Kohlberg stages of children and adults at different ages. In 1974-75 the main addition to our cumulative Kohlberg data has been at the 12-17 year-old and 21+ age levels. The data show that by age 12 there is already a clear preponderance of conventional over preconventional moral thinking and that this is steadily increased until by the early and mid-twenties nearly all moral thinking falls into one or other of the Kohlberg "conventional" categories. Beyond age 25 it would appear that a significant proportion of post-conventional thinking (still only Stage 5) begins to develop, but conventional thinking continues to predominate to a very large degree.

There is a difficulty here in interpreting the results of Kohlberg testing. A

student may be at a relatively low stage on the Kohlberg scale and yet be fairly
reflective in value matters in many of the more important areas of his life.
Accordingly, we must not assume that simply because a person is at one of the
pre-conventional or conventional stages (Stages 1 and 2 or 3 and 4), he does not
reflect on values in many of the ways discussed in section 1, above, and does not
have a rather satisfactory set of values and valuing practices. However, the
Kohlberg data do suggest that the *degree* of reflection and the *extent* to which
people press value questions back to ultimate life goals is less in childhood and
youth than one might consider desirable.

These results, particularly at the high school and 25+ levels are surprising
to many people. It is often assumed that our youth today are rather progressive
and indeed *un*conventional in value matters whereas adults from their mid-
twenties onward sink into a defensive moral conservatism. It would appear,
however, that while teenagers may be pressing toward new frontiers in some very
specific areas such as drug use, mode of dress, and pre-marital sexual relations,
on the average their approach to values is more conventional and less reflective
than that of adults.

It is important not to make too quick and uncritical a transition from the
fact that students are relatively unreflective in value matters to the conclusion
that they must be pushed as fast as possible to a much more reflective approach
to values. Certain kinds of reflection and certain kinds of values are not at
present considered to be acceptable for young people in our society. Students
need to be aware of this fact and take it into account as they reflect on their
values. Students should be exposed to values and helped to pick and choose
wisely and create their own; but they should not be pushed into an approach to
values and a particular set of values, in the name of reflection, that will in fact be
dysfunctional in their lives. One characteristic of a person who is reflective in
values is that he is very aware of and realistic about what values are functional
for given persons (including himself) in a given societal context at a given point
in time. Teachers of values must be realistic in this regard also and avoid unre-
flectively imposing a degree of reflection that in certain problem areas may for
the moment be inappropriate. The fact remains, however, that on the whole
there is a need for students to grow considerably in their capacity to reflect on
values.

6. The "School Program" Model of Value Education

It had been maintained in Beck's *Moral Education in the Schools* (pp. 8-9) that
"with a greater degree of guidance and coordination, more adequate study of
values could begin immediately within the present curriculum structure." It had
been proposed that "the allocation of topics to departments and age levels, the
involvement of particular teachers, and the detailed assessment of the program
could be taken care of by a committee set upon within each school." The
rationale for this interdepartmental, interdisciplinary proposal was "not so much

that value questions should be assigned to their *proper* subject area (where subject areas exist), but rather that they should be assigned to *some* subject area (or teacher, or department) in order to ensure a relatively comprehensive coverage" and at the same time avoid excessive overlap.

Our findings with respect to this approach to value education may be stated rather simply: the great majority of schools are still too compartmentalized to allow the degree of interdepartmental or interteacher cooperation that we envisaged. At the high school level departmental and subject divisions are still deeply entrenched and the reward structure of the school tends to encourage the continuation of this state of affairs. At the elementary school level, insofar as some rotary system has been adopted the problems are similar to those of the high school; and insofar as the "home room teacher" concept has been maintained, there is a compartmentalization between grade levels if not between subject areas (although even the latter may exist *in the teacher's mind*).

We still consider the school program approach (or some variant of it) to be the ideal, but must report that at present one should not pin one's hopes on achieving it. And it is important for people engaged in value education to realize this. For if we tie proposals for improved value education in the school to notions of interdisciplinary, inter-teacher cooperation, we may well fail in the former objective because of current difficulties in attaining the latter. We should be concerned about both problems, but to some extent tackle each separately.

Failing the attainment of a well integrated school program in values, however, the principal and certain other members of a school can be on the lookout for more obvious overlaps and gaps in the school values curriculum. Even within present school organization a few elements of the school program model could be introduced, provided that there was a minimal degree of reporting by teachers concerning the topics dealt with in their classes.

7. The "Organic Fusion" Model of Value Education

Another major focus of our research in 1974-75 was the possibility that "the study of values could be carried on 'organically fused' with the current activities of existing school departments" (see *Moral Education in the Schools*, p.8). The advantages seen in this approach were, first, that it would help increase the interest, relevance and indeed the quality of the study of various school subjects; second, that it would attach certain useful constraints to the study of values; and third, that one would avoid having to introduce "yet another subject" into the school and hence would overcome certain political obstacles both inside and outside the school. (It should be noted that the integrated approach is *not* seen as incompatible with the incidental teaching of values: indeed, our experience has been that the somewhat more systematic treatment of values represented by the integrated approach stimulates incidental discussion.)

We are able to report that there is strong support for the organic fusion approach, or, as we prefer to call it, the "integrated approach," to the teaching of values in schools; but that in practice the incidence of such integrated teaching is not very great. Teachers on the whole consider it to be a good idea, but lack the motivation, curriculum materials, and teaching skills to implement it very widely.

With respect to motivation, the problem is the same as with the school program approach: the reward structure of the school system at present is not such as to encourage teachers "taking time out" (as it is viewed) to deal with value topics. The teacher who is applauded and promoted for being a "good teacher" is still, by and large, the one who doggedly sticks to a traditional school subject and teaches it "well" (that is, with the minimum of "frills," such as discussions of the value issues inherent in the subject). There are notable exceptions to this scenario, and we tend to hear about the exceptions, but the hard facts in the great majority of cases are as we have stated them.

With respect to curriculum materials, our experience is that even the keenest and best informed teachers normally require concrete, highly usable learning materials, initially at least, if they are to engage in more than a minimal amount of integrated value education. Teachers are extremely busy and hence most of them do not have a mind-set to enter a new area of teaching without the support that learning materials can give. Our perception is that there is an urgent need for study materials in the area of values at the present time if sound value education is to become a major component of the school curriculum. Teachers will quickly add to and even abandon these materials as they gain more experience, but most of them will simply not gain the experience if they do not have something suitable to use in the early stages.

8. Teacher Education for Value Education

The third obstacle to value education mentioned in the previous section is lack of teaching skills. This brings us into the whole area of teacher education. The amount of in-service training of teachers for value education that can be carried out through the formal professional development programs of school boards is very limited. The number of days available is small relative to the huge task of both helping teachers become more reflective about their own values and helping them develop teaching skills that will give them the confidence and the ability to take up value issues seriously in the classroom.

One possibility we consider worthy of close attention is that of teacher education "on the job" through the use of study materials that are "teacher educative." We feel that it is possible to develop study materials that will stimulate the teacher who uses them to become reflective about his own values and adopt suitable general strategies in his value education activities. The term "teacher educative" is used advisedly here instead of the term "teacher proof" that might also spring to mind. For we feel that the freedom to adopt or not adopt certain outlooks and strategies would still lie with the teacher; the point is simply that he would have certain new choices opened up to him through the ideas implicit or explicit in the study materials.

Another area of teacher education that has not been adequately explored is that of general education of a society as a whole. Discussions of a kind that might enable a school teacher to do a better job of value education could be carried on in society at large, on television, in newspapers, in paperbacks, in handbooks for parents, in community action groups. We often overlook the fact, for example, that a large proportion of teachers are also parents, and could learn things as parents that would be invaluable to them as teachers. Working through society as a whole also appears an attractive possibility when one recognizes that without general changes in a society's value outlooks, it will be very difficult to achieve value development through that society's schools.

9. Alternative Approaches and Teaching Strategies in Value Education

We have looked at the relative effectiveness and acceptability of various teaching strategies: the theoretical discussion method, the values clarification method, the role-playing method, and so on. Our general conclusion is that (a) different teachers require different approaches and methods, (b) different students require different approaches and methods, and (c) all of the specific approaches current-ly being proposed by educators—McPhail, Wilson, Simon, Kohlberg, the OISE Project—are helpful, so long as no one of them is seen as providing the whole answer, and so long as one's general approach to values and value education is sound. The general approach that we feel must be followed, whatever specific techniques are being used, is the *reflective approach.* And we feel that this approach is compatible with the general message that comes through loud and clear from the modern movement in moral/values education: the students should not have values imposed on them, but rather should (a) be introduced to certain general procedures for arriving at values and (b) be exposed to various ideas and arguments in the area of values as a stimulus to thought. It seems to us that the reflective approach described earlier can be used to implement this basic mes-sage, and within the reflection procedure a synthesis of the various contempo-rary schools of thought on value education can be achieved. In order to illustrate this point, we will look in turn at each of the schools of thought mentioned.

Peter McPhail has argued convincingly that school students need a context in which they may simulate real life situations without many of the insecurities and immediate pressures of real life, a context in which they may engage in social experimentation leading to the discovery of more satisfactory human relationships.[1] He accepts that students pursue fundamental human values such as happiness, fellowship, and fulfillment, but that in everyday life they do not have sufficient opportunities to try out new ways of achieving these values. He claims that the basic motivation is there, but the means chosen are defective.

[1] See "The Motivation of Moral Behaviour," *Moral Education* 2, 2 (1970):99-106; and "To Play Roles or Do Your Thing?" *The History and Social Science Teacher* (Fall, 1975).

Clearly, this position can be related to the theory of value reflection proposed earlier. Through discussions and personal involvement techniques students are helped to being their specific modes of social coping—their means-values—into line with their fundamental human values or ultimate life goals—their end-values.

John Wilson has shown that being moral involves a much more complex set of attitudes, knowledges, skills and tendencies than we have commonly supposed.[2] It is not sufficient for a child to "know" that it is right to be considerate to others. He must have a basic concern for others, he must understand what "others" are like, he must be able to see things from the point of view of others, he must know how to help others, he must have the necessary social skills to help others, and so on. Thus, in accordance with the theory of reflection outlined earlier, a child must acquire relevant knowledge of "the facts of the case," he must recognize within himself a fundamental concern for others along with other basic values, and he must develop specific and intermediate values that enable him to achieve his fundamental values, within the context of the facts of the case. Of course, Wilson goes beyond the theory of reflection into additional aspects of moral motivation, but the approach to moral education inherent in his theory of moral components may be integrated with the theory of reflection.

Sidney Simon, the chief exponent of the values clarification approach, has stressed the importance of being aware of all of one's values—specific, intermediate and ultimate—and being conscious of the consequences of committing oneself to these values.[3] Simon has sometimes been criticized for suggesting that what a child's values are does not matter, so long as he is aware of them and committed to them. However, statements by members of the values clarification school in recent years have suggested that there is a concern for the modification of values as a result of reflection; and whatever the emphasis within the approach may be, the various techniques for facing up to one's values, becoming clear about them, and becoming aware of their consequences can certainly be utilized in a total process of reflective reconstruction of one's values such as was discussed in Section 1.

Lawrence Kohlberg's proposal for arriving at sound values[4] is tied to a theory of moral development which sets what some would see as rather pessimistic limits on the moral insights one can attain in a given problem area at a given stage. However, the general form of the reflective process is much the same as the one I have proposed: values are not imposed, but rather students are exposed to relevant facts, arguments and value ideas and engage in an active process of achieving equilibrium between the various elements of their value outlook. Thus, even if one were to disagree with Kohlberg's empirical psychological claims

---

[2] See especially the "Full List of Moral Components" in *A Teacher's Guide to Moral Education* (London & Dublin: Chapman, 1973), pp. 136-137.

[3] Sidney Simon, *et al.*, *Values Clarification* (New York: Hart, 1972).

[4] See, for example, his "Stages of Moral Development as a Basis for Moral Education" in Beck, Crittenden and Sullivan (eds.) *Moral Education: Interdisciplinary Approaches* (New York: Newman Press, 1972).

about the patterns of moral thought at different ages and stages, one could heartily endorse his non-authoritarian, interactive, reflective approach to arriving at values.

The OISE Project has tended to stress discussion techniques in which attention moves constantly back and forth between value principles and specific examples. It has been felt that while the detailed study of a particular case study or moral dilemma is useful from time to time, it is necessary to review a great many examples, most of them rather close to home, in the course of reflecting on a value concept or principle. Further, it has been felt that while simulation activities and values clarification techniques are undoubtedly useful, progress toward the development of a sound value outlook will be very slow unless individual insights are drawn together in a somewhat explicit manner. Nevertheless, the OISE Project is very concerned to stress (a) that there are many very useful techniques and approaches in value education in addition to the principled discussion approach, and (b) that there is more to value education than arriving at a sound value outlook: one must also learn how to apply one's value outlook in practice (which will in turn lead to a further refinement of one's value outlook). Thus, while the OISE Project also has concentrated on certain aspects of the total reflective process more than others, its position can be integrated into that process as it has been described above.

It would seem, then, that despite differences of emphasis and differences in technique, some agreement is emerging with respect to the value inquiry aspect of value education. It must be an open, reflective, non-indoctrinative process, with exposure to relevant information and various arguments and points of view. The precise list of ultimate life goals provided in Section 1 may not be accepted by all, but the notion that students should be trying to arrive at sound values—specific, intermediate and ultimate—by an open, informed, reflective process is gaining very wide acceptance.

10. Conclusion: Some Problems of Implementation

We continue, then, to advocate the ultimate life goals approach to the inquiry aspect of value education, with some refinement of the reflection process this involves; and we see the school program model and the integrated approach to value education as ideals to be pursued. However, we have found that there are some very real problems of implementation in schools and school systems as they exist at present. As with any practical venture, a number of conditions must be met simultaneously if one is to achieve the ends in view. In particular, in the case of value education, more provision must be made for teacher education; adequate learning materials must be developed; and a reward structure must be established at all levels and by all relevant agencies so that teachers have the processional motivation to engage in value education. At present, value education is still not a sufficiently "respectable" aspect of the teacher's task, from a professional point of view, to attract the serious attention of a large proportion of talented teachers.

PART THREE

THE LEARNING AND HELPING FACILITATOR

HOW TO BE CONSIDERATE WHILE TEACHING CRITICALLY

Robert E. Alexander
Department of Philosophy
Wilfrid Laurier University

It is a truism that the unexamined life is not worth living. Although perhaps less of a truism, it is equally true that the examined life is neither tranquil nor painless. As rational animals we care about holding only those beliefs we think are true. As emotional animals, on the other hand, we cherish our beliefs simply because they are ours. Since our beliefs are not always able to withstand criticism, the feelings associated with those beliefs often end up getting bruised. And when that happens, we have a problem. My essay is a partial response to this.

The critical spirit will be taken as part of a moral problem, and the method for finding a solution, rather than simply as an ideal to be admired. I will try to show how one who wants to be critical can also be considerate towards the feelings of those affected by the criticism. Since this problem typically arises in an educational setting, I will concern myself specifically with *how to be considerate while teaching critically.*

Two qualifications will help to forestall some misleading impressions. First, although the problem will be discussed in terms of the student's feelings being affected by the impact of a critical teacher, this is not the only problematic situation. The same kind of situation occurs when the critical student affects the teacher's feelings adversely, and whenever one's own feelings are affected by self-criticism. Although most of the points made are intended for general application, the explicit discussion will be limited to this one context.

Many of my teachers, classmates, colleagues, students, friends, and family have lived through the tension between caring and criticism, and have played a role in generating these thoughts. However, what follows is not intended as an indirect way of praising or blaming myself or others. It is offered instead as an essay in practical philosophy, as an attempt to articulate the interaction between these two ideals in a concrete setting.

To sharpen the focus, consider the teacher's task. He is not only supposed to help his students learn their material; he is also expected to help them learn how to do something with it, to be able to handle it in various ways. Our interest is in handling material by being critical about it. As long as one of the teacher's purposes is to produce students more critical of statements than they were before, it does not matter what they happen to be about. Whether they are theories, principles, or particular facts, it is essential only that they be capable of being true or false. It is also not very important what level of critical ability is to be achieved or how much of one's teaching effort is taken up with this task. Even if teachers focus their efforts on criticism only part of the time or in small areas of their subject matter, the effects of critical teaching will still be relevant to some extent. Consequently, these remarks should be of interest to parents and primary school teachers, and not only to the obvious case of university professors who teach courses entitled "Critical Thinking."

To be an effective teacher of anything, one must take into account various feelings of the person being taught. For example, noticing that a student is very nervous in front of groups may be important when deciding what form of instruction is most likely to facilitate the student's learning. But no teaching activitity is to be judged only by its success at accomplishing a learning task, even if it is learning to be critical. A person's feelings are an intimate part of what constitutes a person. Consequently, they become an important object of our considerateness for their own sake, and not only for the sake of efficiency. Our concern will be with feelings that are likely to occur as a result of teaching someone in a critical manner, especially feelings that have the character of a "put down."

Assuming that being understanding towards feelings and being critical about truth-claims are equally significant educational goals, an issue that becomes important is whether they can be jointly satisfied. My primary aim is to show how one can be considerate towards feelings without giving up on being critical, even though the two are partially in conflict. Showing in detail that both ideals can be met denies that only two choices are available, each of them unhappy ones. The critically considerate teacher can avoid the pitfalls of two other kinds of teachers: those who think emotions must be ignored to take critical ideals seriously; and those who think criticism must be eschewed to be truly sympathetic to feelings. In the next two sections, these two central concepts will be clarified ehough to give some guidance to their integration and application in the practical educational context in section three.

I

What is critical thinking? Broadly speaking, it is an extension of being rational about beliefs; so, part of what it means to think critically is to have the skills necessary for participating in a rational discussion. As I intend to use the term, a *rational discussion* is a scrutinizing and assessment of the acceptability of claims in terms that appropriately reflect the reasons that bear on them. The acceptability at issue, of course, is that connected with truth, namely cognitive or theoretical justifiability. Acceptability with respect to one's personal needs, the latest school of thought, or the national interest is typically irrelevant. The reasons that bear on logical or mathematical claims will usually be proofs or disproofs, while those that bear on factual or scientific claims will usually be observations. Value and normative claims have their reasons, too, which are more closely tied to human feelings and interests.

Although the point of participating in a rational discussion with oneself or others is to learn *that* a statement is acceptable or not in terms of relevant reasons, this necessarily means that one has learned *how* to obtain such a result. Propositional knowledge depends on procedural knowledge.[1] The required critical skills for rational discussion can be divided roughly into those relating to meaning and those relating to reasons and argument. The former includes: being able to determine or unpack the meanings and senses of words and statements in their context; noticing and avoiding cliches and slogans, as well as emotive, vague, and metaphorical terms; and recognizing different kinds of claims, such as necessary, contingent, and normative-evaluative. The other category includes the abilities to notice and avoid: irrelevant considerations or conclusions; inappropriate weighing of reasons; and expressing claims which are improperly qualified with respect to their support.

The latter sort of skills are valued seriously enough to have the status of intellectual virtues. There is objectivity or impartiality with respect to reasons and their weight, and honesty about how a claim's acceptability stands at the moment. There is also principled open-mindedness, that is, the commitment to follow where the best reasons lead, the converse of which is the capacity to disengage oneself from beliefs or assessments when they are seen to be rationally inadequate. Thus, the ability to engage in rational discussion is hardly dispassionate; in spite of being detached from anything without the strongest rational support, there is strong attachment to whatever has the best reasons.

But these abilities are not sufficient; one could learn how to engage in such discussions with hardly any tendency or readiness to do so. To capture the notion of being critical as a character trait we must interpret them as propensities.[2] The student is supposed to learn *to* be critical when appropriate, not only learn *how* to be critical without ever doing so. Being open-minded, for example, should not be an occasional thing, but a stable attitude towards beliefs.

This may be misleading. One may be left with the impression that being open-minded (understood as a tendency to re-examine claims) implies that one can hold no firm beliefs. This would appear to be a bad result, since it makes a virtue of hesitation and indecisiveness about everything other than being critical itself. To show this is not a necessary implication, we must try, as so often happens, to achieve a delicate balance.

Being open-minded does rule out the unquestioning certainty of dogmatism, but still allows firm convictions. Although we want to avoid closed minds on open issues, we also want to allow for the fact that some issues are closed in the sense that they are taken to be obviously settled one way or the other. Of course we may be mistaken. The possibility of premature closure of a claim's acceptability is enough to require open-mindedness, but not enough to

---

[1]Israel Scheffler, *Conditions of Knowledge: An Introduction to Epistemology and Education* (Glenview, Ill.: Scott, Foresman & Co., 1965), pp. 66-74.

[2]John Passmore, "On Teaching to be Critical," in R. S. Peters (ed.), *The Concept of Education* (London: Routledge & Kegan Paul, 1967), pp. 195-96.

require uncertainty. To be uncertain depends upon more than the mere possibility of being mistaken; what is needed to suspend belief is a special reason that one is likely to be wrong. Being open-minded is not incompatible with having convictions, but only with having convictions one would never rationally discuss.

One more element is necessary for a critical spirit, namely, to be *actively searching* for those reasons necessary to reopen closed issues, as well as those that will close open ones. A person could be open-minded in a passive way, quite content to let others initiate the occasions for rational discussion. But this is part of what it means to be uncritical. It may or may not be very rational to be passive, so on this point criticality diverges a bit from rationality. This tendency of critical thinking to take the initiative is simply the tendency to be creative or imaginative.[3] Although it does not take much imagination to criticize deviation from the accepted beliefs or methods of a given discipline, finding ways of replacing them with better ones usually does. This extra push, the persistence and creativity involved in trying for improvement, is what turns rational thinking into critical thinking, and makes the critical thinker indispensable for moral and intellectual progress.

There may be many ways or methods of instruction that will result in a student becoming critical. After all, this is a factual issue, albeit one which is immensely complicated. The standard assumption, nevertheless, seems to be that one will become critical only and most efficiently by being taught in a critical manner. Critical teaching is a very broad notion; indeed, its comprehensiveness may account for its tacit acceptance as the way to teach being critical. It is narrow enough, however, to exclude some ways of treating the subject matter and the student's verbal or written work.

In other words, one usually assumes that critical teaching includes the example of the teacher, along with his explicit descriptions or explanations of how this manner is a critical one. He should also encourage the student to practice the skills and virtues associated with being critical, thereby eventually embodying them as an active participant, rather than remaining as a spectator. Typically, then, the teacher will engage the student in rational discussion of a claim by asking him such questions as what does it mean, how can it helpfully be restated, what sort of claim it is intended to be, what would count against it, whether a given reason counts against its truth decisively or only in the absence of overriding reasons, and how acceptable it is in light of the reasons considered so far.

Although this is typical, critical teaching does not logically require a method of asking and answering questions by either student or instructor. One

---

[3]"I have introduced the phrase 'critico-creative' thinking, not through any fondness for it, but because 'critical thinking' may suggest nothing more than the capacity to think up objections. . . . The educator is interested in encouraging critical discussion, as distinct from the mere raising of objections; and discussion is an exercise of the imagination." Ibid., p. 201.

could embody the same critical points in declarative sentences. What is necessary is that the pupil's rationality be acknowledged by the manner of teaching, that the pupil be treated as rational. This means that reasons and justifications be given and questions entertained, at least about the subject matter, by either student or teacher.[4] If one is simply teaching, it may be sufficiently acknowledged if assessments and criticisms are offered only on appropriate occasions. I believe, however, that critical teaching makes such acknowledgement continually appropriate, and therefore, requires a stronger or deeper acknowledgement than teaching simpliciter.

II

To *consider* a person's feelings is to take them into account for some purpose or other. For example, they may be used as a basis for predicting what the person might do or for deciding what she needs. It all depends on the purpose we have. To *be considerate towards* a person's feelings, on the other hand, is to act towards them in a particular way. Part of this includes trying to minimize her emotional or psychological suffering. So the purpose is always partly benevolent when being considerate. For instance, even if a doctor has avoided as much physical pain as possible during and after surgery by skillful use of equipment and anesthetic, there is still room for her to be inconsiderate. She could do this by not telling her patient what the unavoidable discomfort will be like, or why it cannot be avoided, or by being unsympathetic about how much it will hurt.[5]

The same thing can happen when the obvious discomfort arising from a situation is emotional and has been reduced to a minimum. There may still be feelings about the discomfort which are being given inconsiderate treatment. It is just as important to be considerate in these circumstances, but it may be harder to do so. The reason for this is that people vary more in their responses to competition, to realizing they are mistaken, to being unable to finish what they start, etc., than they do in response to physical pain. In this context it is not as easy to tell when another is hurting, or how best to be considerate. And since we

[4] Jane R. Martin, *Explaining, Understanding and Teaching* (New York: McGraw-Hill, 1970), pp. 97-8, 105.

[5] When a person happens to be a woman, her feelings have not always been treated considerately, especially her feelings about being equal with men as persons. Our speech has too often used 'he' or 'him' (rather than 'she' or 'her') when the sense of the statement merely means 'one' or 'a person.' In light of this, an earlier draft using only 'she' and 'her' was a way of flagging this systematic (although probably unintended) sexist bias and of righting the balance somewhat. However, it was linguistically jarring enough for some readers (of both sexes) to distract them from the main content of the essay; so it has been reduced to this paragraph and footnote. What is needed (but apparently unavailable) is a singular and neuter set of words which, like the plural 'they' and 'their,' are more personal than 'one.' If generally accepted, it would be an important contribution to being considerate towards feelings while writing, speaking, or teaching critically.

can also have feelings about feelings, the situation is theoretically, as well as practically, very complex.

What should be done in the face of unavoidable emotional or physical distress? One way to cut through the complexities is to take the view that there is nothing more to be done. Precisely to the extent that the distress is at a minimum and what remains is justified in light of all the relevant factors, nothing more should be done. I believe this is a theoretically sound position. Its only weakness arises in practical ways. Without distinguishing between the unavoidable *primary* distress and the feelings about that distress, one may fail to minimize the creation of *secondary* hurtful feelings. Pointing out someone's mistake, for instance, may produce some mild yet unavoidable discomfort. So far this may not be inconsiderate, but it would be if doing so in a brusque or condescending manner added unnecessary distress in the form of feelings of inadequacy or embarrassment.

More significantly, such a distinction may prevent the likelihood of ignoring the primary painful feeling itself. Moderately intense physical pains are unlikely to slip beneath the threshold of awareness when they are ignored. Apart from the interference of drugs or hypnosis, such pains have a way of flooding one's consciousness.' This is no doubt true of intense emotional states, too, except for one fact. They can be hidden more or less successfully from others (or even oneself) if the person involved takes such feelings as wrong, abnormal, childish, despicable, unforgivable, etc. These responses to a feeling of anger, for example, might lead one to misdescribe it as tiredness or depression, or to miss the feeling entirely. In other words, not only is being angry to some extent unpleasant, but the mere fact that one has this particular feeling is the cause of extra distress when seen in light of the view that such feelings are wrong or childish. To the extent that denying the existence of feelings has bad consequences for one's emotional life, paying attention to them has long term benefits that probably outweigh the cost of feeling the primary distress now.

Being considerate towards a person's feelings is primarily a matter of caring, sympathy, or benevolence. The more distressing the feelings are, the stronger the duty becomes. Being considerate has another dimension, as well; it is also a matter of rights. If being a person signifies a special status or dignity, as most of us assume that it does, then we humans deserve special treatment or respect as persons. To move from benevolence to rights is to take considerateness as something we are owed, not simply a gift to be grateful for.

What is it to be a person? The central idea is being an agent with an articulable point of view.[6] A perspective or point of view includes both beliefs and attitudes, feelings being part of the latter category. Feelings about which one can become self-conscious (like hopes and fears, or joys and pains) not only distinguish persons from non-persons; the particular feelings one has differenti-

---

[6]P. H. Hirst and R. S. Peters, *The Logic of Education* (London: Routledge & Kegan Paul, 1970), pp. 91-2.

ate one person from another as a unique individual. Because feelings are an important ingredient in being a person, treating persons considerately with regard to their feelings is one way of treating them with the respect they deserve. Being callous, condescending, or indifferent towards feelings, when wrong at all, then, is an infringement of the person's rights, and not only a failure of kindness.

To digress for a moment, I believe there is also a connection between critical teaching and the right to be treated as a person. Another crucial ingredient in the notion of a person is the capacity to make rational choices in belief and action.[7] To the extent that critical teaching requires a serious acknowledgement of the pupil's rationality, it is automatically a way of respecting his dignity as a person.[8] Although, of course, there are other forms of instruction that acknowledge rationality, or at least do not disrespect it, such respect would be ruled out by some versions of conditioning and indoctrination in spite of their apparent efficiency.[9]

If being considerate means caring, how should this be shown? What sort of actions will be appropriate if one cares about another's feelings? There is no easy answer in light of the complexity and variability of circumstances and feelings, apart from the unhelpful advice to do the caring thing. Nevertheless, the following principles are concrete enough to avoid being trivial, although they remain quite general.

To be considerate, one should express concern or sympathy for the distressing feelings, even when the primary distress itself is unavoidable. The key word here is "express." Sometimes this can be accomplished merely by mentioning to the person that he seems upset, while in other situations some extra gesture of sympathy for what the person is going through may be necessary. This need not, of course, be linguistic expression; some actions speak louder than words.

It might be thought that this principle should always apply, but that is not the case, at least not with regard to relatively short encounters. It is only a *prima facie* principle of considerateness. There are situations where even expressing sympathy, much less solving the problems that resulted in the need for sympathy, would be out of place. Whenever a person's goal is conceived in terms of becoming less sensitive to his feelings or pains, the considerate thing to do is to ignore those feelings. For example, the young adolescent boy who wants desperately to be "manly" may be able to hold back the tears from a hard tackle

[7] For an excellent discussion of the right to be treated as a person, i.e., as one who can make rational choices, see Herbert Morris, "Persons and Punishment," reprinted from *The Monist*, LII (1968) in A. I. Meldon (ed.), *Human Rights* (Belmont, California: Wadsworth, 1970). Alan Gewirth explicates a similar notion of a person as one who acts voluntarily and purposively in his "Justification of Egalitarian Justice," *American Philosophical Quarterly*, VIII (1971).

[8] Martin, *Explaining, Understanding and Teaching*, pp. 207-8.

[9] For a conceptual analysis of indoctrination and some of its moral ramifications in education, see I. A. Snook, *Indoctrination and Education* (London: Routledge & Kegan Paul, 1972).

during football. If the coach were to express sympathy for how much it must hurt, however, he would draw attention to the pain, making it more difficult to keep from crying. In a slightly different situation, the result is the same. When only one partner is in love with the other, for the other to show he is sorry about not being able to reciprocate her feelings of love for him may exacerbate rather than diminish the pain of unrequited love. The considerate thing may be to avoid acknowledging the disparity by words; the facts may speak for themselves in kinder ways.

In the context of close personal relationships, to be considerate often means expressing resentment, hostility, anger, etc. This is appropriate when one is responding to the feelings of the other person which are directed at oneself. Spontaneous expression of anger or fear toward the other shows that one is involved, that the other's feelings are not a matter of indifference. Even though they are negative feelings rather than positive ones, they may be more vital and intense, and therefore more satisfying to both persons in spite of their negative quality. In such situations, expressions of concern and sympathy not only tend to be relatively less intense and more distant, they may also appear to be condescending, and consequently inconsiderate.

To which of these two principles one gives priority will depend on the situation, including how personal the relationship between pupil and teacher is. And even if both are overridden in favor of some other way or principle of being considerate, the important point is to find some concrete ways of realizing this moral imperative which do not simply reduce to ignoring feelings altogether.

III

We are now ready to look at the practical problem of how to be considerate towards a pupil's feelings while critically teaching him. We are interested only in feelings typically generated by critical teaching. Although we ought to be considerate towards feelings however they occur, the impact of instructors in other respects will be ignored here. Throughout this section, the discussion will be following a dual strategy. Some of the remarks will be aimed at diminishing primary distress, while others will be directed at the secondary discomfort, although they will not usually be kept separate. The student I have in mind, while not completely uncritical by any means, is a relative novice at it, perhaps a college freshman.

One effect of being taught in a critical manner is noticing more frequently and vividly than before that one makes *mistakes.* Missing the point, overstating a position, etc., can produce frustrations almost impossible to avoid and blameable on no one. Recognizing an inadequacy can be uncomfortable independently of how one comes to see it or how others are doing in that respect. Nevertheless, something can be done about it.

One way to minimize the occurrence of mistakes, and the resulting discomfort, is to narrow the scope of one's efforts. The less one tries to do, the more likely it will be done well. Of course this can be pushed too hard; trying to avoid mistakes by minimizing risks also minimizes possible gains. To the extent that mistakes are likely to occur whenever one tries not to empty one's critical discussion of all its interest, we need another approach. To handle the mistakes that remain, perhaps it is most helpful simply to be reminded of the other side of the coin. Discovering inadequacies is equivalent to learning, even if it is only that some statement is false or misleading instead of true. Although this is not much by itself, it can often be turned into interesting or more adequate assessments. Learning from mistakes should diminish some of the frustration of having made them in the first place.

Another cause of emotional stress is the lack of *detachment* and flexibility. Part of the uneasiness of a novice is due to the difficulty of fulfilling the expectation of having justifications and explanations available for whatever he means and thinks is true. This may be especially uncomfortable when the opinions probed are religious or ethical, but it is also annoying in factual areas. His ego is not very willing to let go of a belief simply because the better reasons favor a different view. Typically, one's feelings, interests, self-image, etc., are not by themselves relevant to the rational acceptability of a claim; consequently, they are justifiably ignored if one's purpose is simply to engage in a critical discussion. But ignoring such feelings is inconsiderate. If letting his beliefs depend on their critical support is resisted by him simply because of its newness, secondary feelings about this can be diminished by telling him that the unfamiliarity will disappear in time.

Apart from the bruised feelings due to mistakes and emotional attachments by themselves, there is often the additional frustration of a great *disparity* with others. This is particularly relevant in some of the typical ways pupils are compared to instructors. First, there is the disparity due to the teacher's greater critical ability. It is not only true that it is usually he who shows the weaknesses in the pupil's position, but the pupil less often does the same for him. Compared to the student, he usually has better reasons, makes better assessments, misses fewer relevant points, etc.

Secondly, the teacher has a greater degree of detachment from claims and a greater degree of attachment to the reasons for those claims. In this case it is not so much that the teacher is more often right, but that he can better handle being mistaken. This is partly a matter of having made more mistakes as an inevitable part of achieving a relatively high degree of being critical, and consequently, having more time to adjust to making mistakes.

One helpful way of handling these disparities is to de-emphasize the distance between the novice and the teacher. The bluntness of the gap can be softened by the reminder that being critical is largely a matter of practice. Given some motivation and the basic capacities for thinking which most of us have, the critical inequality will begin to narrow with more experience. By putting in the effort and time to try new interpretations, consider unlikely but possible counter-examples, alternate between imagining oneself arguing for the claim, and then against it, etc., his feelings will probably change. He will likely notice himself making less blunders, spotting weaknesses in others' views more often, and becoming more attached to the reasons and less to the beliefs themselves.

Equally significant is the teacher's willingness to publicly admit his own mistakes, whether discovered by himself or the pupil. The student needs his own successes and their recognition by the teacher. But he should also see the teacher's failures. This is not a matter of condescension, of the teacher pretending to be no more practiced than the student himself. It is a matter of doing justice to critical standards no matter whom they affect. Such admissions are also a necessary part of making good on the contention that the teacher is only more likely to be right, or more critical. If there are no instances of the teacher coming off second best, what should be at most a probability will begin to look like an absolute guarantee that the teacher is always right.

This brings us to the last kind of disparity, namely, a difference in *authority.* One kind of authority is troublefree, since in this respect the pupil and the instructor have complete parity. Whether either of them has a reasonable belief does not depend on those it is, nor on who says it is reasonable, but only upon the quality of the supporting reasons themselves. In this sense, authority attaches to reasons rather than persons, so all persons are equal.

With respect to *pedagogical authority,* this does attach to persons and presents a genuine disparity between pupil and teacher. This may be thought to include the teacher's *critical authority.* A person has this sort of authority if his experience (training, practice, performance) justifies the likelihood that his beliefs, reasons, arguments, etc., will measure up to critical standards. We have referred to this previously as the teacher's greater critical ability. Whether this is included or not, something else is also centrally involved in the notion.

The authority of a pedagogue is not the authority of an expert. This is simply the familiar point that one can know something well yet not be able to teach it. To be a teacher one must be a communicator, a translator, or a popularizer of a subject matter or method, and not simply an expert in that area. The latter is a producer of raw materials, but it does not follow that one has the skills of the user that the former does.[10] This means that the teacher must have a dual authority. Diagnosing trouble in the discussion with the student is just as important as diagnosing trouble in the views themselves. The teacher may get by with merely telling, but he is more likely to be successful if he also spends time explaining. Doing this implies that he takes his students' puzzles and misunderstandings into account in ways that are neither necessary nor typical of one who only tells what he knows. He must have special skills as a teacher to mediate between the layman and the expert, skills he does not have in his capacity as an expert.

---

[10]"Competence in one's subject matter is all one needs for telling someone [something]; indeed, it is more than one needs. For teaching someone [something], however, one cannot get along with just this: one needs competence in getting subject matter across to somebody." Ibid., p. 131.

Neither kind of authority causes any special problems not already mentioned, since neither is a guarantee of success, but at best a likelihood. For our purposes, the ideal occurs when the teacher's activities usually measure up to critical and pedagogical ideals, and the student recognizes that they do. To the extent that the ideal is missed, the situation is unfortunate. This is especially so when the activities meet these standards according to the teacher, but not to the student. The difficulty is not so much the mere fact of disagreement, but the occasions when the disagreement takes on the quality of "pulling rank" on the student.

One of the reasons why the pupil may feel the teacher is pulling rank on him is because he is a relative novice. As such he may not easily see the relevance or strength of genuinely good reasons for the teacher's claims or methods even when they are brought to his attention. This makes it almost inevitable that there will be some element of perceived arbitrariness at first.

Another reason worth highlighting is the possible confusion of the above kinds of authority with his *institutional authority.* This concept is not a matter of experience, but of the office or rank one holds within an institution.[11] The authority of the role or job is defined in an institutional context by a set of rights or powers and duties or responsibilities with respect to some goals. The teacher's institutional responsibilities often include activities only loosely related to teaching, such as sitting on committees and monitoring exams. Of course, they also include those bound more intimately with teaching, such as lecturing, explaining, discussing, and tutoring.

To illustrate the different kinds of authority, consider the grading of essays. The critical, pedagogical, and institutional components all play a role. The grade and comments reflect some judgment of truth and strength of argument, some guidance and diagnosis of misunderstandings, and some certification of being qualified or not, perhaps along with the degree of qualification.[12] The latter, like decisions to end discussions, offer courses, require pre-requisites, etc., are made by teachers as officials. They are not intrinsic to the relation between apprentice and master (whether as expert or teacher). As long as teaching occurs in schools with different levels of authority, there will continue to be some legitimate instances of pulling rank.

The student's problems with the teacher as a bureaucratic official is beyond the scope of this essay. Still it should be obvious that those decisions, like any others, can be made and implemented considerately and are fit objects of rational and moral criticism. Our main concern is how and what the teacher teaches. Yet we have seen how closely intertwined they can be. And not each kind of authority will be equally troublesome in a given situation. For these reasons it is crucial to be able to distinguish them.

[11]This point was suggested by Martin's distinction between the activity and role senses of 'teach.' Ibid., p. 101.

[12]For the development of this view, see the "Discourse on Grading" in R. P. Wolff, *The Ideal of the University* (Boston: Beacon Press, 1969).

Critical and pedagogical assessments are based on the teacher's experience, rather than on his institutional power, so they should be treated differently by both student and teacher. The quality of his criticism and guidance are more like predictions about what other critical thinkers and teachers will accept than like sovereign pronouncements from an official. The disparities we are primarily interested in should be reduced to a minimum, although not to zero, when the student realizes this. The teacher's greater experience, when relevant, has an important role to play in the teaching situation without necessarily functioning as a rebuff.

One last problem should be mentioned. Someone might object to the goal of becoming critical independently of how it is taught. The sort of complaint I have in mind is one which might naturally arise or gain support from what has been said so far, namely, that becoming critical is detrimental to other aspects of one's personality. In particular, the detachment necessary to be ctitical seems to be incompatible with the spontaneity and involvement conducive to emotional well-being. Being cool enough to follow the best reasons appears to hinder keeping in touch with one's feelings. Analysing feelings rather than expressing them or responding to them in kind is less than emotionally satisfying. Although a little criticism may be helpful, one can be too critical for one's own good.

The point of this objection is sound, but it may be misconstrued. One can be too critical, for example, by spending too much time thinking and too little time feeling, or by being too disinterested and disembodied while acting. However, this should not undermine the importance of being critical. When and how it is proper and satisfying to be critical, like any other way of acting, is partly a theoretical problem. That is, there are standards and likely consequences to be evaluated. To this extent, the facts and values involved are appropriate objects for critical reflections. It is not true that the only upshot of intellectual scrutiny is to continue intellectualizing; instead, it may be to refrain in specific situations. Nevertheless, the more complicated the issues are, the less likely one will be able to obtain reliable guides to action without critical efforts.

Furthermore, if the major thesis of this essay is correct, then being critical and considerate are not mutually exclusive. For one thing, the caring associated with considerateness has its counterpart in intellectual matters. The passionate commitment to rational standards is not unlike a love affair with ideas. And more generally, the two tendencies can fit together into an integrated whole, since they are personality traits that can remain more or less stable throughout major portions of one's life. The more one narrows the context to actions of a short duration, the more difficult it is to be both sympathetic and critical. But even then it is not impossible to combine them. It should be clear by now that there are still ways of being considerate while being critical.

IV

Being considerate and critical are valuable in any context, but two more points are worth making about the value of being considerate in the context of critical teaching. One thing worth being reminded of is that being considerate is perhaps the most effective way of teaching *how* and teaching *to* be considerate. Any human interaction is to some extent a teaching/learning situation with regard to inter- and intra-personal attitudes. This means that such attitudes as being considerate are supported or weakened even when one's primary goal is quite different, say, teaching a person to be critical. Even if this is not true, and we can act quite neutrally in regard to such moral demands, moral education often suffers from perceived compartmentalization. If it is only thought to take place at home, in the streets, or in religion and ethics courses then it may seem less relevant within other contexts. But in the classroom, it takes little extra effort to teach this along with the subject matter. The pupil receives an educational bonus from a considerate teacher.

Finally, intellectuals and academics tend to be attracted to the ideal of ignoring feelings, probably because of their commitment to impartiality and objectivity. Although this is proper and required of them as critics and theorists, they may overdo it and emotionally harm themselves or others involved. For example, a professor was overheard discussing one of his students with the Dean: "I hope you realize that I take a dim view of personal problems." Now, of course, these problems and the feelings surrounding them are not relevant when it comes to grading a term paper. But we can hope the Dean reminded him that the term paper is not a good model of life, and that ignoring feelings for the purpose of grading should not result in ignoring feelings altogether. When feelings are at stake, merely noticing them helps keep them alive. This is part of the significance of being considerate towards one's feelings, since it presupposes that their existence is recognized.

The importance of being considerate towards feelings while teaching critically is to reaffirm emotional needs in the context where ignoring them altogether is so tempting. The dividend for the pupil and teacher alike is not only more respect and less frustration now, but a healthier emotional life in the long run. Our reflections yield a major resolution of the conflict between the intellect and the heart. In spite of the fact that the examined life is often personally upsetting, it can still be treated considerately.

VALUES AND HUMANISTIC PSYCHOLOGY

Donald Morgenson
Department of Psychology
Wilfrid Laurier University

To say that you and I live in turbulent times, vastly disturbing times is to underscore the obvious or "carry carbohydrates to weight watchers." Vastly disturbing events and urgent issues are brought instantly and insistently into our homes by the mass media. Stripped of their superficialities and their irrelevance, a great number of these events and issues are but manifestations of man's very proper concern with human conditions and with the quality of human life here and now. Indeed, our concern is with the quality of life, not at some distant time but in the attainable future.

Torn by strife and controversy, both internal and external, pressured by numbers, harrassed and challenged by seekers of change, charged with colossal failure, frustrated and discouraged by problems of cosmic proportions, there can be little wonder that today we are unsure of what values we should affirm, unsure as to what form our concerns might take, and unsure of the character of our rather urgent inquiry. Essentially, the questions of greatest importance and relevance in the mid-seventies are questions of values. Perhaps value questions have always been the most central in any age, but the answers to value questions are vital today.

We are in some strange way condemned to be absolutely heroic in our complex world. To exist today means to be confronted by many and complex value choices; to exist is to choose. We are required by the fact of life to face choices and make value decisions. Life does not proceed independently of such decisions. The daily value decisions we make rather quickly seem to add up to a lifetime. In some way, by certain values we affirm life or we deny life. We affirm loving or we deny it. We affirm the humanity of man or we deny it. It is the commitment to man truly alive—intellectually, and spiritually, individually and collectively—that gives urgency to the questions suffering for answers.

Our struggle has always been to give human contours to our age: to devise ideas, symbols and values around which to cluster human experience and creating a truly integrative human heritage. Our commitment has always been to the whole person, no matter how varied or diversified the philosophies or the models we utilize: each of us desperately needs an internally unified set of values.

Only one kind of value counts today and that is the kind which is radical enough to engage this world's basic troubles. If our values cannot do this, then they can do nothing which merits our concern or the world's respect. Efforts dedicated to self-interest, superficial status, prestige and social success are worse than valueless. Value struggles reveal themselves in the attempt to reveal the meaning of our world.

In the records of the trial of Joan of Arc there is a moving passage in which she addresses her judges. Boldly and fearlessly she answered her judge, the Bishop, who was questioning her: "You say that you are my judge. Take care of what you do, for in truth I am sent by God and you are putting yourself in great danger." Yes, we all had better take warning—there may be something sacred and precious about our world and the people of it and we must deal with it humbly and seriously, or indeed *we* may be in great danger.

But need we worry? Conscientious men and women today do not want any easy answers, no trumped up cure-alls, cheap grace, panaceas or peace of mind at any price. But yet we have a world on our hands, burgeoning with unprecedented power, at times terrified by its own momentum, haunted by something that was lost some time ago, assailed by "future shock" and sensory overload.

So our world and the people in it need help not condescension. It needs bold but modest men and women who will put a shoulder under the shadows of a world where life appears to be waning, under lives where the pain of faith itself is enough to break your heart, under the frustrated compassion of the lost whose last hope and trust is simply to be true to one another; but sharing an agony which is great and whose meaning they cannot grasp. Yes, our world needs help, not condescension—help in determining those values which will enhance life and love for us all, values which will enlarge the communities where our lives may emerge full of compassion, commitment and concern.

There are millions around us who have their hungers, terrible and ineluctable; millions who indeed are satisfied with "cheap grace" or pious respectability. They have doubts, shame, pride, humiliations, dreads, but they find it hard to be honest with others because they have not been honest with themselves.

Many critics have described our time as an "Age of Anxiety" (W. H. Auden), a "Century of Fear" (Camus), an age of schism of the soul; a time when we suffer from not only wars, persecution, world-wide famine, and the threat of nuclear holocaust, but also from inner problems fully as appalling: despair, a conviction of isolation, and a pervasive sense of meaninglessness. The prevailing mood has been and is one of profound melancholy and disenchantment. The great values of life are not love, pity, benevolence, and compassion, but strength, ruthlessness and savage acquiescence. Our champions are not Buddha, but Caeser; not Christ but Napoleon; our reality not heaven but the body-strewn battlefield and the life-crushing ghetto. History is not determined by a caring providence or God but by the simple and inexorable laws of growth and decay. Spiritual progress is illusion, freedom an impossibility, the end is, as Ecclesiastes predicts, vanity.

As Matson (1969) as well as others have suggested, dignity and freedom are threatened on all sides today, threatened by what Marcuse refers to as the "one-dimensional society," an attempt to reduce all categories of thought and creative dialogue to a kind of endorsement of the demands of an aggressive and acquisitive society, a society surfeited by and sick of psychological and physical violence. Human dignity may indeed be threatened by the technology of mass society, mass culture, and mass communication which manufactures a *papier mâché* world, in which the "bland lead the bland" hand in hand into a sea of drug-induced tranquility, or are dragged to the edge of that darkling plain where "blind armies clash at night." Freedom of the mind is threatened by the genetic revolution, and our "psychological" liberty and spiritual freedom are threatened by failure of nerve; we sense a chronic inability to live up to the ideals of a truly democratic society, where though difficult, knowing oneself, and believing in oneself is essential to the survival of all men.

We need to revitalize the imaginations of men and women, and stir to activity the consciences of humans everywhere to expose dehumanization wherever it occurs, depersonalization whenever it occurs, and combat those forces which indeed cripple the creative powers of men. As Norman Cousins (1970) has said: "Through dreams, through imagination men can be encouraged to rediscover themselves. Otherwise degradation can be reached wherein even the most stirring visions lose their power to regenerate and redeem men. This point will be reached only when men will no longer be capable of calling out to one another, when the words in their poetry break up before their eyes, when their faces are frozen toward the young, and when they fail to make pictures in the mind out of clouds racing across the sky. So long as men can do these things they will be capable of indignation, they will speak about things which should be changed, and they will ultimately shape their society in a way which does justice to their dreams."

Until we can dream the dreams that can ultimately shape our society in a way that does justice to our hopes, we will continue to suffer from some very specific difficulties.

Loneliness

Loneliness is one of these difficulties. Rather than the optimism which characterized the beginning of the 20th century here in North America, the pessimists of Europe began to influence us all. Spokesmen such as Arthur Schopenhauer (pessimism), F. Neitzsche (nihilism) and S. Kierkegaard's (despair in human existence) combined with scientific discoveries which seemed to erode the foundations of the established religions of the world, generated little optimism. Writers and thinkers such as Sartre, Camus, Mann and Hesse expressed the mood: doubt, despondency and despair.

One of the questions troubling all of us is that of existential loneliness. Nonetheless, in a little known article by Frieda Fromm-Reichman (1959) she noted that loneliness was not even mentioned in most psychiatric textbooks. Ten years later P. Herbert Liederman (1969) reported that the situation identified by Fromm-Reichman had changed little. Liederman's examination of the literature revealed few papers focussing on this very common human condition.

While poets, composers, and artists have spoken of, sung about, and textured the theme loneliness, social scientists have been loudly silent. Some observers have suggested that the entire theme is an embarrassment because psychologists and psychiatrists have no model or theory with which to begin the systematic study of the condition. Perhaps a theory would emerge were we to study it more intensively.

Harry Stack Sullivan (1953) described loneliness as "the exceedingly unpleasant and driving experience connected with the inadequate discharge of the need for human intimacy."

Phillip Slater (1970), author of *The Pursuit of Loneliness* has listed some of the many human desires that tend to be deeply frustrated and thwarted by the North American cultural patterns. One of these is the desire for community. This is the simple desire to live in trust and gentle cooperation with one's fellows in a rather open and obvious (visible) collective entity. Second, there is the desire for engagement or the desire to come directly to grips with social and interpersonal problems. Third, there is the desire for dependence, or the wish to share responsibility for the control of one's impulses and the final direction of one's life.

To a certain extent these frustrations have been spawned by an incredible technology, which by its very efficiency has separated us from one another. Technology has given us separate rooms, our own television, a personal car, but little personal contentment. We have taken a giant step backwards from immediate experience with other human beings and we suffer accordingly. Slater notes: "The poor (in the past) were visible and all around. Psychosis was not a strange phenomenon in a textbook but a familiar neighbour or a village character. The aged were in every house. Everyone had seen animals slaughtered and knew what they were eating when they ate them; illness and death were a fundamental part of everyone's immediate experience."

Everyone knows in those lonely and isolated states, very few of us are listening to each other and this intensifies loneliness. It is said that husbands give half an ear to the conversations of their wives, and wives listen to about half of what their husbands are saying. There are many disciplined attempts at communication, but most of them fail today. Why? Abraham Kaplan has recently said that they are not really dialogues at all. He calls these attempts at genuine communion, "duologues." The duologue, according to Kaplan, is little more than a monologue mounted before a glazed and exquisitely indifferent audience. The teachers talk and the students don't listen, then the students talk and the teachers don't listen. The duologue has its unforgiving rules: you have to give the other his turn; you have to give signals during his turn, like saying "uh huh" or laughing at what he says, to show that he is indeed having his turn. You must always refrain from saying anything that really matters to you as it might be regarded as an embarrassing intimacy. One example of duologue is the televiewer absolutely transfixed before that compelling screen. A perfect duologue would be two TV sets turned on and facing each other.

Kaplan, a devoted student of the Jewish existentialist Martin Buber

(1937), insists that Buber's I-Thou philosophy is based on the conviction that each of us defines ourselves by genuinely engaging other human beings: humanity is a meeting, humanity is communion. Nothing speaks more eloquently of the loneliness and alienation of our age than two humans involved in a duologue— but there is perhaps nothing more beautiful or marvelous than two genuinely engaged listeners. Out of this comes understanding and as Dilthey (1961) has said: "Understanding is the rediscovery of the I in the Thou."

Meaningfulness

Another problem facing us, the resolution of which may have added impetus to the growth and development of humanistic psychology, is the lack of meaning-fulness in our lives today. Individual meaning is of tremendous psychological significance, without which life does indeed seem worthless and empty. Viktor Frankl (1959) speaks of this emotion as the "existential vacuum." Meaning simply gives our lives, individually and collectively a goal, a cause, a purpose, but the meaning is beyond the individual himself ("self-transcendence"). This term for Frankl means that we feel a deep necessity to relate to and dedicate ourselves to something outside ourselves. A search for meaning can lead us out of the current existential crisis into a new discovery of our own life force, that source of love and vitality, which moves us along into a purposeful life of commitment, and dedication to the human spirit.

Clearly related to the lack of meaning in life, lack of self-worth is the growing problem of dehumanization. According to Bernard, Ottenberg, and Redl (1971), dehumanization as a defense against painful or overwhelming emotion involves an inevitable decrease in a person's sense of his own individuality and in perceiving of the humanness of other individuals. The process involves two different but related vectors; (1) self-directed dehumanization, which results in a reduced sense of the individual's own humanity; and (2) other-directed dehumanization, referring to our perceiving others as lacking those traits which are considered to be most human. Reduction in the fullness of one's feelings for other human beings, whatever the reason, impoverishes one's own sense of self; any lessening of the humanness of one's self image may limit our capacity for full relating to other human beings.

The authors list some overlapping aspects of maladaptive dehumanization:

1. Increased emotional distance from other human beings.
2. Diminished sense of personal responsibility for the consequences of one's actions.
3. Increasing involvement with procedural problems to the detriment of human needs.
4. Inability to oppose dominant group attitudes or pressures.
5. Feelings of personal helplessness and estrangement.

The implications for us as individuals are quite clear; even more clear are the implications for our institutions today. Bernard, *et al.*, argue that the actual inhumanities in institutional medicine, education, law enforcement and the administration of justice are often more grotesque than fiction and Ronald Laing

(1967) might remind us that the sanity of society may be madder at times than the madness that it condemns to imprisonment.

As examples of tendencies toward dehumanization in the school system, Charles Silberman (1970) provides us with some observations which clearly indicate that the motto is: logistics first—the lives of children second in priorities. "Administrivia" first—human needs second.

ITEM: A scholar studying curriculum reform visits a classroom using a new elementary science curriculum. Arriving a few minutes before the class was scheduled to begin, he sees a cluster of excited children examining a turtle with enormous fascination and intensity. "Now children, put away the turtle," the teacher insists. "We're going to have our science lesson." The lesson is on crabs.

ITEM: Over an elementary school's public address system comes the principal's announcement: "Children are not using the lavatories correctly. No child may be out of his room for more than three minutes."

ITEM: A first-grade classroom has the following sign prominently posted:

Rules for Classes 1-7

1. Keep your hands at your sides.
2. Raise your hand to speak.
3. Be polite and kind to all.
4. Fold hands when not working.

The sign does not indicate how a child can fold hands that are required to be at his side.

ITEM: In lecturing the assembled students on the need for and virtue of absolute silence, an elementary school principal expostulates on the wonders of a school for the "deaf and dumb" he had recently visited. The silence was just wonderful, he tells the assembly; the children could all get their work done because of the total silence. The goal is explicit: to turn normal children into youngsters behaving as though they were missing two of their most precious faculties.

ITEM: A fourth-grader is discovered by his parents to have abandoned reading E. B. White and the Dr. Doolittle books in favour of Little Golden Books—at his teacher's request. The young teacher—a dear, sweet, loving human being—explains that students are required to submit a weekly book report on a 4x6 filing card. If the student were to read books as long as *Charlotte's Web* or *Dr. Doolittle,* he wouldn't be able to submit a weekly report, and his reports might be too long to fit on the file card. "I urged him to continue reading those books on his own," the teacher explains, "but not for school." The youngster does not continue, of course; he has learned all too well that the object of reading is not enjoyment, but to fill out 4x6 file cards.

ITEM: A fourth-grade Math teacher writes a half-dozen problems on the board for the class to do. "I think I can pick at least four children who can't do them," she tells the class, and proceeds to call four youngsters to the board to demonstrate, for all to see, how correct the teacher's judgment is. Needless to say, the children fulfill the prophecy.

I recall a statement in *Sybil,* by Flora Schreiber (1973): "one is reminded over and over again, that no cruelty is necessary, to destroy another human being; all you must have is the gentle arrogance of being sure you know what is best for other people."

What is revealed in these observations of one institutional setting, the school, is the relatively permanent power of bureaucratic-authoritarian structures. We can explain this enduring power by knowing that the individuals engulfed in these institutions come to believe that authority must maintain itself at any cost in the interest of order, and those within the institutions adjust their moral perceptions so that the macabre becomes reasonable, the bizarre becomes acceptable, the psychological violence is rationalized, and further meaninglessness is generated.

In a very instructive article, Lawrence Friedman (1974) suggests that as we cry for more "law and order" our tolerance for crime will drop dramatically. When our tolerance drops, dehumanization increases, resulting in a greater sense of human meaninglessness.

Tolerance levels for crime are linked to social and economic change. In each historical era society had its own idea of the definitions of crime. In earlier times the ruling classes (most often the middle class) were very hard on crimes against morality. They tried to enforce laws against fornication, blasphemy, nonattendance at church, etc. Idlers, gamblers, etc., were placed in the stocks and pillories. Later the tolerance level shifted and even though crimes against morality remained on the books, they were rarely enforced. People seemed to care less whether or not people sinned privately. But, authorities were less and less tolerant of crimes against property, less tolerant of worker idleness and indolence. An industrial capitalist society cannot abide laziness or malingerers among its workers.

So according to Friedman tolerance for crime is sensitive to real economic needs. Criminal justice will enforce the *status quo.* But behind all of these changes lies a force less economic than sociocultural: a demand that moral domination remain where it is. The middle classes have a moral code, a system of values as well as economic power to uphold. The people feel some satisfaction when their values are the official values, i.e., when the country flies their flag, sings their anthems, enforces their rules. Friedman asks: why prosecute people going barefoot in restaurants, and why the passion over "dirty books" on high school reading lists; why passionately repudiate those men with shoulder length hair?

Going barefoot (and less recently longer and longer hair on men) into restaurants and "dirty books" threatens those who think that their way of life will collapse unless they hold tightly to the "monopoly of respectability." What is at stake here is not deviance *per se*, but flaunting of deviance in the public arena. Parents who become upset over the "dirty books" on required reading lists know in their hearts that their children read books which may be more prurient than *Catcher in the Rye,* for example. What they seem unable to tolerate is OPEN pornography, particularly when it is seemingly peddled by "model citizens," the teachers in our communities. The issue may not be pornography on bookshelves, stage, screen and radio, not pornography, but the apparent legitimization of pornography.

Out of this comes the demand for "law and order," and it may breed a demagogeury which threatens fundamental human rights, and quite clearly there will manifest itself a further maladaptive dehumanization. The "ruling" classes begin to feel that their moral monopoly is breaking down. This insecurity has lowered their tolerance for crime and leads to not only increased demand for law and order but to further systematic dehumanization.

So the more meaninglessness in life, the more inwardly terrified and humiliated people become, the greater the vulnerability to the seductive bigoted promises of demagoguery, we will commit further acts of discrimination and persecution against victims and victim groups. Convinced of the correctness and rightness of their actions, a sweeping indifference results, which permits them (without malice) to write off misery, injustices, and the mass deaths of others as something that "just couldn't be helped" or "they simply deserved what they got"; apathy of epidemic proportions.

Writing of the apathy surrounding the murderous attack on Kitty Genovese, Rosenthal (1964), an editor of the *New York Times,* describes his own reaction:

> ... peculiar paradoxical feeling that there is in the tale of Catherine Genovese a revelation about the human condition so appalling to contemplate that only good can come from forcing oneself to confront the truth ... the terrible reality that only under certain situations and only in response to certain reflexes or certain beliefs will a man step out of his shell toward his brother. In the back of my mind ... was the feeling that there was, that there must be, some connection between [this story and] the story of the witnesses silent in the face of greater crimes—the degradation of a race, children hungering. ... It happens from time to time in New York that the life of the city is frozen by an instant of shock. In that instant the people of the city are seized by the paralyzing realization that they are one, that each man is in some way a mirror of every other man. ... In that instant of shock, the mirror showed quite clearly what was wrong, that the face of mankind was spotted with the disease of apathy—all mankind. But this was too frightening a thought to live with, and soon the beholders began to set boundaries for the illness, to search frantically for causes that were external, and to look for the carrier.

Complicating these tendencies is the fact that we are committed to a model of man as a closed system (homeostasis, physicalism, quantum models of motivation and drive, etc.). Many have argued that the basic striving of man is to find and fulfill meaning and purpose of life. The "existential vacuum" is the mass neurosis of today. Instead of Maslow's "peak experiences" we have "abyss experiences."

In their book, *The Year 2000,* H. Kahn and A. J. Wiener (1967) provided us with a list of possible technical innovations likely to develop fully between now and the year 2000 A.D. Some of these supposed realities were: free choice of the sex of unborn children; free cosmetological alteration, involving changing skin colour, body contours, etc.; chemical management of most mental illness; abolition of senility; cleansing of the gene pool to rid ourselves of hereditary defects; pharmacological substances to modify fatigue, mood fluctuations, and personality traits; postponement of aging combined with rejuvenation of the aged; efficient and dependable methods of behavioural control; human hibernation for predetermined periods of time; dreams tailored to specific individual tastes; genetic techniques such as amniocentesis, cloning, miscegenation (animals and man)—indeed a cybernetic state of psychotechnological bliss. Everyone of these steps along the way, however, should provoke lengthy and heated discussions of ethics, morals, and values.

The attitudes created in our time contribute to meaninglessness. We stress weighing, measuring, analyzing, quantifying, calculating and tend to neglect that which may be intuitive; we stress the pragmatic approach as opposed to more playful cognitive exercises; the outside world is constantly and consistently evaluated for "unknowns" while the dark crisis felt in the heart, silent and painful, remains unstudied. We stress the technical know-how and we are smugly confident about our technical competence. But as T. Merton has said, "We are a society dedicated to the more refined means toward unexamined ends"; behaviours are evaluated as to their economic and scientific usefulness. All of these emphases have left us with the "abyss experience" of meaninglessness. This is the lost reality and humanistic psychology, through the reclamation of value, decision and choice, hopes to re-discover that vital dimension of human existence: meaning. Rollo May (1961) has said: "Existentialism has put decision and will back into the center of the picture." Decision and will to make something meaningful of our lives.

Alienation

Whatever the name we apply to conditions of our contemporary society, all of the terms suggest a deep sense of loss, growing gaps between you and me, distances now perhaps unbridgeable. The terms we have used are: disengagement, anomie, separation, noninvolvement, apathy, indifference, estrangement, disaffection, neutralism, and many others, but what is sensed is a loss of concern, commitment and community. What our spectacular technology has brought us has left us with a sense of unrelatedness, an impenetrable distance from others.

As Sykes (1964) has said: "Although we are chronologically far beyond the day when schoolmen told us with medieval simplicity that alienation meant estrangement from God, we are now confronted with secular accusations that do no less damage to our self-esteem. Rousseau told us and a romantic chorus has echoed that we live alienated from nature; Marx told us and a communist chorus has echoed that we live alienated from society; Kierkegaard told us and an existentialist chorus has echoed that we live alienated from ourselves. . . . We are all in the same guiltlogged boat and usually it is shipping so much water that we lack the time and detachment to find words for it."

Man is alienated from reality and estranged from himself, partly because he has allowed his identity to be deeply submerged in the anonymous, faceless mob. Man is a stranger in the world, the terrain is suddenly unfamiliar, and more importantly he has become a stranger to himself. After his brief walk across eternity he may look back and say sorrowfully, ". . . but none of that was me."

Franz Kafka (1952) speaks to us of our modern alienation and sense of anonymity. He wrote of himself as well ". . . I am separated from all things, by a hollow space and I do not even reach to its boundaries." His characters are often more shadow than substance, i.e., *The Castle, The Trial,* etc.

Many of us painfully identified with Arthur Miller's Willy Loman (*Death of a Salesman*), eternally envisioning that grand million dollar dream, worshipping success, but destined to become alienated from himself and "to fall into his grave like a dog." One of his sons at the graveside said, "Poor Willy . . . he didn't know who he was."

But it is surely as Fritz Pappenheim (1959) argues, far too easy to attribute the modern sense of alienation to history: world wars, the economic changes, the rise and relentless growth of a technology. It is rather a combination of historical antecedents and perhaps the "homelessness" that the existentialists refer to as man's eternal fate.

It is hard to overlook the gathering evidence that people seeking some form of intensive or mild supportive psychotherapy are growing in numbers. They appear to be dissatisfied with the nature and quality of life. It is obvious to many that even those who do not seek help are also feeling alone and empty.

Out of this malaise has arisen a relatively new psychiatric term: "the existential neurosis," which is characterized by feelings of meaninglessness, apathy and aimlessness. As Maddi (1967) has suggested, the existential neurosis like all neuroses has cognitive, affective, and connative components. The cognitive component of the existential neurosis is meaninglessness, or chronic inability to believe in the truth, importance, usefulness, or interest value of any of the things one is engaged in. The prominent characteristics emotionally are blandness and boredom, punctuated by periods of depression which become less frequent as the disorder is prolonged. As to the realm of action, the activity level may be low to moderate, but more important than amount of activity is the introspective and objectively observable fact that activities are not chosen. There appears to be little selectivity, it being immaterial to the person what if any activities he pursues. If there is any selectivity shown it is in the direction of making definite a small expenditure of effort. The picture is one of meaninglessness, lack of choice and apathy.

Perhaps most appropriate here is the Tolstoi's (1960) *The Death of Ivan Ilych.* Ivan knows that he is dying of a horrible disorder and this begins, quite naturally, to affect all that he perceives around him. His visitors, coming to lighten his day, are mostly business friends, whom he ultimately comes to realize are simply performing what they experience as a rather distasteful obligation inherent in their social roles. Not one of these visitors is touched by Ivan's slow and inexorable move toward death. Theirs is simply a social contractual relationship, devoid of any sense of intimacy. Ivan concludes that the same is true of his family members. He begins to think of the past and the truth he realizes then, is that his relationships with these compassionless creatures have been just that: contractual, superficial, and empty of human feeling. He then confronts his "wasted" life realizing that he has always felt devoid of passion, bereft of intimacy, and suffering from a chronic lack of spontaneity and enthusiasm. He renounces himself and those around him who are feigning love, and only then is he capable of feeling genuinely human and fully alive. At this point, most spiritually alive, Ivan Ilych dies. Indeed a heroic but tragic way to die. It is in the midst of this crisis of values, that Ivan Ilych found himself most alive.

It is in life situations like this that questions of value and humanistic psychology can make profound contributions to modern life. Central to modern humanistic psychology is the belief that man can overcome his profound sense of alienation, and meaninglessness. This belief is a call to arms: struggle with the problems of modern life to create a new faith in man, create a new metaphysic, full of faith and hope. Humanistic psychology can help reawaken man's creative powers.

Saul Alinsky (1946) lays it out for us rather plainly. Given the world in which we are currently living, where everything seems to be chronically interrelated such that one feels nothing but helplessness, defeat sets in. From the beginning, the weakness as well as the strength of the great ideals has been the people. Yet there can be no darker tragedy or more devastating tragedy than the death of man's faith in himself and in his power to direct his own future. Alinsky insists that we must learn to respect the dignity of the people so that they will develop self-respect. Self-respect arises only out of people who play a very active role in solving their own crises and who are not helpless, passive and puppet-like.

We *can* transform the social order; if we do not face value issues, we will resign ourselves to living within the social order which continues to separate and divide men, tolerating a way of life which separates us from the natural order and which will ultimately separate us from ourselves.

Humanistic Psychology

The group of psychologists who have attempted to confront the world's ills and have not reneged on commitment are the Humanistic psychologists. The name was selected by a group of psychologists who in 1962 joined Abraham Maslow to establish a new association whose aim was to explore the behavioural characteristics and emotional dynamics of full and healthy human living. Charlotte Bühler (1972) and James Bugental formulated a statement of those characteristics common to this orientation. The Association of Humanistic Psychology, while admitting that not all members agreed to this credo, published these four elements in the brochure of the Association of Humanistic Psychology:

1. A centering of attention on the experiencing person, and thus a focus on experience as the primary phenomenon in the study of man. Both theoretical explanations and overt behaviour are considered secondary to experience itself and to its meaning to the individual.
2. An emphasis on such distinctively human qualities as choice, creativity, valuation, and self-realization, as opposed to thinking about human beings in mechanistic and reductionistic terms.
3. An allegiance to meaningfulness in the selection of problems for study and of research procedures, and an opposition to a primary emphasis on objectivity at the expense of significance.
4. An ultimate concern with and valuing of the dignity and worth of man and an interest in the development of the potential inherent in every person. Central in this view is the person as he discovers his own being and relates to other persons and to social groups.

Essentially, humanistic psychology is a commitment to the human becoming. The term "humanistic" was chosen because it was thought that in time the positive, affirming, explicit value commitment of psychology with that specific orientation would restore "humanistic" to its original positive and healthy emphasis. Also, the different points of view represented by humanistic psychology, such as all versions of existentialism (both religious and atheistic), role theory, self theory, experientially oriented reconstructive therapies, phenomenology, psychosocial theories of cultures, etc., shared one common concern about hope and human kind. The term also focussed conceptual models as well as direction for the "third force."

This so-called "third force" in psychology was a response to two other very significant revolutions within the corpus of psychology. The first, that of behaviourism flashed like a beacon about the time of 1913, and indeed the seismic quake reverberated through the psychological academies. Justifiably fed up with Wundtian introspection Behaviourism reacted to the simplistic structuralist dogmas and threw out not only consciousness but all of the dimensions of the mind. The mind was like Koestler's "ghost in the machine" and had to be exorcised, and purged. Watson (1958) very early on said that he began . . . by sweeping aside all mediaeval conceptions. He dropped from his scientific vocabulary all subjective terms such as sensation, perception, image, desire, purpose, and even thinking and emotion as they were subjectively defined. So the laboratory as well as the mind were swept clean of the cobwebs of that first psychological laboratory in Leipzig, Germany; swept aside by the broom that a "heavyweight" like B. F. Skinner would wield in the days after John Watson.

Now it was argued that overt behaviour, that which could be seen and measured was all that really mattered to the infant psychology struggling along its embryonic way. The early behaviourists borrowed the "conditional reflex" from the laboratories of Pavlov and Bechterev—conditioning was powerful, and control was bewilderingly seductive. Just as man was a machine ready to run, so the behaviourist was no pure scientist but a behavioural engineer, making control a central focus.

The other revolution shaking the foundations of psychology in the past 100 years was that of Freudian psychoanalysis. Both behaviourism and psychoanalysis emerged at roughly the same time, and interestingly enough as a reaction against the simple dogmas of structuralism. But their forms of protest were radically different. Whereas the behaviourists emphasized the environment, focussing on stimuli from the external world, the analysts emphasized intrapsychic conflicts and drives, for explanations of behaviour they depended on stimuli from within.

For Sigmund Freud modern man was very much a creature (victim) of instincts, particularly two instincts: Eros and Thanatos, those of life and death. How these are balanced in an individual determines his mental health and how they are balanced in society determines the quality of life. Life for the individual as well as collective society is a constant struggle between frustration and aggression. So Freud could say, we see man as a savage beast to whom the thought of sparing his own kind is alien.

What is clear, of course, is that man is a victim of his own instincts; he is condemned to death; his actions are determined (psychic determinism). Psychic determinism, not like Watson's or the neo-behaviourists, is a rather strange form of psychogenetic determinism. Whatever the causes or the forces, this left little room for freedom, choice, and subsequent responsibility for man's behaviour.

James F. T. Bugental, in a paper read at a meeting of Psychologists Interested in the Advancement of Psychotherapy (September 3, 1967) outlined in some detail the "humanistic ethic." In prefatory remarks he states that there is in the humanistic ethic an insistence on the right and vital necessity of each individual to be the subject of one's own life. This is in opposition to so much in our culture that tends toward transforming individuals into commodities, objects, or robots. Yablonsky (1972) in the *Robopaths* argues that robots are machine-made simulations of people and he coins the term "robopath" to describe people whose pathology entails robot-like behaviour and existence. A robopath is a person who has become socially dead. He identifies eight interrelated characteristics that help define the robopath:

1. *Ritualism*—Robopaths enact ritualistic behaviour patterns in the context of precisely defined and accepted norms and rules. They have limited ability to be spontaneous, to be creative, to change direction or modify their behaviour in terms of new conditions.
2. *Past-Orientation*—Robopaths are oriented to the past, rather than to the here-and-now situation, or to the future. They often respond to situations and conditions that are no longer relevant or functional. If they are locked into a behavioural pattern, they will follow the same path even though it may ultimately be self-destructive.
3. *Conformity*—In a robopathic-producing social machine, conformity is a virtue. New or different behaviour is viewed as strange and threatening. Originality is suspect.,
4. *Image-Involvement*—Robopaths are other directed rather than inner directed (in Riesman's terms). They are forever trying to be super-conformists. Their behaviour is dominated by image or status requirements set by the surrounding society.
5. *Acompassion*—If compassion entails a concern for human interests of other at

one's own personal expense, robopaths are acompassionate. They appear to be without any compassionate values or social conscience. Their role and its proper enactment becomes paramount over any concern for other people.

6. *Hostility*—Hostility both hidden and obvious is a significant trait of robopaths. People unable to act out their spontaneity and creativity develop repressed, venomous pockets of anger.

7. *Self-Righteousness*—Robopathic behaviour is super-conformist. It is never deviant or against the norms of the social machine. The robopath's behaviour is always right or is considered self-righteous.

8. *Alienation*—Despite the overall appearances of "togetherness," the typical robopath is in effect alienated from self, others and the natural environment.

All of these traits contradict the humanistic ethic. As Sidney Jourard (1967) has said we have problems with the credibility gap, mass produced entertainment is generated for totally passive viewers, education is characterized as depersonalized ("system syndrome") including a mechanomorphic psychology that seeks to reduce the human experience to the banalities of rats, pigeons, and robots.

The central humanistic tenet is a recognition that each individual is the chief determinant of his own behaviour and experience. And for them the humanistic ethic consists of the following assumptions (according to Bugental):

1. *Centered responsibility for one's own life.* Each individual, each person is the single most important responsible agent in his own life. This does not diminish the importance of social imbeddedness, concern for others, the influence of contingencies, but the humanistic ethic insists that these do not displace the person from being the one who mediates all such influences. This is what Rollo May (1959) refers to as "centeredness." You and I are ultimately the only aware influences in determining our own lives.

2. *Mutuality in relationship.* This is Buber's I-Thou relationship. The intent here is a genuine encounter in which the independence and sovereignty of each person is not only respected but is a solid foundation for the meaningful relationship, a foundation which makes possible a deeper encounter, greater caring, and less selfishness. It teaches that we depersonalize and dehumanize at the cost of our humanness and personhood.

3. *Here-and-now perspective.* The third tenet of the humanistic ethic may be designated in a short-hand way as the "here-and-now" perspective. This reminds us that we live only at the present moment; it does not mean devaluing the past and ignoring the potential of the future, but in a very real sense understanding that the past is mute and only the interpretation we make of it today gives it meaning. It emphasizes that we are in this moment doing much that will determine the future and that it is through the ever-flowing and constant flux in the present stream of consciousness that we realize our own potential. A result of this present-valuing perspective, is that we tend to reduce our emphasis on achievement, habitual striving, competitive attainment and deferred living. Some interpret this as irresponsibility, but it is simply a realistic reminder that living truly today is probably the most important opportunity we have and is indeed the best preparation for tomorrow.

4. *Acceptance of all emotions.* The fourth aspect of the ethic is the acceptance of "negative emotions" such as pain, conflict, anger, and guilt. These are all considered a part of the human experience, integral parts of the human condition, fundamental aspects of human nature. In our society, obsessed with the medical model, there is a tendency to see these emotions as evidence of pathology, something shameful, or something radically wrong. Yes, they may indicate that something might be done about such suffering, but these feelings are not alien or disgraceful, but part of the human condition.

5. *Growth-oriented experiencing.* The centering of attention of the individual person, on human dignity, independence, on seeking authenticity, suggests that the humanistic ethic is at root more a value statement about how one experiences life, than anything else. As Bugental states, "Here it is important to recognize that the value orientation is not in terms of traditional good and bad, but is cast in a perspective which respects each person's efforts to do what he can with his life and appreciates his gains in authenticity while regretting or even challenging his dropping back from what is potential."

This ethic centres its values around a perception of each person as worthy in his own right and of genuine relationship as one of life's prime goods. This centering is more evident in the communication that exists among people who share commitment to the humanistic ethic. Apparently this value orientation of humanistic psychology is obvious to students of psychology.

Recently M. S. Lindauer (1967) asked the students in an introductory psychology course to compare humanistic psychology and "conventional" psychology in terms of their orientations. In the table below the terms used by the students are identified as they compared humanistic psychology and conventional psychology.

Humanistic Psychology	Conventional Psychology
1. Whole	1. Fragmented
2. Free will	2. Deterministic
3. Focus on problems; nonscience; role of introspection, experience and intuition	3. Focus on methodology, science, behaviour
4. The individual, the unique	4. The group, the generalizable
5. Does refer to conventional psychology	5. Does not refer to humanistic psychology
6. Abstract, philosophical, subjective, impractical, poetic language	6. Precise, operational, logical, rational, realistic, mathematical language
7. Man	7. Animals
8. Self, consciousness, value emotions	8. Physiology, physics
9. Complex	9. Simple, limited
10. Uplifts man, virtues of man, the positive	10. Debases man, vices of man, the negative

The distinctions appear to be clear to some students and they do seem to favour the humanistic traditions. There are, however, some problems with the humanistic approach.

Irvin L. Child (1973) in *Humanistic Psychology and the Research Tradition*, has stated some of the virtues of humanistic psychology but balances the discussion with an acknowledgement of its defects. The virtuous elements are respect for individual initiative and freedom, and the desire to expand these. Humanistic psychology also has the virtue of fitting what seems to be an enduring and universal value of human life—a regard for individual responsibility. The expansion of individuality is not always valued even through it clearly should be. Humanistic psychology in taking as its basic model the responsible human being, freely making choices among the bewildering possibilities open to him, presents a view of man compatible with this enduring value of human society.

When man studies the earth he is imposing his own values on objects that may be irrelevant to them. When man studies man he is studying "objects," like himself, who are characterized by an orientation toward values. A model that makes values irrelevant to man's behaviour may have bad moral consequences.

Another virtue identified by Child is that humanistic psychology readily leads into the discussion of personal ideals, fulfillment and self-actualization. The openness of humanistic psychology is another of its virtues. Humanistic psychology has a certain readiness to be surprised, an openness to possible facts which a more rigid and closed system might dismiss.

Finally, Child states that the most persuasive virtue is the "intuitive rightness" of the model. In claiming "intuitive rightness" for a human model of man, it is asserted that this model agrees with most people's intuitive impression of what it is like to be a human being and that this agreement is a very important item of positive evidence for the validity of the model.

Pursuing a discussion of the defects of humanistic approach, Child states that one great difficulty with the writings of humanistic psychologist is vagueness. The concepts used are often fraught with ambiguities. It is often difficult to tell what precisely is meant and easy to support that nothing very definite is intended. Terms such as authenticity, existential neurosis, self-actualization often lack precise operational definitions.

Related to the vagueness of the concepts, is the lack of verifiability. Humanistic psychologists often make statements which are not easily verifiable. This is seriously complicated by the apparent lack of interest in verifiability. Abraham Maslow, a leader of "the third force," has often been criticized for his lack of interest in the testability of his concepts. Rarely did he or his students empirically test research ideas suggested by his models.

Child identifies another defect of humanistic psychology: the apparent smugness with which these psychologists approach the understanding of man. Many humanistic psychologists are quite confident about their intuitive understanding of human behaviour. Another defect is what Child calls the "trend toward sentimentality." He compares the descriptions of man by humanistic psychologists to those associated with simple religious optimism, emphasizing the power of "positive thinking" and the infinite capacity of human will to achieve good. Child refers to this as sentimental fantasy. For psychology of any colour or persuasion to retain any usefulness there must be much more to it than this sentimentality. But where else can we look today for a frank and honest discussion of values, in a world confronted by a value crisis!

This crisis of values has some very interesting implications for our youngsters and their socialization experiences. Midge Decter addresses herself to this question in an open letter to the young, published recently in *Atlantic Monthly* (1975). Let me paraphrase her position. She asks the painful question of children: why have our young found it so hard to take their rightful places in the world? Why have the hopes of their parents seemed so impossible of attainment? Our children were supposed to be the executives, the professionals of tomorrow's world; they were to become the artists, the intellectuals; among them we would find our leaders in social reform, business, and politics. They would tend our institutions, and think the influential thoughts and they would add sensitive human contours to our world.

They were bright and gifted, we were told over and over again. Yes, they were gifted and very bright but they (according to Decter) seem infernally content to remain exactly as they were, passive, and unresisting. They have taken themselves out of schools and other institutions by the thousands, and when we asked why we were told that the young were too good to suffer the uninspired, dreary, conventional impositions being made upon their minds and spirits. We were told, rather, that the young would lead us out of evil, heedless materialism, and bring an end to senseless violence, lust, and greed that sickened our society.

So they dropped out and copped out, and we were told that this was so because our children were trying to fulfill a need to return to natural living and natural being. Our children turned their backs on striving for excellence in all things because they were attempting to transcend the nasty competitive drive inherent in the North American way of life; instead they were moving toward brotherhood and gentleness. We worried when our children came close to "blow-ing" their "ever-loving minds" with a variety of pharmacological agents never seen before in the history of medical science: but we were told that when our youngsters were "zonked on grass, cranking up on speed, or mainlining smack" that they were attempting to intensify life's experience, daring to recover the passion and love the world had denied us all.

Midge Decter summarizes her position by identifying three assertions she feels characterizes the young today:

1. The children of today are more than usually incapable of facing, tolerating, or withstanding difficulty of any kind. Their single most important word has been "hassle." To be hassled meant to be subjected to difficulty of an incomprehensi-ble and intolerable sort of something.
2. Our children are more than usually self-regarding. No one working with the young can have failed to notice the serenity, the sublime, unconscious, unblinking assur-ance with which they accept our attentions to them.
3. The third thing to be noticed is that our children are more than usually lacking in the capacity to stand their ground without reference, either negative or positive, to their parents.

She argues, "If our young are self-regarding and we have a sense of failure, it may be because you and I refused to stand for ourselves, for both the correct-ness and hard-earned value of our own sense of life. Our contentions with the young were based on quiet appeal, not on the grounds of natural authority. We failed to make ourselves the final authority on good and bad, right and wrong, and bear the consequences of what might turn out to be a life battle with the young." Even though they may have been the most indulged generation in history, they were also the most abandoned, particularly by those people who endlessly professed how much they cared. According to Decter, we did not believe sufficiently in ourselves, and then we were puzzled by the subtle lack of respect which characterized our young. Our faith in our own values was fragile and hesitant so, too, our youngster's faith: fragile and hesitant.

Faith in our values (or even a discussion of the differences in values held), and a failure to communicate to our young some kind of value system has led to some far-reaching difficulties in today's families. We have been told and we believed that the best atmosphere in which to bring up the young was a value-free context. We came to believe in the neutrality of values.

Humanistic psychology and values education hopes to rekindle interest in and pursuit of value discussions. The implications for the socialization of the child are quite obvious. One objective is a renewed faith in ourselves through open discussions of values.

It is this belief in man which may perhaps turn out to be the most important dimension of humanistic ethic. These beliefs may lead to a new faith in the entire human enterprise, if only as a self-fulfilling prophecy.

In a very important paper Leon Eisenberg (1972) argues this way: what we believe of man affects the behaviour of men, for beliefs determine what each expects of the other. What we choose to believe about the nature of man has important social consequences.

He states: "The Planets will move as they always have, whether we adopt a geocentric or a heliocentric view of the heavens. It is only the equations we generate to account for those motions that will be more or less complex. The motions of the planets are sublimely indifferent to our earthbound astronomy. But the behaviour of humankind is not independent of the theories of human behaviour that men adopt."

He traces the recent history of our attitudes toward the mentally ill. When we assumed that the insane were violent, we chained them to the walls and they raged violently like madmen: we told you so! Later when insanity was equated with social incompetence, the sick were protected and exiled to the back wards of our institutions: the result was the chronicity of the mentally and socially incompetent patients. Self-fulfilling prophecies!

Eisenberg does not want to be mistaken, however! He knows that psychosis is more than social convention; but the course the illness takes is profoundly affected by the milieu in which it occurs, and also affected by the attitudes held by the caretakers in these institutions. We know the profound effects of placebos; we know that in schools children's performances are profoundly affected by teachers' attitudes toward them and their abilities; our confidence in social and political institutions is that which sustains them.

What we have done least well is making a convincing case for the brotherhood of man. Today, the brotherhood (or sisterhood) has become a precondition for our survival.

When people raise value questions, one question seems to transcend other questions: do we have the compassion that our times require? Compassion is indeed a significant moral, ethical, and spiritual issue. It is interesting to note that all of the world's great religions have this compassionate empathy as the central tenet in their teachings. Tussing (1959) cites the following:

> Buddhism—Hatred is not diminished by hatred at any time. Hatred is diminished by love; this is *the* eternal law.
> Christianity—Therefore, all things whatsoever ye would that men should do to you, do ye even so to them.
> Confucianism—Confucious was asked: "Is there one word that sums up the basis of all good conduct?" And he replied, "Is not 'reciprocity' that word? What you yourself do not desire, do not put before others."
> Islam—No one is a true believer until he loves for his brother what he loves for himself.
> Judaism—Do not unto others that which is hateful to you.

Perhaps you and I are involved in something which is quite massive and overwhelming: trying to create and perpetuate a world in which promises are kept. Indeed it is a very important trust. There is a stanza about this in W. H. Auden's poem "The Shield of Achilles." On the old shield in Homer's time, there is a dancing space, and athletes are at their games; on the new shield of the 1970's there is a weed choked field:

> A ragged urchin, aimless and alone,
> Loitered about that vacancy; a bird
> flew up to a safety from his well-aimed stone;
> That girls are raped, that two boys knife a third;
> were axioms to him who's never heard
> Of any world where promises were kept.
> Or one could weep because another wept.

Humanistic psychology has as its goal that central responsibility to create and perpetuate a world where promises are kept.

References

Alinsky, S. *Reveille For Radicals.* Chicago: University of Chicago Press, 1946.

Bernard, V.; Ottenberg, P. and Redl, F. "Dehumanization." In N. Sanford and C. Comstock (eds.), *Sanctions for Evil.* San Francisco: Jossey-Bass Inc., 1971.

Buber, Martin. *I and Thou.* New York: Scribner, 1937.

Buhler, C. *Introduction to Humanistic Psychology.* Monterey: Brooks/Cole Co., 1972.

Child, I. L. *Humanistic Psychology and the Research Tradition.* New York: John Wiley and Sons, 1973.

Cousins, Norman. "The Case for Hope" (editorial). *Saturday Review,* December 26, 1970.

Decter, Midge. "A Letter to the Young." *Atlantic Monthly* 235 (1975):33-38.

Dilthey, W. *Meaning in History.* Edited by H. P. Richman. London: Allen and Unwin, 1961.

Eisenberg, L. "The Nature of Human Nature." *Science* 176 (1972):123-128.

Frankl, V. *Man's Search for Meaning.* Boston: Beacon Press, 1959.

Friedman, L. "Society and Its Enemies." *Nation* 218 (1974):424-426.

Fromm-Reichman, F. "Loneliness." *Psychiatry* 22 (1959):1-16.

Jourard, S. "Experimenter-Subject Dialogue." Cited in Bugental, *Challenges of Humanistic Psychology,* 1967.

Kafka, F. Letter, December 6, 1911, cited by Erich Heller. In *The Disinherited Mind.* Cambridge: Bowes and Bowes, 1952.

Kahn, H. and Wiener, A. J. *The Year 2000.* New York: Macmillan, 1967.

Laing, Ronald. *The Politics of Experience.* New York: Pantheon Books, 1967.

Liederman, P. H. "Loneliness: A Psychodynamic Interpretation." In E. S. Shneidman and M. J. Ortega (eds.), *Aspects of Depression.* Boston: Little, Brown, Co., 1969.

Lindauer, M. S. "Student Views of Humanistic vs. Conventional Conventions of Psychology in the First Psychology Course." *Journal of Humanistic Psychology* (Fall, 1967):128-138.

Maddi, S. R. "The Existential Neurosis." *Journal of Abnormal Psychology* 72 (1967):311-325.

Matson, F. W. "Whatever Became of the Third Force?" Presidential address, Association of Humanistic Psychology, August 29, 1969. Cited by C. Buhler, *Introduction to Humanistic Psychology.* Monterey: Brooks/Cole Co., 1972.

May, Rollo. "Toward the Ontological Basis of Psychotherapy." *Existential Inquiry* 1 (1969),5-7.

————————. "Will, Decision and Responsibility." *Review of Existential Psychology and Psychiatry* 109 (1961):249.

Pappenheim, F. *The Alienation of Modern Man.* New York: Monthly Review Press, 1959.

Rosenthal, A. M. *Thirty-Eight Witnesses.* New York: McGraw-Hill, 1964.

Schreiber, F. *Sybil.* Chicago: Regnery, 1973.

Silberman, C. *Crisis in the Classroom.* New York: Random House, 1970.

Slater, P. *The Pursuit of Loneliness.* Boston: Beacon Press, 1970.

Sullivan, H. S. *The Interpersonal Theory of Psychiatry.* New York: W. W. Norton, 1953.

Sykes, G. *Alienation: The Cultural Climate of our Time.* New York: Geo. Braziller, 1964.

Tolstoi, L. *The Death of Ivan Ilych.* New York: The New American Library, 1960.

Tussing, L. *Psychology for Better Living.* New York: John Wiley and Sons, Inc., 1959.

Watson, J. B. *Behaviourism.* Chicago: University of Chicago Press, 1959.

Yablonsky, L. *Robopaths.* Baltimore: Penguin Books, Inc., 1972.

VALUES AND THE SOCIAL WORKER

Francis J. Turner
Dean, Faculty of Social Work
Wilfrid Laurier University

Social workers have long stressed the importance of understanding and working within the value structure of the client. It is only recently that we have become increasingly aware that the place of values in the therapeutic process is a more involved, subtle and influential factor than we had previously thought. Clearly the final word on this topic has not yet been said; indeed we are probably just beginning to appreciate the importance of devoting careful scrutiny to this component of therapy.

The purpose of this paper is to present some preliminary ideas on this current interest in values and their relevance for contemporary social work clinical practice. It is hoped that this material will be of interest and assistance to educators, especially those with a particular concern about a person's values, how they are learned, modified and developed. This common interest in values by both social workers and educators may well be an important congruence of thought that will serve to bring the two professions closer and thus enhance the effectiveness of both.

Any individual engaged in the practice of one of the human professions is sharply aware that there are many individuals, families and groups in society for whom personal value systems and value orientations are in flux rather than unchanging as we once thought. This phenomena becomes of particular interest to social workers, in that some of these persons in value conflict are turning to social workers for help in dealing with this kind of problem.

This form of help-seeking represents a new task for social workers; a task that in turn creates some uncertainties. The uncertainty emerges from the challenge that this kind of problem makes for a tradition of social work that held that client values were to be accepted and respected and not altered. The therapist, on his part, was to keep his or her values private and rarely were they to be shared with the client lest the client be influenced by these values. Whether social workers did adhere to this value taboo is a moot question at best.

But clearly this tradition is now being questioned. Social workers in clinical practice are finding in their caseloads individuals, groups and families whose stress in psychosocial functioning is directly related to value and value orientation conflicts, sometimes recognized and sometimes not. Thus we can no longer see the client's value system as a private domain. We are being asked to look at it, and get involved in it, and indeed to help alter it. In so doing our own value systems come into play.

It is this phenomenon of being asked to respond to persons with value dilemmas that has resulted in the current reevaluations of the place of values in therapy. In the remainder of this paper some dimensions of this reevaluation will be discussed.

Since this area of thought is an emerging and developing one terminology is not uniform in professional communications; thus before proceeding some clarification is necessary, especially in regard to the term value orientations. In this paper my use of the term *value orientation* is close to Kluckhohn's and Strotbeck's (1961) use of it. In my view it approaches the concept of *value systems* as used by Milton Rokeach (1973), although he questions that this use of the term would fit his concept of value systems. I am comfortable that it does.

Value orientations refer to those pragmatically oriented, preferential choices almost automatic in operation that assist individuals to develop patterns of selection from the vast array of daily decisions and choices. Value systems or belief systems are more conscious but less directly operationalized. If there is a difference between value orientations and value systems it might lie in the idea that value orientations are somewhat less obvious than belief systems.

Every person, in the process of social interaction, during the course of a single day faces a wide spectrum of alternative behaviours from which to choose to meet the demands of the many roles in which he or she is engaged. A significant number of these decision-making situations involve the following areas; our relationships with other people, the nature of activity, time, and relationships with material things. Many of the decisions that we make are spontaneous, with little or no observable conscious reflection. If this were not so our lives would consist of an almost unbearable number of decision-making processes. Our ability to act in this virtual spontaneous manner is the result of our having internalized a set of attitudes that represent an ordering of priorities in the significant life situations mentioned above. It is this set of attitudes that in this paper are called value orientations.

In the following pages the question of values and values orientations will be examined from a four-fold viewpoint: the value bases of therapy; the values of the therapist; the value problems of the client; and the value orientation of the client to therapy.

The Value Base of Therapy

In the professional literature heavy emphasis has not been placed on examining the value assumptions which underlie modern psychotherapy. Thus even less has been put on whether a change in this base is taking place. One of the underlying assumptions of this paper is that indeed a change is taking place.

In spite of the paucity of research a strong case can be made that up to the recent past the value basis of much of North American psychotherapy reflected the first-order value orientation profile of society as described by Kluckhohn. This profile posits that North American society reflected a "future oriented," "doing," "individualistic," "man over nature" first order value orientation. Therefore, an approach to therapy that reflects this orientation would be "future oriented." Indeed this was the case. Up to the recent past, one could see in therapy a future orientation in the stress that was put on seeking solutions to current problems to insure future developmental goals and future achievements. Therapy was also "doing oriented" in that the client was expected to work on his problems and the work was seen as hard work, maybe even painful. Therapy, in addition, was "individualistic oriented"; certainly there was some group work practiced but the focus of therapy was on individual change. Finally, therapy reflected that "man was to conquer over himself and the world of nature" and not to accept the status quo or the influence of nature on him.

But it appears there has been a dramatic shift in this profile and in the seventies therapy now appears to strongly reflect a new profile. Again using the Kluckhohn scheme I suggest that the following profile now underlies much current therapeutic endeavours. Today's therapy favours a strong "present orientation" in which interest in a client's past and future is given much less stress. Similarly, there is much emphasis on experiential therapy in much of current therapy. This emphasis strongly reflects a "being orientation" in place of the earlier problem solving and doing approach. The recent dramatic shifts away from one-to-one therapy to group therapy and family therapy reflects a therapeutic shift to a "collateral value orientation." In addition, increasing interest in transcendental meditation and other approaches to therapy based on eastern mystic philosophies, as well as the growing importance of existentialism indicate a move to a "man with nature" orientation rather than our former "man over nature."

Clearly at this point these are only speculations briefly identified and should be subject to further critical examination. But it is an important point because it is presumed that a practitioner's choice of an approach to therapy and his or her attitudes to therapy are differentially influenced by his or her individual value orientation profile.

The Values of the Therapist

Along with the shift in the kinds of therapeutic styles that are currently in vogue, shifts that are presumed to be related to a societal reordering of value orientations, it is clear that therapists in general and social workers in particular have also had to come to terms with their own and society's value changes. Although codes of ethics that regulate the practice of social work have not changed dramatically, social workers as individuals have had to meet and come to terms with the same questions as members of society and like many others have had to learn to live with unanswered value dilemmas about critical ethical issues. Thus such things as civil authority, duties to one's country, one's neighbours, and one's significant others, questions of life and death before birth and at the end of life, are clearly topics where earlier moral certitude no longer

exists. This uncertainty is puzzling, troubling and painful for the mature therapist whose self image customarily includes a sense of comfort and completion.
That is a sense that one's moral development was complete and matured. Such
completion was, of course, not in a rigid inflexible format. In an Eriksonian way
it was accepted that throughout life there was on-going growth and development; thus some shaping and tuning up, some enhancement, some enrichment
was accepted and desired as an attribute of the mature person. But this concept
did not include the possibility of serious and indeed fundamental challenges that
required dramatic reordering of ethics and values. Such reorientations that leave
in their wake uncertainties and dilemmas were not expected to be a part of the
comfortable mature person's psyche.

Troubling as these personal struggles may be, society expects that a prac-
ticing professional will be able to internalize these struggles and keep one's own
private conflicts out of the therapeutic situation. This is indeed not a new
challenge to professionals; we have long been accustomed and experienced in the
application of a therapeutic rubric that cautioned against the imposition of
personal values on a client. Probably we have never followed fully this dictum;
indeed most clinicians are aware that clients' attitudes and views on many life
areas are influenced through the therapeutic encounter. This is especially so
when the worker has comfortably integrated a particular value set. But when the
worker is not comfortable in a value position and is aware that the client may
expect him to be so, there is a further stress put on the helping relationship.

Value Problems

Thus a new phenomenon in clinical practice has emerged that has made this
style of value neutrality untenable. It is the emerging trend, mentioned in the
beginning of this article, that there are many persons for whom the current
phenomenon of changing values is itself the source of serious psychosocial stress
for which professional help is sought. Thus social workers are increasingly dealing with clients with serious psychosocial problems in which there is a significant
component of value stress sometimes recognized and sometimes not. The clients
referred to here are persons and families diagnostically within the range of
normal functioning yet in need of skilled help. Clearly the problems become
even more complex when a value problem emerges in persons who are also
experiencing stress from other sources, either internal or external. For the purpose of this paper we will restrict our remarks only to persons clinically assessed
as normals.

Although the data on this trend in clinical practice are scarce, already a
patterning of some of the emerging problems can be described. First, there is
the person who is experiencing stress clearly related to their being in a transitional value situation but not recognizing the stress originating from this source.
This person may not even be fully aware of the extent of the shift that has taken
place in themselves and even much less aware that this value change is causing

personal concern and stress in other life areas.

A second type of value problem that has been identified is seen in those clients who, unlike the group mentioned in the preceding paragraph, have recognized that there has been an internal altering of values and a resulting shift in the concept of desirable and responsible behaviour. The principle motive that influences such clients to seek help is their inability to follow through on the implications of this inner change. Examples of this are seen in persons strongly attracted to the possibility of changing careers, changing life styles, terminating or beginning relationships, but unable to follow through comfortably in seeking these emerging new life goals.

A third cluster of problems with a value base consists of those persons who recognize the shift in themselves, and are prepared to follow through on the implications of the shift. The problems arise when it is found that significant others in the client's life are not ready to accept the implications of the changes. This problem appears to be prevalent in many of the marital situations that show up in our practices. Thus we see marriages where there have been several years of a reasonably stable, apparently healthy, relationship between essentially mature persons. Nevertheless, conflicts of a serious nature begin to emerge as one or both partners begin to change attitudes toward broad life objectives, role perceptions, or moral conduct. This type of conflict requires persons to reassess such differences, their implications for self and others, and often to make difficult choices about the future of the relationship, be it with a spouse, other segments of the family, or with significant others in one's life.

No doubt there are other clusterings of cases with linked similarities. The three groups thus far identified serve to establish the existence of the type of case referred to here.

The Value Orientation of the Client to Therapy

The theory and practice of psychotherapy has always considered the concept of resistance a significant component of the helping process. Thus it was understood that although one part of the client would be consciously aware of the hurt and suffering being experienced and of the need for help, another part of our complex personalities would resist the help being sought out of a fear of the unknown, and a resistance to let parts of us be seen by others.

In addition to unconscious resistance we have also been aware of clients resisting change when help was perceived as not being sought voluntarily or being imposed on the client. It now appears that we could have another type of stress in the therapeutic relationship that is much like resistance in that it impedes progress. This relates to the stress that may arise from a different view of therapy by worker and client.

In the past we have tended to see the process of therapy itself as being a unitary process with a clear value base. But as was suggested above, if this was ever true, it is no longer. Clients and therapists do have a range of value orientations to therapy and such diversities must be taken into account as a part of the process. Thus some clients expect therapy to relieve hurt immediately, and without self-understanding; other clients expect therapy to give them understanding of themselves and others in their lives; still others expect therapy to help them to uncover and come to terms with influences from their past. These are only a few examples; many other orientations and expectations of therapy could be identified.

In a similar way therapists have a diverse range of attitudinal orientations to the therapeutic process. Because of this orientational spectrum it is inevitable that some of the orientations between client and therapist could represent a good fit that could enhance the therapeutic process. On the other hand there are undoubtedly other value clusters that represent a poor fit that would inhibit or indeed preclude the possibility of a successful therapeutic process. Clearly, this phenomenon of differing value orientation towards the therapeutic process must be given serious consideration. To fail to do so could well result in the establishing of roadblocks for an effective helping process. Such roadblocks could easily be misunderstood or unrecognized.

Therapeutic Learning

One of the advantages of any new development in a profession is that new learning and new understanding comes from the struggle to find responsible and effective ways to deal with the new phenomena. And so in this instance we have already learned much. Some of this learning has been an enrichment of what has long been known; in other instances the learning represents new insights and understandings of human behaviour. Also some of the learning has been related to identifying what we don't know.

Thus, we have learned that ethical and value systems are not as stable and unchanging as we have traditionally thought. Whether philosophers and educators held this view or not, social workers have considered that ethical codes and value systems had a fixed and permanent component to them. Our recent experiences with clients have made us more aware than before of the ability of individuals to make dramatic and fundamental shifts in standards and behaviour. This in turn helps to reinforce in us an optimism about man's ability to change, adapt and mature.

In a related way we have also learned that this ability to adjust to new norms and values is not as age-related as we had once thought. Indeed, some of the most flexible people observed in recent years have been old, and some of the most conservative and value constricted are among the young. This observation should lead us to be more open about our perceptions of the characteristics of the various ages of growth and development. In particular we now have further evidence to support the idea that the period of aging can indeed be a period of ongoing growth and development.

A further learning component in dealing with value stress relates to behaviour in crisis situations. There is no doubt that the intensity of stress created on some clients in value transitional situations results in crisis reactions of various intensities. As theory postulates, one of the advantages of a crisis situation is the opportunity it provides for the maturational process to continue. As a person's accustomed coping mechanisms prove to be inadequate in crisis, there frequently results a resurgence of earlier unresolved issues from the person's developmental history. When these components of unfinished developmental work are recognized by the alert therapist there is an opportunity to work on them, thus aiding the client in moving to a more mature level of functioning.

A particular facet of such reawakened developmental material relates to the concept of superego development and moral development. In the ego psychology literature on superego development, stress has been put on the censoring, restricting, and inhibiting components of the superego. In general the concept has had a negative quality to it. What is frequently overlooked is that the concept of superego development includes components of a person's attitude towards himself, his perceived self-esteem or lack of it, his attitudes to authority, firstly to parents and later to all authority.

> The superego goal for the maturing person is the development of a psychic structure that fosters the establishment of norms, attitudes and identities in a way that is increasingly autonomous. This stance permits an individual throughout life to set his own life rules and attitudes and to select the societal systems by which he will be influenced, rather than be directed with little autonomy. (Turner, 1975, p. 287)

Generally it has been suggested that this process is complete by early adulthood. By then a person has developed a functioning value system and self-image that can accommodate both his sense of autonomy and the expectations of the significant others and societal systems in his life space. But as we have said we know now that a person's value systems can be seriously upset and diametrically altered in many current situations. Thus, because of the close connection between a person's value orientation and their developmental history it is increasingly clear that challenges to a person's values touch very directly issues related to a person's early developmental history.

It is this psychodynamic component of value development that increases the intensity of value stress and can complicate what, on the surface, appears to be a mature discussion of the implications of value changes. Such dynamic factors become even more complicated when the client includes adolescents, experiencing their own identity issues, and still more complicated when the adolescent's parents are themselves in value conflict. This in turn becomes even more complex when some of the value issues are related to sexual mores in view of their close connection to psychodynamic developmental history. And to cap this area of potential confusion, add to the above the possibility that the therapist is also experiencing value stress in his or her own life.

Implications for Treatment

The above is not an effort to present an exhaustive review of the situation but only to give some general dimensions to the clinical challenge resulting from a societal situation of dramatic value transition. If these dimensions have validity then it can be established that a professional in a psychotherapeutic role has six specific tasks related to problems where value stress is a factor, in addition to his other case management responsibilities.

1. The first of these is related to the diagnostic component of practice. Because of the high probability of value stress in current society it is important in assessing a client, his situation, his needs and wishes, that the social worker keep to the fore the possibility of value stress being present in the client's life. This is especially important because of the concomitant high possibility that the effects of value stress may not be recognized as a precipitating factor. Value stress may be present and unrecognized as a complicating factor in situations where other problem components are more easily recognized.

2. The secondary task of the social worker in clinical practice has been referred to earlier. It is the need of therapists to be alerted to the possibility that unresolved issues of a developmental nature may be aroused in situations of value stress. If these reactions that have their origins in the past are not properly recognized then it will be impossible to understand fully the current situation and thus to intervene appropriately. At this time all the various interconnections between current value stress situations and earlier developmental history have not been identified, although the role of the developing superego has been described as being one of the important interconnections.

3. In a less problem-focussed sphere, but of great therapeutic importance, the third specific task related to the topic of values is to include in the overall case study an effort to understand the client's value orientations especially as they relate to problem solving activities. As was suggested in the earlier part of this paper it is highly likely that a person's value orientations will effect the extent to which he or she is, or is not, identified or comfortable with a particular modality of treatment or theoretical approach to treatment. If this is so, it may well be that the therapist not only has to assess the problem areas accurately but also to assess the kind of intervention that is the best fit for the client; e.g., reality therapy versus psychodynamic therapy, short-term versus long, individual versus group, to mention only a few of the dependent variables.

4. The above three tasks have stressed understanding the client. However, since the social worker may be also experiencing value stress in his or her own life there is a new dimension present in the clinical role. It is the need to be continually seeking awareness of what is happening in the therapist's own life from the viewpoint of values. This stress in self-awareness, of course, is not a new dimension to social workers. What is new is the possibility that the social worker may also be caught up in value struggles, that in turn may have reactivated early psychodynamic material. If so, there is always the possibility that the worker cannot objectively assess particular situations.

5. In a similar vein the worker must also be aware of his own orientations to problem solving, therapeutic modalities, and theoretical systems of helping.

That is, the worker must attempt to insure that the profile of intervention selected is not unduly influenced by his or her own value preference for some interventive strategies over others. Unrecognized preferences for one approach to practice over another may well lead to selecting approaches that do not fit the client's own orientations to therapy and thus a new stress in the client's life is created.

6. The sixth task of the social worker is to be aware of the possibility of using external resources to assist specifically in helping the client come to terms with value conflicts. This could mean a different use of the clergyman, the philosopher, and the educator than have been customary up to the present. I am quite certain there are many persons who could be greatly assisted if they could find the opportunity to struggle with their specific value dilemmas with a person with special knowledge, interest, and skills in dealing with such questions. The social worker can indeed deal with the stress and anxiety caused by the effects of value changes but is not ordinarily equipped to provide assistance in the how of dealing with value problems.

In this vein we can move beyond the therapeutic role and discuss the preventative role that is possible in this area of values. Obviously educators who have moved into values education have identified the extent of the need of persons in society to learn skills in valuing; that is, of learning how to deal with value issues in their own life. I think it well behooves social workers to look into these expanding resources as potential resources both for their clients and indeed for themselves.

Summary

In this paper we have identified the effect of the current flux of values and value orientations on social work practice. Without attempting to exhaust the question, two important areas for the clinical social worker have been identified; the client's and worker's own values orientations related to problem solving and help seeking, as well as the more obvious situation of value stress.

An underlying theme of the paper is that the kinds of situations met in social work practice of a value type have strong similarities to those situations met by the educator. Indeed this might well be an area where the two professions can come together, understand each other better, and even collaborate in this crucial psychosocial area.

Social workers have not exploited fully the conceptual richness of value concepts. It has been thought that values were something the client had and the worker hid. Indeed this approach is no longer viable. To ignore it could result in our underserving our clients. We are now beginning to understand that even the existence of social work as a phenomenon in current society is a reflection of society's values towards problem solving; a value that is far from being universal in its acceptance.

References

Kluckhohn, Florence R. and Strotbeck, Fred L. *Variations in Value Orientations.* Evanston, Ill.: Row Peterson and Co., 1961.

Rokeach, Milton. *The Nature of Human Values.* New York: The Free Press, 1973.

Turner, Francis J. "Effect of Value Reevaluation on Current Practice." *Social Casework* (May 1975).

EPILOGUE

WHERE ARE WE AND WHERE MIGHT WE GO IN VALUES EDUCATION?

John R. Meyer
Faculty of Education
University of Windsor, Ontario

"Change" and "process" have been dominant concepts in the scholarly literature of most academic disciplines. No less have educational theory and practice been influenced by these concepts. The reactions of a major segment of the public are indicative of a quest to return to the last stable state. The essays by Debrock, Morgenson, and Turner have suggested the impact of such change in values upon various professions. Our work with parents, teachers, administrators, and trustees is a constant reminder of Brown's (1971) words:

> The most primal risk is that one will change. And the status quo is comfortable. Security, no matter how false or how well sustained by the denial of reality, seems preferable to "what might happen."

Several risks have been taken and changes made in values education since the last report (Meyer, 1975). It is again time to capture most of these changes in a descriptive overview of the state of the art in applied research. In a second part, it seems appropriate to comment on some current problems and future prospects.

Where Are We?

The projects and applied research activities that I am most familiar with are in Canada, Great Britain, and the United States. There is interest in New Zealand and Australia but little formalized into specific projects.

1. Canada

The core of activity has been in Ontario. This is an ongoing effort since at least 1968 when the Mackay report, *Religious Information & Moral Development*, was presented and when the Ontario Institute for Studies in Education initiated a conference and a pilot study in moral education.

During the past twelve months, the following events have occurred:

- Publications on various aspects of values education were produced
    - Brian Burnham, "Human Values Education: The New Dynamic in Program Development," *Education Canada* (Spring, 1975).
    - John R. Meyer, "Values Education: Some Reflections on a Pilot Project in Southern Ontario," *Comment on Education* 5:4 (April, 1975).

— *Moral/Values Clarification: A Comparison of Different Theoretical Models* (Toronto: Ontario Government Bookstore, 880 Bay Street, 1975).

— Special issues of: *The History and Social Science Teachers* (Fall, 1975); *The School Guidance Worker* (Nov./Dec., 1975).

— *Values Education: A Resource Booklet* Toronto: Ontario Secondary School Teachers' Federation, 60 Mobile Dr., Toronto, 1975).

- Local educational jurisdictions have either initiated or continued their efforts to develop materials, inservice select staff, and provide consultative services. The London, Halton, Hamilton, Scarborough, and the York County jurisdictions have been particularly committed to some or all of these aspects.

- The Ministry of Education has promulgated a guideline for the first six grades or levels of the elementary panel. *The Formative Years* has many references to education in human values and one special section. Professor Litke explores this in some depth in this volume. This has generated considerable interest at the local level.

- Professional Development for teachers through workshops and academic programmes has been widespread. Local jurisdictions, faculties and colleges of education, and professional associations (OSSTF & OPSMTF) have promoted such activities. In many cases, experienced teacher teams have been requested from both the Halton-Hamilton project and from OISE. The academic programming has developed at the undergraduate level at Wilfrid Laurier University (currently 3 courses) and OISE and Brock University continue a component in their M.Ed. programmes. Interest has been expressed in the faculties of education at Ottawa, Queen's, Western, Windsor, and Lakehead Universities.

- Preservice programmes for students in training for the teaching profession have emerged in optional courses at Toronto and Hamilton. Most of the departments in foundational subjects seem to offer one or more courses in values education.

- Annual conventions of professional associations have included one or more sections on the subject. The Ontario Education Association, the Ontario Association for Curriculum Development, the Ontario Guidance Association, and the Canadian Education Association have been a few of those sponsoring sections. Another invitational conference, featuring McPhail, Meyer, and Hersh and special workshops conducted by experienced teachers, was sponsored in St. Catherines, Ontario, by several local jurisdictions, the Ministry of Education, Brock University, and the OISE field office.

- Several publishers in Ontario have taken the initiative to promote the development and publication of learning materials at both the elementary and the secondary grade levels.

- Local values education projects in the Halton, Hamilton, London, and Scarborough Boards or jurisdictions have established positions for consultative staff of at least one experienced teacher who will devote all their energies to assisting their colleagues in various grades. This is, indeed, remarkable at a time of retrenchment for educational budgets.

- The joint project involving the neighboring jurisdictions of Halton and Hamilton will continue their efforts in two specific directions: Halton will disseminate materials at the K-6 levels and coordinate it with other core curricula, and Hamilton will extend their implementation to include the elementary and vocational panels on a family of schools basis. It may result that an experiment will be attempted at one or two schools to create the "just school." An evaluation phase will be continued and augmented with a student population of considerable size.

The goal of the project includes the four complementary objectives of promoting values development through the components of:

(1) *AWARENESS* to one's own and others' values

(2) *SENSITIVITY* to the feelings, attitudes, and values of others

(3) *MORAL REASONING* about value-laden issues

(4) *ETHICAL ACTION* which expresses or affirms prosocial behaviours.

When controversial issues arise either in an incidental manner or by structuring the curriculum, the teacher will monitor the environment so that certain expectations in values development will be promoted.

The specific objectives or learner outcomes that are expected may be grouped under the four complementary components of the curricular framework:

AWARENESS—This implies that the learner will be able to:
— Explore and discover a personal value system
— Clarify his/her personal and social values
— Establish priorities of values
— Observe the actions of self and others based on principles or values
— Recognize value-laden issues
— Express feelings openly
— Feel positive about oneself
— Appreciate individuality and diversity
— Identify some sources or influences of values
— Identify 6 value categories-concepts and one or more themes of each.

SENSITIVITY—This implies that the learner will be able to:
— Experience empathy towards the values, feelings, needs of others
— Role-play and demonstrate some social skills
— Recognize the strengths and weaknesses of self and others
— Respond in more mature ways to levels of social-perspective-taking
— Express greater degrees of moral reciprocity

— Relate personal values to peer and/or societal values and value systems
— Demonstrate and receive affection, influence, respect, responsibility, well-being, wisdom to and from others.

MORAL REASONING—This implies that the learner will be able to:
— Analyze personal value conflicts
— Reflect on moral judgments and actions
— Interpret value-laden personal and public issues
— Use moral reasons and evidence for principled behaviours or actions
— Demonstrate critical thinking skills in resolving moral dilemmas
— Integrate values , into a system that is reasonably consistent and coherent
— participate in analysis and problem solving
— Express increasingly more mature and adequate responses to conflict situations
— Apply decision-making and valuing skills to moral problems.

AFFIRMATION—This implies that the learner will be able to:
— Express personal and social values in actions
— Apply the conclusions of the reasoning process
— Test social skills through involvement in school, family, or community projects
— Initiate efforts to cope with injustices that are resolvable
— Exert influence in a constructive manner in conflict situations
— Present evidence that is clear and consistent with universal principles for the justification of one's position
— Demonstrate or express the extended or suggested activities of one or more of the current modules.

The evidence from the experiences of the past few years indicates that these four components are necessary for a holistic framework. Social growth and education is multifaceted. It has been demonstrated that when any one of the components is isolated and becomes the prime or exclusive focus, then negative reaction and little growth or development occurs. In the social sciences the last component has been severely neglected and it is much of the expression of the other three. Fred Newman (1975) has made a case for this at the secondary level when he advocates the goal of "environmental competencies." Johnson and Ochoa are wrestling with a social action curriculum at The Florida State University. The public at-large calls for improved citizenship qualities from the learner clients.

The Ontario Institute for Studies in Education has shifted its emphasis to teacher-educator awareness and skill development in values or moral education. A small team has concentrated on providing workshops and seminars for those engaged in the training of teachers at the faculties and colleges of education throughout Ontario. The project will produce a manual or handbook that will be useful to this sector of professionals.

Pockets of activity do exist in other provinces of Canada but information is limited. Alberta is digesting a lengthy evaluative report on the new social sciences curriculum which contains a large section on valuing. British Columbia is concluding a struggle with a rightest group wishing to establish a "values school" that would teach only Judaeo-Christian values. The maritime provinces are slowly promoting interest by means of an interested core of inserviced teachers. The College of Cape Breton continues to offer education courses in values in their summer programme and in conferences.

Few educational jurisdictions have really placed a priority on developing and implementing curricular programmes in affective education to the extent of those aforementioned Ontario Boards.

II. Great Britain

Since 1967, the Schools Council has commissioned projects in moral education under the direction of Peter McPhail at Hughes Hall, Cambridge University. The project for 13-16 year olds devised curricular methods and teaching materials to help students adopt a considerate style of life, i.e., to adopt patterns of behaviour which take other people's needs, interests, and feelings into account as well as their own. It was interested in both attitudinal and behavioural change. The materials were published in packets by Longman of England and then in North America by Argus Communications. The project concluded that adolescents learn much of their behaviour by social experiment and that behaviour is contagious so that the principal moral influence on adolescents is the treatment that they receive from others.

The second project for 8-13 year olds recognizes that moral education should begin when children experience their first social encounters. In a survey, children responded to open-ended questions regarding their behavioural reactions to pleasant and unpleasant experiences caused by others. The results indicate that social learning involves moral situations and nurturant relationships. There will be a variety of learning materials forthcoming.

III. United States of America

Again due to the many changes and the lack of specific information, my description of developments in the U.S.A. will be cursory. The California Association for Moral Education continues to provide a forum for a network of state activities. As usual, there is a continuum from one extreme to the other, i.e., the value clarifiers to the cognitive developmentalists.

The Massachusetts centers continue their respective dimensions, i.e., the humanists and clarifiers at Massachusetts University and the developmentalists at Harvard and Boston Universities. Much of the work of the latter group is described in the special issue of *Social Education: Cognitive-Developmental Approach to Moral Education*, 40:4 (April 1976), guest edited by collaborator Ted Fenton at Carnegie-Mellon University.

In New York State there are two projects worth watching, namely, SEARCH, organized through the Humanities curriculum section at the State

Department of Education and Tom Lickona's work at SUNY at Cortland. After several years of anticipation, a major publication has appeared that should certainly give more credibility to the field. Lickona has assembled twenty essays under three divisions: theory, research, and social issues. It would appear that this book, *Moral Development and Behavior* (Holt, Rinehart & Winston, 1976) will be more meaningful for the advanced student and specialist than for the practitioner in pre-university classrooms.

Another development from New York is the publication of *Moral Education Forum* (Hunter College, 695 Park Ave., New York, N.Y. 10021) under the general editorship of Lisa Kuhmerker. This commenced in rough form two years ago at Harvard. Now it appears in a polished format with input from a list of well-known associate and contributing editors. This promises to be a very productive vehicle for much of the news that is generated by the field throughout most of the world.

Two projects that are directly related to curriculum development and the production of learning materials are the Religion-Social Studies Curriculum Project from Florida State University and the "Skills for Ethical Action" project from Research for Better Schools, Inc. Rod Allen is completing the 4-6 grade level materials for field testing and Argus Communications will be publishing the 1-3 level materials under the title, *Learning About Religions/Social Studies*. The SEA project at RBS is now being field tested at the 7-8 levels. The materials are highly directive and encompass more than 30 lessons. They emphasize personal feelings, ethical sensitivity, and moral reasoning that should promote ethical action. There is concentration on improving communication and decision-making skills.

Another more recent project commissioned by the National Institute of Education is *Planning for Moral/Citizenship Education.* Research for Better Schools, Inc., is contracted to develop planning recommendations for research, development, and dissemination with the ultimate objective to develop moral/citizenship educational programs which will have an impact on American schools and society consistent with democratic values and principles.

The National Endowment for the Humanities has granted support for a moral education curriculum development project at the College of Stuebenville (Ohio) under Robert Hall and John Davis. Their prior research was published in *Moral Education in Theory and Practice* (Buffalo, N.Y.: Prometheus Books, 1975).

There is also a federally funded project at the K-12 grade levels in the school district of Tacoma, Washington.

Where Might We Go?

Though a plethora of studies and publications continues to confront us, there are a number of problematic areas that need a great deal more attention. Frequently one discovers that a hidden agenda or unnamed assumptions underpin certain projects in values education. It would be a real service to this emergent field if all or some of the following issues would be carefully examined.

(A) DEFINITIONS: There is a vast panorama of definitions for a value. There are an equal number of explanations for the interconnections of the affective domain, values, beliefs, morals, decision-making, and most of the components of a larger picture. It may be too early to expect much precision but writers need to be more explicit how they use terminology. Practitioners are easily perplexed by such imprecision and flexibility.

(B) LEARNING THEORY: Developmentalism or structuralism appears to satisfy the desire for an appropriate theoretical basis for values or moral development. However, there are relatively few longitudinal studies that impressively substantiate the positive effects of cognitive development and its impact or transference to prosocial behaviours. The demands for accountability, justification, and "product" tend to prevail in socializing circles. Somehow we need to be able to provide more tangible and hard data to ensure that what interventions are introduced will achieve the expected outcome. There are specialists working on this problem but what they need is more time and support.

There is an imperative to somehow involve the community more in gaining their support and cooperative efforts. The clamor for a return to the "basics" has the potential of diverting attention away from the concerns for affective education. The awareness of values education as a very powerful vehicle for logical or cognitive growth needs to be voiced strongly. The basics will be greatly enhanced if and when the values education framework is implemented.

(C) MORAL AGENTS: It is even perhaps more important to understand a particular philosophical frame of reference that holds that the human person and the public school are both moral agents. Parents and organized religion are also moral agents, i.e., sources of socializing in morality that effect the learner. It is not always clear who is responsible for what influences. Certainly the parents are primarily responsible but in many instances and for great periods of time they entrust this responsibility to the schools and to teachers. More recently, there are some trends that create conflict between two legitimate moral agents by both thrusting schools into the role of a parent (*in loco parentis*) and legally preventing disciplinary acts (Berger, 1976).

The assumption is that the school is a moral agent that has the responsibility to promote moral development as well as logical and social perspective-taking development. A bigger issue is HOW this shall be accomplished, i.e., whether by default or by design with preparation, focus, and resourcefulness. One might extend the argument and claim that the school which defaults in values development is a very real partner in the harvest of anti-social behaviours. This is also to say that a person who has not developed a reasonable and functional system of values is a personal and social hazard.

The territory of school responsibility includes the development of shared or unifying values and of personal values which contribute to the fulfillment of the intrinsic worth and dignity of the individual (Meyer, *SGW* 1975). If we are truly convinced that movement from heteronomy to autonomy is a desirable and attainable goal, then the "key issue is to bring the facilitation of autonomy from the unconscious, unplanned level to the level of conscious awareness" (Dittman, 1976).

(D) EVALUATION: Another crucial task for on-going development is that of refined evaluation by means of a variety of sophisticated (valid and reliable) instruments. I have already alluded to the demands of accountability and justification of programme. The analysis of learning materials in values education is refined (Superka, 1976). Kohlberg and team are completing another revision of the moral dilemma and reasoning scoring (see Gibbs, *et al.* herein). Burnham (1975), Damon, and Rest (1975,'76) are refining and completing their studies in moral issues surveys and interviews. Sanders is experimenting with several instruments closely allied to learning materials.

What we still lack is a comprehensive package that will assess all the major preconditions for morally mature action or behaviour over the range of school years from K-12. Wed this type of development to longitudinal studies and classroom interventions and you have compatible, credible, and productive marriage.

(E) COLLABORATION & ADMINISTRATION: One clear sign of the times in those countries in which values education is operative is that fiscal restraints are forcing a shift in priorities somewhat detrimental to the typical implementation patterns. This is not adverse to the health of the programme provided one is creative in suggesting new alternatives for development and implementation. We should not be permitted to "reinvent the wheel" by duplicating the development of materials or by perpetuating dependence on less effective methods of inservice.

Pressures have been applied to steer a course of action that demands collaboration and the discovery of alternatives for ways of doing things. It is evident that in highly structured and hierarchical jurisdictions, there must be conviction, commitment, and priority at the top eschelon. The support systems will then be guaranteed for the most vital person, the classroom practitioner, so that teacher commitment will be nourished. At the school level, the principal must see his/her role as one of a programme leader and implementer. Progress is made not because it is "fashionable" or the political thing to do but because human development in values education is what education is really all about. The notion of "faddism" or separateness cannot be tolerated.

Sometimes the right mixture of representation on an advisory committee can provide a marvelous buffer unit and a powerful leadership influence. We certainly need to get trustees, parents, administrators, teachers, and students together for the beginnings of the just school and just community or society concept.

It is not clear when and how the just school concept will be effective. It may be a direction that will prove the most effective prototype or model for extensive impact in an entire school district or jurisdiction. Again that takes time, tremendous collaboration, considerable inservice or retraining, concensus on objectives, stability, and perseverance.

Some ventures in values education are working with degrees of achievement. More opportunities are required to provide both development and implementation. We can rejoice that we have come this far in the company of so many concerned and dedicated educators and learners.

References

Berger, M. L. "Student Rights and Affective Education: Are They Compatible?" *Education Leadership* 33, 6 (March 1976):460-62.

Brown, G. I. *Human Teaching for Human Learning.* New York: Viking Press, 1971.

Burnham, B. "The Important Considerations Survey: A Measure of Moral Reasoning Power." *The School Guidance Worker* 31, 2 (Nov./Dec. 1975):33-8.

Dittman, J. "Individual Autonomy: The Magnificent Obsession." *Education Leadership* 33, 6 (March 1976):463-67.

Meyer, J. R. "Projects and Prospects: Applied Research in Values Education." In J. Meyer, B. Burnham, and J. Cholvat (eds.). *Values Education.* Waterloo, Ont.: Wilfrid Laurier University Press, 1975.

————. "Is Values Education Necessary and Justified?" *The School Guidance Worker* 31, 2 (Nov./Dec. 1975):40-5.

Newmann, F. M. *Education for Citizen Action: Challenge for Secondary Curriculum.* Berkeley, Ca.: McCutchan Publishing Corp., 1975.

Superka, D. P. *et al. Values Education Sourcebook.* Boulder, Col.: Social Science Education Consortium, Inc., 1976).